Learning from the Other

SUNY SERIES

SECOND THOUGHTS: NEW THEORETICAL FORMATIONS

DEBORAH P. BRITZMAN, EDITOR

Sharon Todd, *Learning from the Other: Levinas, Psychoanalysis, and Ethical Possibilities in Education*

Marnina Gonick, *Between Femininities: Ambivalence, Identity, and the Education of Girls*

LEARNING FROM THE OTHER

Levinas, Psychoanalysis, and Ethical Possibilities in Education

Sharon Todd

State University of New York Press

Published by
STATE UNIVERSITY OF NEW YORK PRESS
ALBANY

© 2003 State University of New York

All rights reserved

Printed in the United States of America

No part of this book may be used or reproduced in any manner whatsoever without written permission. No part of this book may be stored in a retrieval system or transmitted in any form or by any means including electronic, electrostatic, magnetic tape, mechanical, photocopying, recording, or otherwise without the prior permission in writing of the publisher.

For information, address
State University of New York Press
194 Washington Avenue, Suite 305, Albany, NY 12210-2384

Production, Laurie Searl
Marketing, Anne M. Valentine

Library of Congress Cataloging-in-Publication Data

Todd, Sharon, 1962–
   Learning from the other : Levinas, psychoanalysis, and ethical possibilities in education / Sharon Todd.
     p. cm. — (SUNY series, second thoughts)
   Includes bibliographical references and index.
   ISBN-13: 978-0-7914-5835-8 (alk.paper) — 978-0-7914-5836-5 (pbk.:alk.paper)
   ISBN-10: 0-7914-5835-0 (alk. paper) — 0-7914-5836-9 (pbk. : alk. paper)
   1. Levinas, Emmanuel—Views on education. 2. Education—Moral and ethical aspects. 3. Intersubjectivity. I. Title. II. Series.

LC269.T63 2003
370.11'4—dc21

2003050526

10 9 8 7 6 5 4 3 2 1

In memory of my father,

George Todd,

from whom I learned to see the world

in subtle shades of grey.

CONTENTS

ACKNOWLEDGMENTS — IX

INTRODUCTION:
LEARNING *FROM* THE OTHER:
A QUESTION OF ETHICS, A QUESTION FOR EDUCATION — 1

ONE   "BRINGING MORE THAN I CONTAIN":
ON ETHICS, CURRICULUM, AND LEARNING TO BECOME — 17

TWO   BEING-FOR OR FEELING-FOR?
EMPATHIC DEMANDS AND DISRUPTIONS — 43

THREE   A RISKY COMMITMENT:
THE AMBIGUITY AND AMBIVALENCE OF LOVE — 65

FOUR   STRANGELY INNOCENT?
GUILT, SUFFERING, AND RESPONSIBILITY — 91

FIVE   LISTENING AS AN ATTENTIVENESS TO "DENSE PLOTS" — 117

POSTSCRIPT:
WHERE ARE ETHICAL POSSIBILITIES? — 141

Notes   147

Bibliography   165

Index   173

ACKNOWLEDGMENTS

This book has been written across many continents and time zones, each place having contributed something unique to my experience of writing in situated contexts. In addition to what I have learned from these experiences, my colleagues, friends, and students have had the most impact on the form and content of my ideas. First and foremost, I thank Deborah Britzman, not only for giving me the opportunity to publish my work in her series but for the generosity and warmth of her intellectual friendship, which contributed greatly to my finding a home in the academy. Upon taking my first position at York University, Sharon Murphy encouraged me to design a graduate course on ethics and education, which led to the conception of this book. I am quite grateful for that opportunity. Alice Pitt read various pieces of writing and suggested resources along the way; her wonderful dinners got me through some long days. I thank Michaela Hynie for her provocative conversations—over many cups of coffee—that kept my thinking moving in new directions. I am also indebted to Lisa Farley for easing the difficulties of my life over the past couple of years with her characteristic sensitivity as well as for providing a careful reading of the manuscript. Many thanks to Margaret Manson on whom I could always count for sustenance in those times of difficulty with the writing—and with life in general. Trent Davis offered his routine thoroughness in pulling the notes together, and his ongoing questions clarified my own thinking. Thanks also to Stan Nemiroff, who helped me fine-tune some of my ideas at an early stage. Roger Simon commented extensively on a previous version of chapter 1, and Paul Standish offered editorial advice on an earlier version of chapter 4. I am also grateful to the anonymous reviewers of the manuscript who provided most thoughtful readings and allowed me to engage my work with some distance. I also wish to thank the Social Sciences and Humanities Research Council and the Faculty of Education at York University for their financial support in allowing me to research various chapters. In pulling together the final draft of the manuscript, I was a guest researcher at Örebro Universitet in Sweden, and I thank colleagues there for providing me with a home away from home. Portions of this book have been read over the last few years at various conferences and seminars from which I have benefited from some engaging discussion: the Philosophy of Education Society, the American Educational Research Association, Uppsala Universitet, Örebro Universitet, the Conference on the Internationalization of Curriculum Theory and Philosophy of Education in Baton Rouge, and the Bergamo Conference on Curriculum Theorizing. Finally, I extend my loving thanks to my partner, Carl Anders Säfström, whose emotional intensity and responsiveness infuse the words I write here with a "breathlessness of spirit."

Material in various chapters has been published elsewhere. Parts of chapter 1 first appeared in "'Bringing More than I Contain': Ethics, Curriculum, and the Pedagogical Demand for Altered Egos," *Journal of Curriculum Studies* 33, no. 4 (July 2001): 431–450 (www.tandf.co.uk). Portions of chapter 3 have appeared in "A Fine Risk To Be Run? The Ambiguity of Eros and Teacher Responsibility," in *Studies in Philosophy and Education* 22, no. 1 (January 2003): 31–44. Chapter 4 was based on material from two articles: "Guilt, Suffering, and Responsibility," in *Journal of Philosophy of Education* 35, no. 4 (Fall 2001): 597–614, and "When Is Guilt More than Just a Petty Face? Moving from Liberal Guilt Toward Reparation and Responsibility in Education," in *Philosophy of Education 2000*: 357–364.

INTRODUCTION

LEARNING *FROM* THE OTHER: A QUESTION OF ETHICS, A QUESTION FOR EDUCATION

WHAT, OR WHERE, is ethics in relation to education? Ethics, insofar as it potentially offers us a discourse for rethinking our relations to other people, is central to any education that takes seriously issues of social justice. It seems crucial, then, that any philosophical investigation into the ethical possibilities of education—which is how I characterize this present work—cannot only *not* ignore the exigencies of present social conditions, but it must make those exigencies central to its conceptualization of the relation between ethics and education. The magnitude of violently lived realities of homelessness, poverty, sexism, racial injustice, and genocide is, to me, the very reason why ethics not only demands immediate attention, but why education needs to concern itself with ethics. It is only by anchoring ethics and education to the tangibility of people's lives and their interactions that we might then explore hopeful possibilities for living well together.

One way such anchoring has taken place is through what might be loosely defined as social justice education; here I am thinking of a wide range of pedagogies that seek to ameliorate social harm wrought through inequitable practices and structures. Social justice education has been and continues to be marked by a moral concern with those who have been "Othered" and marginalized through discriminatory relations that are seen as violent, both in symbolic and material terms. Often defined through social categories of identity, difference, and community, this figure of the "Other" occupies a special, and central, place in both theoretical and practical approaches to such pedagogical initiatives.

This preoccupation with the "Other" within education may also be seen as part of a broader cultural turn to ethics in recent years. Congruent with social justice initiatives, this ethics has largely defined itself by appeals to the possibility for a nonviolent relation to the Other.[1] Not only in education, but in theoretical enterprises such as literary studies, political theory, cultural studies, and anthropology, this ethical turn involves thinking about the ways in which we define otherness and how our engagements with otherness leave intact or challenge the very differences that categorize the Other as other.[2]

French philosopher Alain Badiou is critical of this turn to the category of the other in ethics, pointing out its pervasiveness (and, to his mind, perniciousness) within current philosophical and popular discourses.

> Whether they know it or not, it is in the name of this configuration that the proponents of ethics explain to us today that it amounts to "recognition of the other" (against racism, which would deny this other), or to "the ethics of differences" . . . or to "multiculturalism." . . . Or, quite simply, to good old-fashioned "tolerance," which consists of not being offended by the fact that others think and act differently from you. . . . This commonsensical discourse has neither force nor truth.[3]

For Badiou, viewing ethics as a relation to the other is yet another experiment in muddled thinking, since its focus on the category of the other actually constitutes an evasion of the truths that could be marshalled to counter evil. However, what this turn to ethics in recent years has opened up, in my view, is the possibility for inquiring into the meanings the other holds for us; it has introduced complexity (as opposed to the simplicity that Badiou intimates) into how and why difference matters to any ethical project. Thus my primary concern here is to explore how ethics and education might be rethought together as a relation across difference. This means attending to what it is we mean by otherness and difference, on the one hand, and the kinds of factors that shape a relation to difference, on the other hand.

Within the terms of social justice education, the "Other" is seen to be the consequence of social, economic, or political disaffiliation, and thus to *be* "Other" signals that which is undesirable by virtue of its formation within oppressive circumstances. It is an attribute obtained through material, ideological, and discursive practices, and it is therefore viewed as a construction of time and place. Otherness, as a philosophical concept, however, is often of a different order. It is not so much an undesirable *attribute* of being, or social position, but instead it signals a radical alterity that is independent of social forces. Difference is, one might say, an ontological given.

Turning to the work of Emmanuel Levinas, the French-Jewish philosopher perhaps most well known for his ethics of alterity, this book explores what otherness as an absolute and unknowable difference has to offer to an ethical orientation for social justice education. Writing his most significant works in the aftermath of the Holocaust, which took a devastating personal toll,[4] Levinas's work speaks profoundly to the inevitable responsibility each one of us has to the other we meet. Influenced by, and yet critical of, phenomenology and existentialism, Levinas's thought locates the possibility for nonviolent forms of relationality in the immediacy of the self's encounter with the Other, an encounter that is eminently social: "in the very heart of the relationship with the other that characterizes our social life, alterity appears as a nonreciprocal relationship. . . . The Other as Other is not only an alter ego: the Other is what I myself am not. The Other is this, not because of the Other's character, or physiognomy, or psychology, but because of the Other's very alterity."[5] What is ethical, or nonviolent, becomes an attentiveness to and the preservation of this alterity of the Other. It is this Levinasian understanding of the Other as infinitely unknowable that is my first point of departure here. One of my tasks in the following pages is to propose ways that this understanding of otherness as absolute (that is, always already a given) can help educators think about the many differences that are effected through power and social location. What I am suggesting is that social justice education might consider ways of dealing with the concept of difference outside terms of oppression in order to respond ethically to the range of lived experiences of oppression. For with this turn to alterity, there opens up two fundamental questions for social justice education: first, are we (as researchers, teachers, and readers) enacting violences upon others as we engage their stories and narratives of self-identification, despite our best intentions? That is, in seeking to learn *about* them, can we be negligent of learning *from* them? And, second, if so, how might we attend to the Other and preserve alterity as a nonviolent alternative while working toward the aim of social justice?

The orientation of the present work takes seriously the challenges posed in thinking about the unknowable Other as a beginning for ethics while attempting to avoid the dangers of falling into trite categorizations that simply uphold, rather than explore, what precisely the other has to do with ethical possibilities in education. Guided by the question "What constitutes ethical possibilities in relation to learning from others?" this inquiry operates on a number of assumptions that are, like all assumptions, challengeable. That there is a possibility for ethical interaction between individuals in contexts of gross social inequity, that social differences between us do matter in considerations of ethics, and that these have some significance in relation to learning are all ideas that cannot presume to have theoretical or practical transparency. Yet I propose that there is an obligation to examine what these assumptions have to offer us in rethinking what we do when we engage in pedagogies of social justice. This obligation not only grows out of the abhorrent social conditions mentioned above, but out of the very fiber of social justice education itself. For it is precisely in the context of the educational struggle for more just social relations—where an encounter with difference, or otherness, is the *sine qua non* of pedagogical practice—that an elaboration of ethics as a relation to otherness becomes integral to its very project.[6] Indeed, given that social justice education is an attempt to achieve nothing less than the radical reformation of specific social relations (and attitudes toward those relations), it seems inevitable that we need to question what kinds of relations support nonviolence toward others as we engage in the nitty-gritty of pedagogical activity.

In exploring pedagogical relations, then, as being important for the pursuit of ethical possibilities within social justice education (and, indeed, all education), it seems necessary to discuss how they evoke certain feelings, emotions, and affect that may or may not sustain nonviolent forms of relationality. Psychoanalysis has taught us that what transpires in the everyday practices of education between teachers and students, and students and curriculum, involves complex layers of affect and conflict that specifically emerge out of an encounter with otherness. Feelings of guilt, love, and empathy, to name but a few, powerfully work their way in and through pedagogical encounters, and they do so not via conscious intent or purpose but in startling and unsettling ways that, in turn, fashion one's engagement with the Other. Thus one's capacity for response is shaped by factors that often lie outside one's control. It is in the *relating* to an unknowable Other through the adventure of learning (and teaching), that teachers and students become *psychically* implicated in the very possibilities for ethical interaction. The present work contends, in fact, that the discourse of ethics in education must grapple with the everyday vicissitudes of unconscious affect in confronting what cannot be known as it explores the conditions for nonviolence. This psychoanalytic orientation constitutes my second point of departure, and through it this work attempts to render visible the ways that pedagogical encounters with difference incite psychical complications that have ethical consequences for social justice education.

Readers familiar with both Levinas's work and the project of psychoanalysis will no doubt recognize the difficulties inherent in my project here, especially given their conflicting understandings of the subject. While these tensions will be discussed in detail later, what is important to emphasize at this stage is that together, in my view, they offer insight into how the surprising and unpredictable forms of relationality that arise in the immediacy of an encounter with difference carry profound relevance for ethical interaction. At issue is not only how the learning encounter acts as a site or milieu *in* which good relations across differences are developed—where goodness is always already a preestablished ideal—but as a process *through* which ethical relationality to otherness becomes a possibility. This means, of course, that my own view of where ethics lies in relation to education diverges from a typical application model of theory to practice. To get a fuller sense of this divergence requires a closer examination of how the relation between ethics and education is usually understood.

ETHICS, KNOWLEDGE, AND THE HAZARDS OF INSTRUMENTALIZING EDUCATION

Ethics frequently signifies two major things for education: a programmatic code of rules or principles and a branch of philosophy that has importance for theorizing educational issues.[7] It is the first of these that is most often deployed in discussions about moral action and what role education plays therein. When seen as a system of moral regulations, laws, or even guidelines, ethics inevitably renders education as instrumental to its purpose. Whether it concerns one's duties in light of a Kantian categorical imperative or one's rights and obligations under a Rawlsian liberal democracy, education becomes the medium through which laws and precepts are passed on, are taught and learned as so many other pieces of knowledge. Moral education becomes identified as that domain of educational knowledge that can aid students in the practice of living. Of course, such living requires that students not only need to know about certain principles but also need to live as though they mattered, assuming particular habits of mind. This means that ethical knowledge is a particular kind of knowledge that supposedly brings with it a commensurate change in how one lives.

On the other hand, when ethics is seen to be framed within understandings of social interaction, and when education is seen to be a generative process where knowledge itself is not absolute but socially constructed, the connection between ethics and education lies in its advocacy of certain principles of relationality. Attention is paid, for instance, to the importance of cooperation (Dewey) or care (Noddings), and emphasis is placed on how such interactions form an ongoing ethical practice that promotes "better" social conditions. Although these principles are significantly different in their privileging of the situational aspects of ethics, and are thus much more closely allied to my own orientation, ethics still enters education from the outside, as it were, since "appropriate" forms of interaction are deduced from quite specific definitions of the concepts of democracy and care, as opposed to a more general possibility that nonviolence can take on many different forms of relationality.

As it comes into contact with education, ethics as a discourse about principles becomes transformed into an applied morality. By this I mean that education frequently becomes a practice through which ethical principles and ideals are made into concrete moral obligations, duties, and the like, and responsibility itself is based on the degree to which such obligations are fulfilled. As an organized system of teaching and learning, education is often viewed as the unarticulated yet necessary condition for ethics to fulfill its practical mission, for ethics to become part of the domain of concrete human relations. Within this line of thinking, it is by teaching and learning principles and appropriate ways of behaving that ethics is brought closer to the everyday problems and dilemmas that vex us, thereby making ethics itself an educational project. Indeed, Zygmunt Bauman is pointed about what happens when ethics falls into the hands, as it were, of "philosophers, educators, preachers," the "ethical experts" of our time:

> Only ethics can say what *really* ought to be done so that the good be served. Ideally, ethics is a code of law that prescribes correct behaviour

"universally"—that is, of all people at all times; one that sets apart good from evil once for all and everybody.... The authority of ethical experts is legislative and juridical at the same time. The experts pronounce the law, and judge whether the prescriptions have been followed faithfully and correctly. They claim to be able to do it because they have access to knowledge not available to ordinary people—by speaking to the spirits of the ancestors, studying the holy scriptures, or unravelling the dictate of Reason.[8]

So what are we saying when we insist on instrumentalizing education in relation to ethics as a programmatic moral code? Do we risk putting educators in the position of experts who are "in the know" while ignoring the way moral relations transpire through the lived realities of everyday life, relations which require no specialized knowledge, and perhaps no formal knowledge at all? And what does this say about experts' attitudes toward the "ordinary people" who, ostensibly, are waiting for knowledge to be bestowed upon them so that they might then "become" moral?

In instrumentalizing ethics through education, or, rather, in viewing education as an instrument for ethics, there is a tendency to read ethics as a problem of knowledge. Ethics often is construed in educational terms as, "what and how do we need to know in order to live well together?" The ethical question thus gets rerouted along an epistemological path. What constitutes the "right" kind of knowledge becomes highly significant to teaching and learning encounters. Consequently, education becomes focused on two things: how best to encourage the acquisition of ethical knowledge through teaching, and, how best to embody, or model, ethical principles and concepts. Education, then, is seen to be about applying ethical concepts: it is a kind of knowledge in practice.

In challenging these assumptions, I am not suggesting that concepts of social justice, equity, respect, or fairness are insignificant to how we live together, both within and outside classrooms. Quite the contrary. As part of this book was written on a visit to Sri Lanka, I am all too aware of the horrible human cost of civil war and the very necessity of education as embodying a hopeful appeal to more democratic and just civil practices. And, I am very aware of struggles within North American communities to understand and combat the devastation wrought by youth violence and hatred, particularly within a growing context of right-wing hostility against the poor and marginalized, which has created further divisiveness within the educational system. Thus I am not advocating that we simply dismiss concepts as irrelevant to the moral project of education. But I do want to caution against the assumption that education can be a panacea, can be a full response to these issues, as though it can innocently reconstruct the world with better curricula, for this underestimates the powers and hazards of education itself as a practice: the very force of education to change lives and instantiate new modes of relationality is where its dangers as well as its aspirations lie. One has only to consider the wrecked lives of natives in residential schools in Canada, or the key position education has occupied in colonial histories, to see this point quite graphically. When it comes to ethics, the danger is that whether one teaches ethics as a set of abstract principles, or attempts to teach ethical relations (such as empathy) in order to lead students to interact more appropriately, or teaches through modeling and example, education risks becoming a form of rhetoric, a practice in the art of persuasion that already presumes that those who are subject to it do not already know what they need to in order to act morally.

As Derrida warns us, "rhetoric may amount to the violence of theory, which *reduces* the other when it *leads* the other, whether through psychology, demagogy, or even pedagogy which is not instruction."[9] If pedagogy is not instruction, Derrida intimates, then it is a rhetoric which does violence because it seeks to shape, influence, and "lead" the other in a particular direction without consideration for persons as distinct subjects of difference. That is, in the name of justice, respect, or equity, a pedagogy that is not instruction performs the very violence it is supposedly working to ameliorate. But one cannot simply solve this problem by claiming refuge within a nondidactic pedagogy, for it is in the very nature of how ethics is conceived in relation to education that poses the real problem for how we understand teaching and learning.

It would seem that in order to avoid the rhetorical violence of pedagogy, ethics ought to be freed from the clutches of epistemological certitude: that is, perhaps we need to consider the ways in which ethics is something other than acting on knowledge. Yet to pose the possibility that ethics might have a different relation to education, that is, a relation that lies outside the sole domain of knowledge, is to put into question a foundational idea of much of ethical philosophy: that our moral actions, our capacity for acting in the name of what is right, good, or simply better, are premised on our knowledge of what is right, good, or simply better. To challenge the connection between ethics and knowledge, to break the complicity between epistemological claims and moral action, would instantiate, of course, the proverbial thorn in education's side, for we need not only imagine Socrates' admonition long ago—that virtue cannot be taught because teaching is impossible—might have some truth in order to be troubled. In bringing the ethical possibilities of education into touch with the very tangible experiences of violence, the mere suggestion that we might unhitch ethics and knowledge appears highly problematic, if not downright flippant and irresponsible. Could not all these violences be marshalled as evidence that it is precisely because we do not have the right kind of knowledge at our disposal that we are capable of committing such acts against each other in the first place? Could we not (simply) get to know the other better, teach ourselves to be more empathic, learn to care for and about the other, and/or act more in accordance with principles of justice, respect, and freedom in order to make the violence of our lives disappear?

On the surface, of course, to suggest that knowledge, or enlightened thinking, may not be the moral guarantor of our times, and that education may not be an innocent purveyor of knowledge, but caught up in the very practices of violence that it seeks to remedy, gives us great cause for worry, for education will seemingly find itself ethically afloat without the hope for a moral project to anchor it. This is, in my view, simply not desirable, for the very project of education, particularly social justice education, needs to offer an alternative to what it renders unjust, inequitable, and harmful. The issue is, rather, how to problematize the triangulation of ethics and education through knowledge without giving up on the capacity of education to be transformative as an ethical practice.

REPOSING THE ETHICAL QUESTION OTHERWISE

One way to achieve this is to reframe our attention to the Other, to difference, without appealing to knowledge *about* the Other. The idea that we only need to get to know someone in order to be able to act responsibly (and responsively) toward that person is a common way for people to talk about one of the conditions for ethical interaction. In education in particular, this getting to know the other (e.g., teachers getting to know their students through their experiences, cultural backgrounds, etc.) often becomes the premise for building relationships that better meet the needs of persons involved. Indeed, there is some commonsense appeal to this. How often has each one of us thought that if we had only known the full story, we might have acted differently, been more sensitive, or paid closer attention to the other person?

This learning about the Other, however, suggests two things: that otherness *can* be understood and that learning about others is pedagogically and ethically desirable. Attempts to work across differences in social justice education often gain their ethical strength from deconstructing center and margin, inclusion and exclusion, and self and "Other." Anti-racist projects, for example, seek to make transparent the discourses that marginalize people through their positioning of certain racial and ethnic groups as "Other." Curricular and pedagogical initiatives frequently focus on the untold histories, narratives of self-identification, and demands for recognition of the "Other" in order to disassemble the structures of power that distort, if not outright destroy, certain individuals and their communities. Framing our ethical attention to difference as a question of knowledge implies that the more we know about "Others," the better we are able to understand how to respond to them, how to be more responsible, and how to de-"Other" them.

This present work is a serious questioning of whether knowledge *about* ethics, or knowledge *about* the Other, can deliver us from moral quandaries about treating each other responsibly across our social differences. Shifting our understanding of the Other as that which manifests an ontological difference (rather than a socially defined one) means that we cannot assume that knowing leads to better ethical reflection, and that de-"Othering" is a worthy moral aspiration.[10] The Levinasian understanding of the Other as an unassimilable and unknowable alterity means that the I and the Other lie in a relation of nonreciprocity, where they come together only ever as strangers to each other, a fundamental strangeness that secures the hope for ethicality.[11] Thus, rather than see our ethical attention to the Other, to difference, as a problem of cognition, I want to investigate, following Levinas,[12] the conditions that make ethical attentiveness to strangeness possible in the first place. Indeed, so-called ordinary people do live their lives morally in relation to others, without knowing anything either about ethics as a programmatic moral code or about those others with whom they interact in any definitive way. In focusing on conditions instead of principles, codes, and rules, ethics might be considered in terms of those *moments of relationality that resist codification*. That is, various modes of relationality create moments of nonviolence insofar as they define our ethical attention to otherness in ways that cannot be codified into prescriptions for practice. What I am suggesting here is that it is the disruptive, unpredictable time of attentiveness to the Other where ethical possibility lies. It seems to me that it is precisely because our capacity to relate to others is premised on our susceptibilities, vulnerabilities, and openness to the Other, and not on knowledge, that forms of relationality resist containment within rational appeals to principles, or through any ethics understood as a codified system. That is, the conditions for relating to one another carry tremendous ethical weight and do so outside the systemic bounds of rules or regulations. Teaching, then, would not be focussed on acquiring knowledge about ethics, or about the Other, but would instead have to consider its practices themselves as relations to otherness and thus as always already potentially ethical—that is, participating in a network of relations that lend themselves to moments of nonviolence. In this sense, the way in which we engage the Other becomes a central question *of* ethics and *for* education.

Of course, education very much needs to be about knowledge, and the content of curriculum is indeed worth struggling over. My point is merely that this alone cannot define what is potentially ethical within education. Turning our attention to the conditions for ethical possibility means giving up on the idea that learning about others is an appropriate ethical response to difference. Rather, if we place susceptibility, vulnerability, and openness at the core of relationality, then the question that begins to emerge is how we learn *from* the other. This focus on learning *from* means having to consider not only *what* we learn when we learn—narrowly defined, this would simply place the emphasis once again on the content of learning; rather, the shift I am making here involves investigating what is at stake in the *process* of learning from, and what the Other signifies in such a relation. What happens to ethics and education when learning is not about understanding the other but about a relation to otherness prior to understanding?

LEARNING FROM PSYCHOANALYSIS AND LEVINAS

The distinction between learning about and learning from is one Freud made in an essay, "On the Teaching of Psychoanalysis in Universities."[13] While Freud's mention of it is confined to a single sentence, it is the entire purpose of the project of psychoanalysis to learn from and not merely about one's own attachments to others—to people, ideas, and objects—in order to purchase insight into one's condition in the world. With respect to education, both Deborah Britzman and Adam Phillips have written on the significance of this distinction, and they have elucidated a double sense of learning *from* in psychoanalytic terms: how they have learned from Freud (and psychoanalysis more generally) in order to consider what is involved in learning from an other.[14]

In drawing out the importance of difference for education, Britzman explicates more fully the earlier distinction made by Freud. She writes:

> Whereas learning about an event or experience focuses upon the acquisition of qualities, attributes, and facts, so that it presupposes a distance (or, one might even say, a detachment) between the learner and what is to be learned, learning from an event or experience is of a different order, that of insight.... Learning from demands both a patience with the incommensurability of understanding and an interest in tolerating the ways meaning becomes, for the learner, fractured, broken, and lost, exceeding the affirmations of rationality, consciousness, and consolation.[15]

Learning from an Other, then, is a psychical event, one caught up in the interplay between what lies outside and inside the subject, what lies interior and exterior, so that the encounter with otherness becomes the necessary precondition for meaning and understanding. Equally important, however, are the kinds of connections, disjunctions, and ruptures that this brings to the learner. The subject who learns from the Other cannot find an easy way of keeping itself separate from the Other, and making such distinctions becomes an (almost) unbearable task: "What becomes the ego and what becomes the object? What belongs to me and what belongs to the other? These questions often dissipate into the angry gesture of us and them, where it is they who are making my life miserable, not me. Psychoanalysis resides within these difficult tangles of implication: how *the me lives in that and the that lives in me*."[16]

This view of learning from implicates the subject in a relation to the Other that is not predictable or calculable; that is, the subject cannot know beforehand how she will respond, or what unconscious bits of affect are going to emerge in the context of any particular encounter. There is thus a kind of trauma in encountering what is outside the subject, because that outside threatens the stability of the ego. In confronting difference, the subject brings to the scene of learning its own history of affect, which then becomes woven into the fabric of the present. Melanie Klein's work reveals, as I discuss in chapter 1, that it is the very anxiety over encountering difference that both leads to the possibility of learning and presents learning with its fiercest form of resistance. Precisely because the Other is seen to be that which disrupts its coherency, the subject tumbles into uncertainty, its past strategies for living challenged by the very strangeness of difference itself. That is, the very instability of the ego that is necessary for meaning to develop also signals an implicit riskiness to learning that involves not simple cognition, as might be the case, for instance, in coming to know that 2 + 2 = 4. Rather, the stakes for the subject are higher. In gaining insight, one risks altering the very parameters of self-perception and one's place in the world, and risks losing, therefore, one's bearings and conventions. And this riskiness manifests itself through the dynamics of affect mobilized in order to, for example, defend against, identify with, or disavow the Other in the learning encounter.

But looked at from the other side, so to speak, learning from is also, in its very approach to the Other, not only a question of what the subject who learns undergoes or what she brings to the encounter but fundamentally a question about the alterity of the Other. While Levinas agrees that learning is a traumatic event (what he refers to as a "traumatism of astonishment," where the subject's self-identity is indeed ruptured through learning), he parts company with psychoanalysis in his insistence on what an encounter with difference means for the possible preservation of alterity. For Levinas, learning from is a profoundly ethical event because the very encounter with difference, with the Other, is a passive one, one in which the learner is openly receptive to the Other. Such openness signals for Levinas an unavoidable responsibility for the Other, placing an encounter with the Other in the time of ethics. It is the very responsibility born of passivity that enables a nonviolent relation to the Other to emerge. Thus, for Levinas, it is the disinterestedness, the noninvestment of one's conscious ego—and one's psychical past—that allows for the preservation of the Other's alterity. It is not that Levinas refuses the importance of affect, in fact, the ethical subject for Levinas is preeminently rooted in sensibility. As Simon Critchley explains, "The subject's affective disposition towards alterity is the condition of possibility for the ethical relation to the other. Ethics does not take place at the level of consciousness or reflection; it rather takes place at the level of sensibility or pre-conscious sentience. The Levinasian ethical subject is a sentient self (*un soi sentant*) before being a thinking ego (*un moi pensant*). The bond with the other is affective."[17]

There are two elements to learning from that are important to highlight here: first is the ethical dimension of this encounter with difference; second is the way affect participates in the encounter. However, as we have seen, for psychoanalysis, such affect is precisely what gets in the way, so to speak, of ensuring that the alterity of the Other is preserved. This is particularly the case when affect troubles the learner's ego, and when the borders delineating outside and inside become unclear. For Levinas, however, affect is not about the baggage that is brought to the encounter but about the potentiality to be moved in such a way that the self becomes egoless in facing the Other. Affect thus binds the self to the Other in such a way that the distinct singularity of each is maintained. Given these radically different orientations, how might these discourses be brought into conversation?

BUILDING ON TENSIONS

Levinas and various proponents of psychoanalysis may seem to have little to say to one another with regard to ethics and education. To be clear, Levinas premises the conditions of ethics—the conditions of a nonviolent relation to the Other—upon a self-Other relation that is free of those screens and filters through which we encounter other people: defensive posturings, moments of identification, interpretations or knowledge of the Other. Instead, Levinas proposes that the ethical self-Other relation is a relation of disinterestedness between two distinct beings, a relation that is not caught up in the egoism of the self, nor in knowledge about what is right, but where the self is passively open to the Other. It is this very passivity that is necessary in order to counteract the potential for violence that always exists in our relations to one another; moreover, it is in this openness and vulnerability to alterity where the self encounters the infinite possibilities of the future. Levinas writes, "I do not define the other by the future, but the future by the other."[18] Thus the future for Levinas is only made possible as an element of time as it comes into relation with the present.[19]

In contradistinction to this, psychoanalysis insists that our relations are indeed laced with threads of affect and psychical complications, where defenses, identifications, and ambivalences continually erupt in spite of our best intentions. Unconscious slips of the tongue, projected anger, and erotic desire are no strangers to the self-Other relation, seeming to make it impossible to think about the conditions of ethics as being based on selfless activity. As Freud postulates, past violences suffered by the individual continually play themselves out in indeterminable ways in our present encounters, while simultaneously we continually remake the past through a projection of the present.[20] In this sense, our ethical capacity is necessarily tinged (if not saturated) in the temporal interplay between past and present.

What demands mention up front, then, is the fact that psychoanalysis and Levinasian ethics are fundamentally incommensurable discourses. In offering a theory of the subject (and thereby making the otherness of the other knowable at the level of discourse), psychoanalysis performs, in Levinasian terms, a violence upon the subject through its very act of thematizing. That is, as an interpretive theory, it risks the danger of claiming to know the Other, which creates a host of expectations that foreclose on those elements of openness and surprise necessary for preserving alterity. On the other side, Levinas insists on a pre-originary passivity toward the Other that guarantees ethicality. For psychoanalysis, this understanding of the subject ignores the ways the unconscious is active in constructing reality, and not only in receiving it. Thus, psychoanalysis, to put it bluntly, is not an ethical discourse in Levinasian terms, and Levinas's egoless passivity is simply a naive impossibility for psychoanalysis.[21]

It would appear on the surface, then, that one would either have to hold the Levinasian view of an egoless passivity that precedes knowledge of the Other or the psychoanalytic view of the unconscious and the ego's capacity for insight in order to think through the possibility of ethics in education. What I wish to consider here, however, are the ways in which these two views may be held in tension—without collapsing their significant differences. Both discourses offer education a way of thinking through the relationship between self and Other that refuses to ignore affect as significant not only to learning but to engagements with difference. Moreover, both view the fragility of the self as the source of traumatic wounding when it encounters difference, acknowledging that the Other disrupts one's self-identity. And, finally, both view the relation between self and Other as basically nonreciprocal and asymmetrical. As Noreen O'Connor writes:

> Levinas and Freud both consider that the relationship between human beings is the most crucial issue to be elucidated in order to counter violence and heal suffering. Freud, despite the mechanistic and pseudoexplanatory character of his metapsychology, nevertheless shares with Levinas an emphasis on the primacy of heterogeneity or asymmetry of human relationships.... Psychoanalysis highlights the fact that the time of each human being is not the time articulated by historiographers; rather, it is constituted by the individual's relationships to other people. What is at issue is the difference yet relationship between people, separation and individuation.... Without elaborating a model of genetic development of the psyche in terms of a drive economy, Levinas nevertheless also concentrates on the separation and yet the vulnerability of the "self."[22]

Although these similarities are precisely why I draw upon both discourses here, I nonetheless read the tensions between Levinas and psychoanalysis as not something to be dissolved but something to be mined for the way in which they offer different temporal perspectives on learning from the Other: one gesturing toward the future promised by the Other, the other recognizing traces of the past in present encounters with difference. In this regard I am not trying to integrate these two views theoretically but to work within and through their very differences. Investigating the importance of relationality for ethicality means, then, exploring the ways in which people come together, both with definite histories that shape the reception of and response to the Other, and with the kind of surprising openness that exceeds these histories. This doubled view paints a more complex picture of what occurs in classrooms in the here and now, one that might inform an ethical time of nonviolence, a time that is infinitely momentary.

CHAPTERS AND THEMES

The first chapter lays out the difficulties inherent to learning, focusing on a view of education as a violent process of "learning to become" through an encounter with difference. Here I outline how a relation to otherness is a prior condition of learning and understanding and suggest that there are moments of nonviolence that interrupt this process to be found in various modes of relationality that constitute one's response to difference. Each of the following four chapters then focuses on a particular mode of relationality in order to highlight the complex nature of learning from difference and to probe where the conditions for ethical possibility might lie. Empathy, love, guilt, and listening are considered here in turn; the order of their appearance is generally suggestive (although by no means definitively so) of their increasing significance for promoting conditions of ethical attentiveness, and each mode of relationality is explored in terms of its relevance for learning from the Other. Although all the chapters are thematically linked, the ones on love and empathy are particularly close insofar as I argue that the configuration of otherness and togetherness that empathy presumes has more to do with our capacity for love than empathy allows for. The chapter on guilt highlights its disregarded place in social justice education and acts as a reconsideration of guilt's moral significance as a learning from the Other. Chapter 5 contends that listening as an attentiveness to the narrative presence of the Other promotes conditions of nonviolent learning. Specifically, I argue for listening to the Other *in time* as a quality of relationality that attends ethically to the multidimensional nature of signification. Importantly, each chapter enacts its own learning *from* through close readings of key Levinasian and psychoanalytic concepts. Overall, three themes are woven throughout the various chapters. Each of these underscores a particular understanding of the relation between ethics and education as one that is fundamentally rooted in difference.

First is a view of education as a site of *implied ethics*. An implied ethics means that educational practices, technologies, discourses, and relationships always already participate in a field of ethical signification, that is, a domain or realm in which nonviolent relations to the Other are possible (even if not inevitable). As a site of implication rather than application, working across difference means attending to the specificity of relationships in our classrooms. An implied ethics requires paying close attention to what we do when we engage in practices of teaching and learning, and it means exploring the ways in which our engagements across difference promote conditions for nonviolent relations. If responsibility is inescapable because of the "impossibility of indifference to the Other,"[23] then our interactions with one another profoundly matter to our understanding of ethics. How a teacher handles, for instance, a student's response to traumatic literature carries not only pedagogical but ethical significance. What dynamics are at stake in the teacher's response to the student, or in the student's response to the literature? What, essentially, is the quality of relationality across difference? This brings me to my second theme.

A recognition of the *quality of relations* plays an important role in sifting out moments of nonviolent relationality. Attention to the quality of relations, as opposed to the types of relations, focuses on to what degree the relations we *actually* engage in (rather than identifying what types we *should* engage in) enhance or compromise the persons involved. Returning to Levinas's conception of alterity, what is morally significant is whether the otherness of the Other is supported within these relations. Equally meaningful is how it is possible to preserve alterity in the face of the vicissitudes of our (psychoanalytic) egos. Thus an important aspect of focusing on the quality of relations means examining to what extent we are open to the Other, and how social structures affect the conditions for enabling this to happen. Am I responsive to the Other in such a way so as to maintain alterity as a distinctive mark of relationality within the larger social frameworks of institutional settings?

Third is the idea that to *teach responsibly—and responsively—one must do so with ignorance and humility.* That is, knowledge about the Other is truly an impossibility on two counts. Ontologically, otherness is precisely that which defies our own sameness and exists in a relation of exteriority to the self. Furthermore, even from a sociologically oriented understanding, otherness resides in fantasies, desires, creativity, and passions that remain the Other's alone. And although psychoanalysis attempts to render the unconscious knowledgeable at the conceptual level (psychoanalytic theories, of course, do say something of substance about the unconscious), a fundamental precept that it teaches is how the unconscious as a creative force, what Cornelius Castoriadis refers to as a "radical imaginary,"[24] remains unassimilable to conscious thought. To follow Levinas, when I think I know, when I think I understand the Other, I am exercising my knowledge over the Other, shrouding the Other in my own totality. The Other becomes an object of *my* comprehension, *my* world, *my* narrative, reducing the Other to me. What is at stake is my ego. But if I am exposed to the Other, I can listen, attend, and be surprised; the Other can affect me, she "brings me more than I contain."[25] Insofar as I can be receptive and susceptible, I can learn *from* the Other as one who is absolutely different from myself.

It is through a consideration of these three themes that this book represents a reworking of some of the ethical assumptions embedded within social justice education. While all three are important for framing our ethical attention to difference, I have placed more emphasis on the third idea, that we can and do learn from others. It is this learning from, which emerges when we let go of our need to know, that offers, in my view, the best hope for working across our specific social differences. Obviously I realize that when we learn *from* we do learn *something,* and we do not always approach the Other from an egoless passivity. Yet the specifically *ethical* possibility of education, this possibility for nonviolent relation to the Other, can only surface when knowledge is not our aim. Instead, learning *from* as opposed to *about* allows us an engagement with difference across space and time, it focuses on the here and now of communication while gesturing toward the future and acknowledging the past; it allows for attentiveness to singularity and specificity within the plurality that is our social life. It is only when we learn *from* others that we can respond with the very humility necessary for assuming responsibility. And moving toward such an ethical horizon of possibility seems to me to be what social justice education is all about.

ONE

"BRINGING MORE THAN I CONTAIN": ON ETHICS, CURRICULUM, AND LEARNING TO BECOME

WE READ SIMON WIESENTHAL'S *The Sunflower* in a graduate seminar I teach on ethics and education.[1] The central story consists of a grueling meeting that Wiesenthal has with a dying member of the Nazi *Schutzstaffel* (SS) while himself an inmate in a concentration camp. The SS man, Karl, has asked that a Jewish prisoner be brought to him so that he may be granted forgiveness for his participation in a mass murder involving a number of Jewish families. Wiesenthal is chosen from among the prisoners to be the man's confessor, and he listens with outrage, horror, and anguish to the soldier's detailed account of the murder. Yet Wiesenthal is also witness to the man's deathbed suffering, and his listening is punctuated by tiny gestures of ambivalence. At one point, in a moment of self-surprise, he shoos an irritating fly away from the dying man's face, an act that Karl is too incapacitated to perform himself. Wiesenthal takes his leave of the death room without offering the soldier any consolation, any forgiveness, and he is later haunted by lingering doubt about his inaction. A few years after his liberation, Wiesenthal seeks out the man's mother, uncertain as to whether he will reveal the truth about what he knows of her son. He decides to remain silent in the face of her grief, allowing her illusions to predominate over his own complicated feelings of sympathy and moral outrage. Told with the hindsight of many years' distance, Wiesenthal asks his readers to consider what it means to forgive, and whether he did the right thing in not granting the soldier his dying wish.

Rather than focusing solely on forgiveness, the class explores the moments of ethicality within the story, the moments of ambivalence that make possible different configurations of moral action, discussing how Wiesenthal represents these moments in narrative form. We discuss the relationship to community, to trauma, and the vulnerability of what Levinas would recognize as "face-to-face encounters," both between Wiesenthal and the dying SS man and between Wiesenthal and the man's mother. Students generally discuss the difficulties they face in reading, and rearticulating what they read, in light of the enormity of suffering present on so many levels. Most significantly, it is also Wiesenthal's continued ambivalence about his response to the SS soldier that students often have very strong feelings toward, ranging from empathic attachment to guilt to condemnation.

I reflect on this here to raise some fundamental questions about what we ask students to accomplish in staking out a relationship to a text, particularly one so filled with the pendulous vicissitudes between pain and suffering, on the one hand, and dignity and hope, on the other.[2] What do students risk in encountering a story, an idea, an other? What do they risk in forming a symbolic relationship to knowledge, and to curriculum, more generally? And what are our responsibilities to students as teachers in asking them to read and, indeed, to respond?

For students, insofar as curriculum involves introducing them to new encounters, it also asks them to change their views, perceptions, assumptions, and modes of thinking. This suggests that in asking students to produce meaningful relations to texts, ideas, or representations, we are not only engaged in a "provocation of semiosis,"[3] but we may be provoking an ontological crisis of sorts.[4] What appears to be at risk, therefore, is the self itself, or, more precisely, in Kleinian terms, the ego, developed through its continual negotiation with external reality.[5] For instance, how could articulating a relation to the ambivalence in Wiesenthal's story be so difficult (after all, it is *his* ambivalence he is writing about) if it were not for the possibility that such articulation would be risking something beyond the story, risking something beyond what is familiar, risking a relation with an other outside of the self? I wish to explore here the idea that it is in this act of symbolizing—of making meaning in relation to something outside of the self—where the conditions of ethicality and being come together. What might be the place of curriculum and teaching in this relation between otherness and ego? Does learning itself mean having to face a difference that is "not me"? Does learning mean becoming someone different than what one was before?

LEARNING TO BECOME AND THE PEDAGOGICAL DEMAND FOR ALTERED EGOS

Pedagogy starts at age zero and no one knows when it ends. The aim of pedagogy (or *paideia*)—I am of course speaking normatively—is to help the newborn hopeful and dreadful monster to become a human being, to

help this bundle of drives and imagination become an *anthrōpos*.... The
point of pedagogy is not to teach particular things, but to develop in the
subject the capacity to learn.[6]

As a philosopher and political theorist, Cornelius Castoriadis opens up the question of pedagogy, of learning and teaching, to the conditions of a person's becoming. He proposes that along the trajectory of subjecthood, from one's beginning as a "hopeful and dreadful monster" to one's finale in death, pedagogy turns on the ability of the nascent subject to change, to alter, to become something other than what it was. The subject accomplishes this self-alteration through its capacity to negotiate meaning in the world in relation to the objects and persons around it. Castoriadis draws attention to how subjectivity is instituted, that is, how the nascent human subject is eminently pliable and is potentially fitted into any social order into which it happens to be born. But Castoriadis is also a psychoanalyst, and as such, he speaks of the project of becoming in terms of the development of the ego, glossing the famous Freudian adage, "Where Id was, there Ego shall become." What it means to learn, for Castoriadis, is to learn to become an ego, and it is in this process of learning where the subject is both shaped by and yet resists the forces of social circumstance.[7]

Like Freud, Castoriadis suggests that "learning to become" is an inherently violent activity where the social environment exacts a traumatic price from the psyche. The subject, through making symbolic connections to its environment, must relinquish its own unconscious desires and drives in the service of sociality. It renounces, represses and sublimates its "bundle of drives" in a struggle to negotiate with what is always necessarily outside and other to the subject itself. It is precisely through this negotiation that the subject learns to take pleasure and delight in the external world, and it learns to control itself, as best it can, for the purpose of making relationships to others. For Castoriadis the psyche is thereby necessarily coerced into becoming a being—a social individual, an ego—through the social institutions (e.g., the family, school, and religion) that furnish the subject with meaning, that impose limitations upon the subject's desires and drives.[8] Yet for Castoriadis, there is always a residue, a psychical remainder that cannot be subsumed into the social order and that allows for the possibility that subjects will make meaning and learn in unpredictable ways.

In some ways, Castoriadis's radical insight is both simple and familiar: the subject *learns* to become a being in relation to others it encounters, learning values, behaviors, and modes of thinking within the nexus of culture, language, and social relations. However, rather than taking a naive view of this process, Castoriadis sees that this is an inevitably violent demand that society places on its subjects. Through social institutions, society exerts a force upon the subject to become, for example, a worker, citizen, or consumer (or, in other social-historical circumstances, feudal lords, peasants, or anointed kings).

Thus, insofar as education is a socializing institution *par excellence,* what Castoriadis underscores here is not only the need to speak of the violence *in* education, but the violence *of* education.[9] It is important to signal that I am employing neither a metaphorical usage of the term nor one designed to erase the differences between specific acts of violence (e.g., neglect, humiliation, fear, abuse, torture). Indeed, acts of violence such as these are of a completely different order, for suffering is here inflicted through hatred, cruelty, and indifference. My emphasis here is on the inevitable external force that has the power to subject, that compels us to learn and become. In this sense, education, by its very socializing function and by its mission to change how people think and relate to the world, enacts a violence that is necessary to the formation of the subject (this is, after all, what is meant by "formation"). Following the metaphysical formulations of Derrida and Levinas, on the one hand, and the psychical formulations of psychoanalysis, on the other hand, violence is a necessary condition of subjectivity. Thus the question is not so much whether education wounds or not through its impulse to socialize, but whether it wounds excessively and how we (as teachers) might open ourselves to nonviolent possibilities in our pedagogical encounters.

Castoriadis's portrayal is helpful in examining a major assumption underlying education, and social justice education in particular: that educators teach in the hope that others will learn and change. Yet at the same time, it challenges education's innocence. Learning to become depicts well the ontological stakes in processes of learning, both in terms of the benefits of change and the high prices to be paid in terms of the coercive nature of subject formation. It echoes the comments students often make when they begin to think and experience their own lives differently through new ideas, concepts, and relationships to other people. It is not uncommon, for example, to hear even adult students say, "I have never thought of myself this way before reading this book," or "My life has changed as a result of taking this class." My own educational history speaks to such moments of elation. These declarations of change, however, are often accompanied by statements of struggle in making a relationship to a knowledge that is outside the subject; students wrestle with the otherness and difference that are presented to them through the curriculum and through the bodies of teachers and students they encounter. Building on Castoriadis's view, such difficulty suggests that there is something profoundly at risk in coming to know, involving renunciations and sacrifices that are sometimes too great to bear. Students often feel that once they struggle to know something, they can never be quite the same again. And as if this struggle were not enough, the process continually returns, refusing to offer consolation for very long. Egos are not formed, nor are desires done away with once and for all. The ego is never finished but always incomplete, not "an attained state but . . . an active situation."[10] This means that the ego is continually vulnerable to the potentiality of violence, to the recurrence of learning to become.

Thus, pedagogically speaking, the simplicity of Castoriadis's insight is deceptive, for although it seems to depict, in a straightforward fashion, the ontological possibilities of learning, it also highlights the ethical aspects of learning itself, insofar as learning is accompanied by a certain violence to the subject. Moreover, this violence is occasioned not only by the content of what one learns but by the structure of the demand to learn itself. To illustrate this point more thoroughly, let us turn to a pedagogical interaction often held up as a paradigm of learning, namely, Plato's *Meno*.

A PEDAGOGICAL DEMAND IN THE GUISE OF A QUESTION

"Can you tell me, Socrates, whether virtue is acquired by teaching or by practice; or if neither by teaching nor practice, then whether it comes to man by nature, or in what other way?"[11] Meno's question is the opening line in Plato's drama of teaching's limits. It teases and provokes, inciting Socrates to address the relationship between teaching and ethicality. The crux of the Socratic position in Plato's dialogue is a refusal of the possibilities of teaching virtue. Socrates turns teaching away from didactic pronouncement, turns learning away from factual acquisition, and concludes that virtue is not something that can be taught because learning and teaching are themselves impossible. Meno's incredulity echoes our own: "How do you mean that we do not learn, but that what we call learning is recollection? *Can you teach me that this is so?*" (81e, emphasis added). Caught within Meno's demand to teach that which cannot be taught, Socrates replies, "You are a rascal. You now ask me if I can teach you when I say there is no teaching but recollection" (82a). Shoshana Felman remarks that Socrates "inaugurates his teaching practice, paradoxically enough, by asserting not just his own ignorance but the radical impossibility of teaching."[12] But is the performance of his practice congruous with his assertion?

The teaching practice that Socrates inaugurates involves an encounter with Meno's slave boy in an attempt to prove to Meno that learning is recollection and that teaching is, by extension, impossible. We are made witness to a lesson within a lesson. In a subtle bit of irony, Socrates' "teaching" of the slave itself becomes an object lesson for Meno. "Pay attention then whether you think he is recollecting or learning from me," states Socrates (82b). The subsequent interaction with the slave boy takes on the twofold burden of teaching both the boy and Meno. On the one hand, questioning the boy supposedly substitutes for teaching him, yet the *performance* of questioning reveals itself as a teaching: teaching occurs in the guise of a question. On the other hand, Meno is instructed by example, not by question: he is to learn by *observing* Socrates *perform* the question.

What I wish to consider, through a close reading of the text, is how this double performance of Socrates' questioning provokes a demand for alteration;

it acts as an instantiation of subject formation, of learning to become, for both Meno and the boy, a becoming that is fundamentally about the asymmetry between self and other, between teacher and student, in this case. What is important to investigate, for my purposes here, is not only what Socrates *says* (*à la lettre*), but his *saying:* teaching through questioning has both rhetorical effect and ethical command. Socrates cannot simply be taken at his word.

A NARRATIVE OF LEARNING, OR THE TYRANNY OF THE QUESTION?

The scene with the slave boy narrates three moments in the path of learning to become for the boy, and each of them revolves around a series of lines to be geometrically organized. Initially, Socrates' questioning is simply a rephrasing of a truth statement, to which his pupil responds in the affirmative, the response having been embedded in the question itself: "A square then is a figure in which all these four sides are equal?—Yes indeed" (82c). In his various replies to further questions, the student knows that he knows, and he finds a degree of naive certitude: a belief that certainty is attainable through the teacher's question.[13] Meno, too, as witness to this event, is convinced of the boy's knowledge and of Socrates' powers as a teacher.

The pedagogical experiment continues at an increasing level of complexity, that is, the pupil is asked to perform functions that are not apparent in the phrasing of the question. The boy begins to stumble, trying to calculate what length of line is needed to form an eight-foot-square figure, and he finally gives the erroneous answer of three feet. Through Socrates' persistent questioning, the boy realizes he has given the wrong answer:

Socrates: How much is three times three feet?—Nine feet.
Socrates: And the double square was to be how many feet?—Eight.
Socrates: So the eight-foot figure cannot be based on the three-foot line?— Clearly not. (83e)

This inaugurates the second step in learning. Socrates identifies this point at which the pupil is at a loss as a *necessary* "fall into perplexity." Here the slave boy understands that he has given the wrong answer. In one of his numerous asides to Meno, Socrates says, "Do you think that before he would have tried to find out that which he thought he knew though he did not, before he fell into perplexity and realized he did not know and longed to know?" (84c). Socrates sees his questioning as provoking a crisis, what Melanie Klein acknowledges, as we will see, as the anxiety necessary to provoke the emergence of the ego. Such falling into perplexity, into a crisis, or into a state of anxiety, indicates not merely an ignorance on the part of the subject but an *acknowledged* state of ignorance: "as he [the boy] does not know, neither does he think he knows" (84b). Socrates has, in effect, made possible a shift in the boy's thinking about his own learning, and sees this as necessary to the pursuit of knowledge itself. An alteration of the subject is required in order for there to be a continuation in the pursuit of knowledge and of new understandings: we must know that we do not know so we can pursue what there is to know.

Similarly, Meno is equally unsure of what he is witnessing. What seemed to be certain (that the boy knows) is no longer the case. Socrates' parenthetical remarks to Meno at the point of the slave's perplexity attempt to console Meno over his own confusion. Socrates prompts him repeatedly to, in effect, pay attention: "Look then how he will come out of his perplexity while searching along with me. I shall do nothing more than ask questions and not teach him. Watch whether you find me teaching and explaining things to him instead of asking for his opinion" (84c-d). Both in its substance and rhetorical drive, Socrates' speech massages Meno's worries, while on the other hand he continues to subject the slave boy to a new round of questions.

The climax of the scene ushers in the third phase of learning. Socrates draws for the slave boy a series of diagonal lines cut through each of the four squares they have been working with.

Socrates: Each of these lines cuts off half of each of the four figures inside it, does it not?—Yes.

Socrates: How many of this size are there in this figure?—Four.

Socrates: How many in this?—Two.

Socrates: What is the relation of four to two?—Double.

Socrates: How many feet in this?—Eight.

Socrates: Based on what line?—This one.

Socrates: That is, on the line that stretches from corner to corner of the four-foot figure?—Yes.—Clever men call this the diagonal, so that if diagonal is its name, you say that the double figure would be that based on the diagonal?—Most certainly, Socrates. (85a-b)

The pupil here becomes certain of his knowledge, has become convinced, as Meno is after him, that he can come to know that which he did not know. Indeed, both "students" are surprised and, by the end of the brief encounter, are convinced that knowledge was theirs to recollect from the start.

We witness this trajectory of coming to know as perhaps the pedagogical event *par excellence,* an event that calls upon us to take delight in the power of the teacher to facilitate and give birth to knowledge "in" an other, without recourse to didactic procedures. Socrates' own insistence that his act of questioning is a nonteaching event, is a practice of midwifery, obliges us, however, to rearticulate what we have just witnessed.

The three movements of learning that Socrates' teaching narrates—naive certainty, acknowledged ignorance, and certainty of knowledge recollected—

do not, however, easily map on to the performative aspect of Socrates' questioning. The narration consists of a pedagogical scene that is continually refused by the teacher to even *be* a scene of teaching. For Socrates, teaching is impossible precisely because what there is to know is not transmissible, but recollected. Learning is made possible for the slave boy only because Socrates refuses teaching itself, refuses the grammar of didacticism where the imperative reigns over the interrogatory, the expository over the exploratory. Plato serves up the irony of teaching in the very consummate figure of the teacher, Socrates: the good teacher is someone who does not teach, or more appropriately, who does not see oneself as teaching. Socrates is the teacher, who, like the perfect murderer, makes it appear that teaching has not taken place, who leaves the scene without a trace, and who, moreover, is convinced of his own innocence.

This innocence, however, seems spurious at best and might serve to illustrate to all educators the need to be attentive to the demand for alteration that structures the conditions under which we come together to teach and learn. Performatively speaking, in a pedagogical scene where teaching is supposedly absent, where the teacher is an innocent facilitator, Socrates exhibits himself as a crafty questioner, a skilled wordsmith who carefully scaffolds the possibilities of response. Questions pregnant with insinuation offer the boy a means for organizing, quite literally, what begins as a series of lines drawn in the sand. The slave boy develops new opportunities for symbolizing lines and their values, and he alters his understanding as he proceeds to be questioned. In fact, the questioning pursues him relentlessly until this alteration comes about, until he thinks geometrically, so to speak. Socrates offers him words in the place of lines, offers him geometrical and mathematical relationships where he apparently saw none before. Despite his assertion that teaching is impossible, that questioning is not teaching, the artful rhetorician nonetheless structures a number of possibilities for the boy's subjectivity.

Most obvious, perhaps, the boy's position as a slave is a mode of being that is continually underscored through the act of questioning. The boy is very much unlike the interlocutors that people Plato's dialogues, such as Meno himself, and Socrates addresses the boy *solely* through the medium of the question. This sets up a set of discursive rules where the slave is only to speak when asked: the questions are crafted in such a way as to limit the opportunities for further engagement (e.g., "does it not?," "consider it this way," as opposed to "what do you think?" or "why might this be the case?"). The slave boy comes into being *through* the question: the boy's performance as a slave is the complement to the teacher's performance as questioner.[14]

Just as important, for the purposes of exploring the process of learning to become, the boy learns to recognize himself as a learner. Moving from the fall into perplexity into the realm of certitude, he becomes a subject of pedagogy, a subject that has learned to become a subject of learning. Under the tyranny of the question, the relation between what he knows about geometry and what he knows about himself is regulated. Yet by proclaiming the question to be innocent, Socrates obscures the fundamental structures of alteration and asymmetry that are present between teacher and student. These are the very structures necessary for the boy to assume his position as a learner.[15]

Meno's learning, while following a similar path—naive certainty, acknowledged ignorance, and certainty in knowledge recollected—is, however, significantly different in one respect: it comes about from the supposed *witnessing* of the questioning. Functioning as proof, as evidence of learning as recollection, the encounter presumably speaks for itself. However, throughout the encounter, Socrates interrupts himself and offers Meno a language for interpreting what he is seeing. Just as these asides to Meno function to objectify the slave, they also function to make Meno a subject of pedagogy and convert him to Socrates' view. Here we see the art of teaching as persuasion. The lesson with the slave boy cannot—and will not—speak for itself but requires the intervention of the teacher to disrupt its discourse. To learn from the lesson that learning cannot be taught requires Socrates to *teach*, to *tell* Meno that learning cannot be taught. Plato's figure of the teacher as nonteacher is indeed ironic! The object lesson Socrates devises suffers under the weight of its own intentionality to instruct: a naked didacticism and demand for alteration are revealed under the guise of the question. Thus, what I am suggesting here is that while these two pedagogical experiences are carried out differently, there is a violence located in both of them insofar as they force each student to become a subject of pedagogy through the demands of becoming a learner.

THE HOPE OF NONVIOLENCE

To say that violence occurs despite the teacher's intentions, despite whether or not one acts as facilitator or with extreme didacticism, seems to leave one with little hope. Learning to become occurs within a teacher-student relation, where the struggle to symbolize and make meaning takes place within complicated dynamics of communication. However, what I wish to suggest here is that it is also precisely in our relationality with others where hope is to be found. Consider, for instance, the following example written by a student teacher reflecting upon an experience in a first-grade class.

> At the beginning of the morning children change their outside shoes to inside shoes, take off jackets and place them along with their knapsacks on coat hooks in the classroom cupboard. At 8:50 A.M. students are sitting on the carpeted area of the classroom and stand for *O Canada* that is announced over the P.A. system. The students have been instructed not to move or talk. I hear crying from a girl that is standing at the back of the room. The host teacher ignores the crying and continues to sing *O Canada* with the rest of the class. I walk directly to the girl that is crying. I ask the girl if she is hurt. She says "no." I then ask the girl why she

is crying. She says, "I could not go to the washroom because we can't move during *O Canada*." I notice her legs are rubbing against each other. I whisper in the girl's ear if she is wet. The student says "yes." She cries louder. The host teacher continues to stand and looks away from me as I look at him. I take the girl and we walk outside the class toward the health room. (student essay, December 1998)

Explored from Castoriadis's point of view, the girl portrayed here has learned to become a student who obeys the rules and procedures around a particular activity. Part of what is demanded is that the student control, however unsuccessfully in the final analysis, her own desires and needs in the service of performing a social ritual, the singing of the national anthem. In her own words, what she has learned is "I could not go to the washroom because we can't move during *O Canada*." The ego here understands the limitations and restrictions placed upon it by an external force: the school routine, the teacher's rules. She symbolizes that relationship in a particular way, associating the singing of the anthem with bodily stillness and control. Such symbolization displays a mode of understanding that incorporates the coercive impulse of education, where subjectivity is forged within the demands placed upon it, and, as Klein writes, such symbolism "is the basis of the subject's relation to the outside world and to reality in general."[16] The turn to language to explain her subjection simultaneously signals her entry into subjecthood.[17]

In retelling the incident, it is also evident that the student teacher is struggling to symbolize her relationship to the girl, to the host teacher, and to herself. By writing her scenario in the present rather than past tense, she is doing more than merely describing *un temp perdu;* instead, her retelling suggests an ongoing engagement with a past that continues to haunt her present. That is, the incident is not simply an event that has passed without comment, like so many others that occur throughout her day, but participates in her negotiations of what it means to be a student and a teacher. Does becoming a teacher necessarily mean learning to make certain concessions to rules and routines that might be hurtful, at times, to students in the class? A mature and thoughtful woman, she, too, is subject to an event that has challenged her sensibilities, that is demanding of her to participate in something—and become someone—to which she is utterly resistant and from which she attempts to distinguish herself. The scene captures a certain understanding of the culture of schooling, and it is the student teacher's continual resistance to rules at the expense of human relationships that marks her (ambivalent) entry into this culture. The witnessing of the event provokes a crisis to which she responds by retelling it as a story where she is not like the host teacher: she approaches the girl who is in tears and thereby disobeys the established rules and routines. In her resistance, and in her attempt to work through the crisis this incident has provoked for her, she in effect splits teacher as an institutional figure from teacher as a compassionate person. However, what is of particular significance for my purposes here is not an interpretation of the content of her retelling (e.g., the splitting, the distancing from the teacher), but how the act of retelling attempts to capture her experience of learning as a form of coercion. That is, learning to be a teacher at this point is akin to learning to act like a teacher and, as this incident revealed to her, such learning is placing certain (undesirable) demands on who she is.

Thus the coercive force of education is here doubled: in seeking to articulate a position for herself that can only be caught within the tensions of being part teacher/part student, the student teacher offers a narrative that both reveals the violence of learning to become a teacher and the violence of learning to become a student. The retelling, as a form of symbolization, suggests, like the girl's own symbolic articulations, that learning to become (and the future toward which it beckons) can be fraught with anguish and traumatic awareness.

There is, however, another moment present whereby the girl's learning to become a student and the student's learning to become a teacher are disrupted by another event: their relationship to each other. In this instance, there is another mode of relationality in evidence. The interaction between the girl and the student teacher inserts another possibility in the girl's understanding of herself in relation to the anthem and makes it possible for her to imagine that there are other forms of social relation available to her. Similarly, the reaching out of the student teacher to inquire into the young girl's situation suggests a capacity for a relationality not premised on control or coercion. There opens up the potential for a nonviolent relationship, a relationship that is not based on denying or repudiating the student's needs (bodily needs, in this case), but is rooted in a response that is quite particular to the situation at hand.

In working with the idea that pedagogy is a process of learning to become that involves violence, I wish to consider below the ways nonviolence might also be evident in pedagogical interactions more generally. More to the point, I ask what are the conditions for ethicality, even in the face of such ontological violence?

LEARNING TO BECOME AND THE QUESTION OF ETHICS

As both the above examples imply, the idea that pedagogy is about the demand for learning to become crystallizes both the dream and the nightmare of education itself. On the one hand, it touches on the hope that people can think differently, can change the way they relate to one another, and can form new understandings of themselves and the world that make possible the very act of teaching and learning. As Britzman writes of education, "it demands of students and teachers that each come to something, make something more of themselves."[18] There is an implicit rising to the occasion, as it were, a demand for a certain kind of being in the classroom. On the other hand, the demand for learning to become carries with it a great burden, for if pedagogy is about the becoming of the subject, then it can become a tool for the most oppressive ends. Questions of a normative nature inevitably arise: Who is it that we, as educators and citizens, desire people to become?

Indeed, philosophically speaking, exploring the place of ethics in education often begins from this normative point of departure: What values are to be invoked in educational encounters? How might students be educated to become better citizens, more responsible moral subjects, or people who can live and work better across social differences? Roger Simon notes that pedagogy is not just about the teaching of morals, but is itself a "moral vision."[19] Normative questions are often central in helping to define and reflect upon an educational project.

However, posing normative questions has the tendency to make ethics programmatic in its orientation to education: a set of duties or obligations that if well enough defined and well enough followed will produce the ethical behavior desired. Bauman remarks of men and women living in a postmodern world, "we look in vain for the firm and trusty rules which may reassure us that once we followed them, we could be sure to be in the right."[20] Education is seen as a fulfillment or failure of prior principles of goodness and rightness—prior, that is, to the actual face-to-face encounters between teachers and students. In such an understanding, ethics comes to education from the outside. It asks education, often through appeals to empathy, or reason, or politics, or moral imperative, to become a better practice, to think about how it imagines its ideals; it also asks education to consider what students have to learn and how teachers and students need to act in order to ensure the realization of such ideals. What it often forgets is the uncertainty and unpredictability of the pedagogical encounter itself.

But what if one begins from a slightly different place? What if one begins with the "messy and ambiguous" nature of human reality?[21] What if one reflects upon the failure and uncertainty of the demand for learning to become? As Adam Phillips suggests, "people can never know beforehand, neither can their teachers, exactly what is of personal significance"; students insofar as they have unconscious desires "choose their own teachers . . . [an individual] picks out and transforms the bits [s]he wants, the bits that can be used in the hidden projects of unconscious desire."[22] Thus at the same time pedagogy demands that its subjects "learn to become," in practice, there is a great deal of uncertainty and unpredictability to the pedagogical enterprise. People bring a host of idiosyncrasies and unconscious associations that enable them to resist, transform, and create symbolic attachments that pedagogy cannot predict or control. Could the host teacher, in the above example, predict that the girl would so rigidly attach to the idea of bodily immobility that she would forfeit her own bodily needs? It may not be surprising, but is it a sure thing?

Instead of asking what education ought to be, what if educators ask what makes ethics possible in education in the first place, particularly in light of the latter's uncertainty and its ontological entanglements with learning to become? What makes education receptive, perhaps even vulnerable, to ethicality? Taking my cue from Levinas, who holds that ethics consists in the nonviolent relationship to the Other, in the particular relation the self has to another person, I look at the specificity of relationships within the pedagogical encounter as possibilities for ethics.[23]

Shifting the focus from education as a scene where one ought to apply this or that principle to a scene where the conditions or contingencies of ethicality may be found means no longer simply thinking *about* education in relation to ethics; rather, it means thinking about ethics *through* education. This means exploring the day-to-day details of pedagogical encounters to see what they might offer in putting forth an understanding of education as a site of *implied*, rather than *applied*, ethics. To explore this idea of an implied ethics more fully necessitates reading teaching-learning encounters for the way they promote conditions for ethicality as they promote conditions for being, both of which involve relationships between self and Other.

TEACHING AS "BRINGING MORE THAN I CONTAIN" AND LEARNING AS RECEIVING

Levinas is helpful in fleshing out pedagogical encounters, for he centers otherness at the very heart of teaching and learning. But what he means by otherness is important to highlight here, for it does not simply mean a sociological "Other" who is marginalized or maligned, nor does it simply signify another person who, as a subject, resembles myself. Simply put, for Levinas "the Other is what I myself am not."[24] In Levinas's view, self and Other exist as radically distinct beings; the Other is not "like me," nor am I "like the Other."[25] Moreover, whatever psychical bridges a self does make with the Other, such as identification or empathy, merely serve to underscore the chasm that in fact separates the two. What is important for my purposes here is that it is in the very break between self and Other where Levinas locates both the conditions for ethics and the possibility for teaching and learning. Like Castoriadis in this regard, it is that which is outside the subject that provokes learning and alteration: the Other ruptures a sense of unified being.

Levinas suggests that teaching is about staging an encounter with the Other, with something outside the self, whereas learning is to receive from the Other more than the self already holds.

> It is . . . to *receive* from the Other beyond the capacity of the I, which means exactly: to have the idea of infinity. But this also means: to be taught. The relation with the Other, or Conversation, is . . . an ethical

relation; but inasmuch as it is welcomed this conversation is a teaching *[enseignement]*. Teaching is not reducible to maieutics; it comes from the exterior and brings me more than I contain.[26]

Note here how teaching and learning are conceived as an ethical relation, not because of some prescriptive injunction, but because there are present two distinct beings who come face to face in an encounter. For Levinas, teaching and learning, like ethics, lie in the "insurmountability of the duality of beings."[27] The Other signifies a limitless possibility for the self, and it is by coming face to face with such limitlessness that the self can exceed its own containment, its own self-identity, breaking the solitude of being for the self. In this view, teaching is only possible if the self is open to the Other, to the face of the Other. Through such openness to what is exterior to the I, the I can become something different than, or beyond, what it was; in short, it can learn.[28]

This view of teaching as "bringing more than I contain" is antithetical to the Socratic method that so predominates dialogical approaches to educational practice, where teaching is viewed as "bringing out of the I that which it already contains." The latter is, of course, more familiar: a pedagogy of recollection and self-knowledge, where the teacher as midwife facilitates the birth of students' knowledge. As discussed previously, in the Socratic view, learning supposedly happens almost in spite of the teacher. It is the skill of the teacher to elicit that which is already inside the subject, not the social encounter per se that matters. The maieutic method erases the significance of the Other and claims that learning is a recovery contained within the I, rather than a disruption of the I provoked by the Other in a moment of sociality. Levinas writes, "This primacy of the same was Socrates's teaching: to receive nothing of the Other but what is in me, as though from all eternity I was in possession of what comes to me from the outside. . . ."[29] However, as we have seen, this is also a fiction in terms of how the question itself comes from outside the subject via the Other.

In contrast, what is important to Levinas's view is that it is sociality—the encounter with the Other who is radically distinct from the self—that enables the self to learn and to change. By recentering the importance of teaching, Levinas compels educators to think about their responsibility in terms of this otherness, something that the Socratic view, because of its emphasis on what is self-same, cannot. By posing otherness as a condition of learning, Levinas's view underscores the point that teaching cannot abandon its ethical significance or run away from the possible consequences it generates.

Pedagogy seesaws between the "bringing more than I contain" that teaching aspires to and the "receiving beyond the capacity of the I" that learning strives to achieve. Within this movement, of course, there are many surprises and shifts, and the roles marked out for teachers and students are not so rigid as perhaps they first appear. Heuristically, Levinas's focus on the centrality of otherness to teaching, learning, and ethics lends insight into the demand for alteration that pedagogy makes, and it enables teachers to begin to consider what responsibilities they have toward those they teach. This is not to suggest that students do not have responsibilities themselves; their capacity to receive and to be open to difference is certainly an ethical response, according to Levinas. But the question that remains for educators is how, in the face of the violence that is implicit in the pedagogical demand for learning to become, might we be open and responsible to the Other?

Here is the crux of the tension. The subject can only become an ego if it is forced to repress or sublimate certain wishes and drives in the service of sociality, yet it must also be open, or receptive, to what is outside itself in order for this to occur. Teachers, as the vehicles through which the pedagogical demand for learning to become is made real for students, cannot escape their role—they require students to make symbolic attachments and meaning out of the curriculum they present, and in doing so they cannot escape a certain degree of coercion. It is not simply by repressing this coercion, by convincing ourselves that education is otherwise, that those of us committed to the project of education will arrive at ethical solutions that avoid this coercion. In fact, taking refuge in education's innocence denies the possibility of asking ourselves ethical questions, for it is precisely because violence is inherent to learning to become and because teachers and students are continually vulnerable to each other in the face of this violence that the question of nonviolence can even be raised. As Levinas himself writes, it is the potential to do violence that suggests its own reversal: "The face is exposed, menaced, as if inviting us to an act of violence. At the same time, the face is what forbids us to kill."[30] Or, elsewhere: "Only beings capable of war can rise to peace."[31]

For teachers, perhaps participating in a nonviolent relation to the Other means having to become a learner oneself, opening up oneself to the rupture of being that the face-to-face encounter entails. "The face is a living presence; it is expression. . . . The face speaks. The manifestation of the face is already discourse."[32] That is, ethical relations may rest in the teacher's own capacity to be receptive to the discourse of the face, to hear and listen for the meanings that students work out for themselves. Recall in the example above how the teacher could not face the girl or the student teacher; one can never know what motivated this turn away from the face but can simply note that in turning away, the teacher could not receive the girl's vulnerability, or be open to the meaning she construed between her body and the anthem, and thus foreclosed on the opportunity for response.

Thus far, what is at stake here for teachers are two layers of interaction. On the one hand, there is the demand for learning to become, where teachers have a social obligation to offer students opportunities for encountering difference—to bring more than the I contains. As has been discussed, however, the meanings students make are not cast beforehand, nor can teachers assume that fulfilling their obligations is not harmful. On the other hand, there can be a receptivity to what is unpredictably returned to the teacher: the meanings that students make and the vulnerabilities that accompany them. What I am suggesting here is that if educators demand that students make relationships to curriculum, and if these relationships are always uncertain and open to failure, then the place of ethicality in education lies in the failure of the demand for learning, what Britzman refers to as "social, ontological, and epistemological breakdown."[33] It is here, in the moments where students struggle for meaning, struggle to make sense out of and symbolize their relationship to curriculum, where teachers are called upon to be receptive, where a nonviolent element to the teaching-learning relationship may be allowed to enter.

Klein's 1930 case study, "On the Importance of Symbol Formation in the Development of the Ego," outlines what this failure looks like and the impact it has on the ego development of a four-year-old autistic boy, Dick.[34] Klein has much to teach her readers about her role as a pedagogue, insofar as it is her function as a psychoanalyst to help the child make meaning and symbolize his world. At the same time, Klein also offers her audience a window through which to see how this harsh process is also inflected with an openness and receptivity to the vicissitudes of Dick's vulnerabilities. As well, the case study highlights the work in which Klein and Dick are engaged when the demand for learning to become is front and center. The study also gives educators reason to pause, for in asking students to alter themselves, do teachers instigate a replaying of the students' earlier struggles with ego formation outlined by Klein?

LEARNING FROM KLEIN AND DICK

Klein's case study is a foray into how the subject learns to become an ego. The journey she embarks on is quite compelling, for Klein depicts not only the difficulties, trials, and anxieties that face Dick, but she reveals something of her own role in inducing these difficulties and her attempts at allaying them. For these reasons, looking in detail at Dick's ego development may help educators understand some of the structures that emerge within the educational setting itself. Klein notes three movements in becoming an ego: initial nonresponsiveness; induced anxiety; and finally, the turn to symbolization in order to tolerate this anxiety.

Klein describes Dick as a four-year-old boy who functions, in terms of vocabulary and emotional relations to his surroundings, at the level of a fifteen-month-old child. He fails to communicate any feeling and is now thought to have been an autistic child at the time of his analysis. Klein offers an account of how the ego comes into being for Dick through his ability to form symbols and make meaning. During his first session with Klein, Dick refrains from all outward emotional activity, be it hiding, shying away, crying, or playing. He runs around Klein as "if I were a piece of furniture" (222). Klein concludes her initial portrait of Dick with the claim that "Dick's behaviour had no meaning or purpose, nor was any affect or anxiety associated with it . . .

[his] ego had ceased to develop phantasy-life and to establish a relation with reality" (222, 224). She regards him as being absolutely incapable of aggression, and he refuses to chew up his own food, seemingly unwilling to allow even this little aggression into his life. Although she continually reminds the reader throughout the narrative that the child was affectless and disinterested, she nevertheless also notes his interest "in trains and stations and also in doorhandles, doors and the opening and shutting of them" (224), a point to which I shall return below.

Because of Dick's incapacity to symbolize his fantasies through play, Klein notes that she has to shift her technique.[35] Instead of focusing on what the child acts out through his play, Klein must find a means of provoking play and thus symbolization and fantasy. "His lack of interest in his environment ... [was] only the effect of his lack of a symbolic relation to things. The analysis, then, had to begin with this, the *fundamental* obstacle to establishing contact with him" (225, emphasis in original). Her analysis becomes focused on disrupting Dick's enclosed sense of self, and she begins a strategy that, to put it in Levinasian terms, brings him more than his I can contain, or, as Klein would put it, induces anxiety. This marks the second phase of Dick's learning to become. The demand is the familiar pedagogical one, tinged with coercion: to provoke the child into making meaning.

Klein takes the rather brazen step of placing two trains on a table before Dick, stating that the big train is "Daddy train," the little one "Dick train." This move acts as more than a provocation, appearing invasive and coercive, perhaps even "brutal," as Lacan would suggest. To quote from Klein: "Thereupon he picked up the train I called 'Dick' and made it roll to the window and said 'station.' I explained: 'The station is mummy; Dick is going into mummy'" (225). Dick then runs into the dark hallway between the entryway doors of the room and says the word "dark." After repeating this several times, Klein reports:

> I explained to him: "It is dark inside mummy. Dick is inside dark mummy." Meantime he picked up the train again, but soon ran back into the space between the doors. While I was saying he was going into dark mummy, he said twice in a questioning way: "Nurse?" I answered: "Nurse is soon coming," and this he repeated and used the words later quite correctly, retaining them in his mind. (225)

However, it is in the third analytic visit where Dick begins to make a sustained symbolic relation, marking the third phase in learning to become. Instead of running between the doors after picking up the train, Dick hides behind a piece of furniture and becomes seized with anxiety. It is at this point that he, for the first time, calls out for Klein to come to him.

This is the turning point in the analysis, the moment when Dick begins to formulate a relation to the outside world, occasioned, according to Klein, by his intense anxiety. This then leads Dick to an increased vocabulary and a heightened sense of emotional investment in Klein and his nurse. Indeed, Dick begins to play, begins the work of symbolization. The work of making meaning through play is a strategy that allows Dick to tolerate his anxiety. The ego work that he is engaged in brings with it the pain of having to accept difference, to receive that which Klein has to offer him, which is always already outside himself. As Levinas might say, Klein has ruptured Dick's own containment. Now, in a face-to-face relation with difference, Dick struggles to overcome (what Klein would call a "working over") the profound vulnerability aroused by his anxious state.

The analysis continues, and Dick begins to act out his fantasies with regard to his parents. As Jacobus notes in her close reading of the case study, at each turn Klein, with "characteristic literalness," gives him "signs in exchange for toys."[36] Klein retells Dick what he is doing, interpreting his play as he performs it, rather than waiting for patterns of repetition to emerge in the play itself. This is how she describes the modification of her technique:

> In general I do not interpret the material until it has found expression in various representations. In this case, however, where the capacity to represent it was almost entirely lacking, I found myself obliged to make my interpretations on the basis of my general knowledge.... I succeeded in activating anxiety and other affects. The representations then became fuller and I soon acquired a more solid foundation for the analysis, and so was able gradually to pass over to the technique that I generally employ in analysing little children. (228–229)

Her technique centers on giving to Dick words that activate anxiety and affect. Klein believes that it is only through such crises that Dick can begin the process of becoming. But she also gives him something more. She introduces him to significations that come from the Other and therefore places him in a potential social relation—and an ethical one. Dick, through his receiving "beyond the capacity of the I," beyond what he is at present, begins to make a relation with his own unconscious desires and conflicts; at the same time, he makes a relation to the otherness that is Klein.

This is crucial, for not only does Dick establish a relation to the outside world via a relation to the Other that is Klein, but he also must establish a relation to the otherness of the unconscious. What Klein demonstrates here is that the latter relation cannot take place prior to the former. It is through the Other that is Klein, through the social relation, that Dick's own relationship with himself is provoked. This suggests to me that it is not only Klein's words that are important but the very presence of two beings that conditions Dick's receptivity of words.

But what does this suggest about Klein's role as a pedagogue? What can educators learn from her? One certainly can see the ruthlessness of her invasive strategy. At least in her recounting of the analysis, Dick is pushed continually toward making a relationship to the words she offers, anxieties are incited, and she fosters sublimation through her abnormally persistent interpretations of his fantasies. These are the key ingredients in Dick's developing symbolic relationships to his surroundings. Learning to become is indeed presented as a violent process, where Dick not only struggles to enter into a social relation with the Other but does so with profound affective difficulties, evident in his calling out to Klein in utter despair. But even in this case, where the violence of pedagogy, of learning to become, is so transparent, there is nonetheless evident a mode of interaction that swims against the current of Klein's seeming invasiveness, and it concerns Dick's initial interest in trains, doors, and handles.

There is no question that Klein brings Dick more than he contains, that she "teaches" him; she infuses the trains and doors with a signification that is truly "outside" what Dick is capable of articulating on his own. As Jacobus writes, "This all-too-literal naming is the glue that makes language 'stick' to the trains, door handles, and *dark* of little Dick's imaginary. Klein's words 'graft' the Oedipus complex onto little Dick's arrested symbol-making capacity."[37] However, the "grafting" only takes root because it already builds on a nascent interest. Dick has some—albeit tentative—capacity to begin the work of semiosis through his interest in trains, doors, and handles in the first place. What is of particular note to education is that in some measure Klein has been receptive to this interest and uses it in order to create a logic or structure for Dick's fantasies to take hold. Moreover, she alters her own technique, her own mode of symbolization, in order to do so. She gives Dick a social relation with difference, a signifying structure, to which he attaches his fantasy life and works through his anxiety.

In some ways, then, Klein is receptive to the otherness Dick returns to her.[38] She is open to working with the defenses Dick presents, and while we might say she errs on the side of giving Dick too much to handle (pun intended), of creating excessive anxiety, what Klein is also able to recognize is that it is Dick who has made meaning with the tools and structures she has offered him. Thus it is in Dick's failures to become, his hesitations, anxieties, indifferences, and *non sequiturs,* where Klein's openness reveals itself. As a psychoanalyst, she knows that Dick must learn to tolerate his own anxiety through symbolic attachments, but she also knows that she has a role to play in bringing him more than he can contain, and perhaps more than he can bear to know. Hers is not a maieutic method, where she is but eliciting that which Dick already knows, but a pedagogy of provocation and disruption that responds to the specificity of Dick's interests and needs. She listens for possibilities of slippage in meaning, in the breakdown of communication, in the glances he gives her, and in the associations of word and action made through play, and she returns them to Dick, returns them through the discourse of the Other. I want to return to a claim made earlier, that it is not the words themselves that provoke Dick's anxiety and subsequent symbol formation but the fact that they come via the Other, via the presence that is Klein.

To recall Levinas: "The face speaks. The manifestation of the face is already discourse"; and "Discourse is ... the experience of something absolutely foreign ... a *traumatism of astonishment*. ... This absolutely foreign alone can instruct us."[39] It is just such a traumatism that Dick received and one that, in my view, our students may at times receive from us.

Klein's case study suggests to me that teachers, in trying to encourage students to engage in meaning-making activity, take a number of risks, the incitement of anxiety being a major one. What she helps educators understand, in my view, is the *delicacy* of engaging students in their interests, in offering them interpretations or theories of their experiences, in providing for them a structure through which they might think themselves in relation to the world. That is, even when teachers do offer interpretations and structures through texts, films, and the like, and even when they refrain from offering personal beliefs, curriculum nonetheless largely comes via the Other that is the teacher; it comes from that which is foreign, risking, to echo Levinas's words once again, a "traumatism of astonishment." This traumatism is not just about being "bowled over" or being in awe of something but about being traumatized, about risking the security of one's self-identity, about facing the possibility of becoming altered. It is thus precisely within this context of risk that the delicate nature of teaching arises. But what might attending to the delicacy involved in teaching look like?

Klein, one could argue, employed anything but a delicate touch, instead forcing upon Dick her own prescriptive interpretations in order to provide a structure for meaning to take hold. Yet as I have suggested, her interaction with Dick is not reducible to the words she says to him; she is also open and, therefore, subject to Dick's unique responses of fear and anxiety. She goes to him when he calls; she plays with him when he enters the analytic session; she responds to the looks he gives her; she talks to him when he is at play and, at times, she cuddles him when he is overwrought. What teachers might learn from Klein, and psychoanalysis more generally, is not a "laundry list" of behaviors replicating Klein's actions but a concern to be attentive to the range of possible responses students generate out of their own positions of vulnerability and to be sensitive to the profound singularity of the situation at hand. That is, the quality of one's response to another's particular vulnerable condition is central and not merely incidental to learning; this is particularly so since teachers, as the ones who "bring more than I contain," are implicated in this very vulnerability in the first place. Understanding teaching as a delicate engagement means that the emphasis is not on specific strategies or behaviors for "optimal" interaction (this would be not unlike an applied ethics with a set of rules to determine behavior) but on an attentiveness to the exposure and riskiness that students face in their everyday experiences of learning (an implied ethics where what is ethical about interaction is to be found within the pedagogical realm itself). Thus such an understanding means, on the one hand, accepting the fragility of students' identities as they seek to develop meaning for themselves with ofttimes heightened emotional intensity (e.g., the beginning teacher who is genuinely fearful of the students she is about to teach; the young child who anxiously awaits the teacher's approval for getting the right math answer; the graduate student who falls thoroughly in love with an idea). On the other hand, such an understanding also requires acknowledging that one's teaching, as a relation to otherness, is precisely what provokes (but does not determine) such fragility and intensity to begin with. The delicacy of teaching, then, with its emphasis on responding to the unique Other, is at once a curricular and an ethical matter.

PEDAGOGY, CURRICULUM, AND ETHICAL POSSIBILITIES

Where does this leave educators in contemplating the possibility for ethics in education? Where might this lead in terms of thinking about the nature and place of curriculum, particularly within social justice education?

Earlier I explored what an "implied ethics" might mean for education, that is, looking to the particularities of the pedagogical encounter, the relationships between teachers and students, between Klein and Dick, to see what might be learned from them regarding the ethical significance of education. As discussed, even within a pedagogy that is structured by a demand for learning to become, a learning that, often under the rubric of "socialization," is not so innocent or painless as educators would perhaps like to believe, there is nonetheless a place for ethical encounters. There are two pedagogical contingencies that lend ethical significance to an implied ethics for education.

First, there is the uncertainty of the pedagogical encounter itself, where the meanings students create for themselves cannot be foreseen, where learning to become is not a seamless project of success. As Klein's case study demonstrates, the miscues, associations, and interests found in Dick's play, and his failures to become an ego, compel her attention and responsiveness and lead to a change in technique. This attentiveness to unforeseeable detail and meaning also holds for the educational realm. It is from an "initial position of uncertainty," as Lynda Stone suggests, that "openness, humility and trust" become possible.[40] As teachers and students, we tentatively come together in anticipation of an encounter of which we cannot predict the outcome; the exchanged looks, the tones of voice, the artifacts of curriculum, the passion of opinion, the indifference to a question, the time and space to be negotiated, the desire for love and recognition, all of this and more comprise the tiny yet colossal details that shape and shake the ground upon which educational edifices are built. Thus such uncertainty in our interactions carries serious ethical weight, for if such uncertainty is inevitable, then the quality of response to the Other is rooted in shifting social relations rather than in solely abstract adherence to ethical rules or principles. Moreover, in terms of an implied ethics, such uncertainty compels educators to develop thoughtful approaches to the Other rather than to carry out a set of predetermined behaviors that tell teachers "this is what you should do." While some guidelines are unavoidable (and legally necessary), mere rules alone do not ensure ethical, nonviolent interactions.

Yet a second contingent feature of implied ethics is the relation the self has to the Other, which signals the importance of sociality and ethicality to education and also highlights that it is through this sociality that a different relationship with one's self may be established. Words, information, and teaching are not disembodied within the pedagogical encounter but are made available through the Other; as such, the encounter speaks to the necessarily social aspect of teaching and learning. As I have argued, it is the potentiality of this relationship to do violence that makes it susceptible to ethics right from the start. Moreover, as Dick's analysis revealed, the kind of provocation and disruption to self-identity that the Other brings to the I sets the conditions, in the form of anxiety or traumatism, for profound alteration of the ego; anxiety itself becomes an otherness to which the subject has to make a relationship. As a way of thinking about ethics through education, the self-Other relationship is crucial in understanding how profoundly teachers can be implicated in the lives of their students—often unwittingly, of course—and it enables teachers to reflect on how their everyday responses are always already ethically laden.

What I have been outlining here is, of course, a critique of the Socratic model in education, whereby learning is rendered through a process of dialogue and questioning. This midwife model is often a cornerstone both for progressive and critical approaches to education: the teacher is merely there to guide students to discover knowledge for themselves. This appears to be a model of limited pedagogical intervention, beginning from students' own interests and building from there. But as we have seen, what is omitted from this account of midwifery or facilitation is how the questions always come via the Other, via an Other that is not reducible to the self. That is, the epistemological emphasis on self-knowledge blankets over the dialogical relation as a social and an ethical relation between two nonsynchronous subjects. Dialogical exchange is not seen to be about confronting otherness but about eliciting the implicit knowledge the student already has. Learning thus neither dislocates nor interrupts; it merely gives definition to what is already there.

Instead, what I am suggesting here is that learning is accompanied by a receptivity to the Other, by a receptivity to the difference that is returned to the learner through the practice of teaching. As Felman's commentary on Lacan indicates: "Coming from the Other, knowledge is, by definition, that which comes as a surprise."[41] In this way, learning occasions states of affect that are disturbing and, perhaps, painful, making teachers and students incredibly vulnerable to one another. Thus being open or receptive to an other suggests a mode of relationality that may be very difficult to sustain. My own position, however, is that responsiveness to the Other can counter the harm wrought by pedagogy's own demands for alteration. Perhaps receptivity and total nonviolence are not humanly or psychologically always possible—after all, teachers have defenses too—but if educators are going to live well in the uncertainty of their classrooms and interact in less harmful ways that respect the otherness of the Other, then are they not compelled by virtue of their roles as teachers who do "bring more than I contain," who do provoke and disrupt the security of students' selves, to be responsible, to be responsive? As stated above, such receptivity does not only concern the Other but affects one's relationship to one's self. In this regard, then, part of the ethical relation involves an openness to considering one's own anxieties and defenses and how they appear in the self-Other relation.

At the risk of losing sight of the place of curriculum in pedagogical encounters, particularly since the content of curriculum is such a struggled-over terrain in social justice education, what is recentered in this discussion is the place of teaching and its ethical significance. Indeed, I have implied that it is important to think curriculum through teaching, just as I have been thinking ethics through education. Curriculum, in this view, is neither only a cultural or political instrument divorced from the concrete practices of teaching, nor is it a solipsistic rendering of personal or autobiographical knowledge. Instead, curriculum passes through the very sociality of self and Other, replete with uncertainties and diverse contexts. Moreover, it is precisely because it passes through this social relation that curriculum can become a tool for the most oppressive ends, in spite of best intentions. That is, it is not only the "content" of curriculum that matters but the articulatory practices through which difference is symbolized, as I have discussed at length elsewhere.[42] From the perspective of the learner, curriculum comes via the Other that is the teacher in the form of new ideas, concepts, and texts; yet the meaning he or she makes out of such material can never be secured beforehand. As a feature of such self-Other interaction, curriculum lends substance to the process of learning to become: it is the symbolic raw material that students use, discard, or rewrite in making meaning for themselves. Curriculum is thus fundamental to the symbolic elaboration necessary to ego formation.

Yet in thinking curriculum through teaching, curriculum also participates in the pedagogical contingencies for ethicality already outlined: in both the uncertainty of meaning and the self-Other relation. With regard to the latter, curriculum cannot appear as a mirror in which students simply see themselves reflected. This would, in effect, serve to erase otherness, each self looking only for its own reflection, reading texts, and listening to people to see how they are "just like me." On the surface, this view of curriculum I am elaborating seems to fly in the face of calls for a more inclusive curriculum, where social justice is premised on just such a capacity to see the commonalities between people, or when underrepresented and misrepresented groups seek to include curricular materials that more adequately reflect their reality and with which they can identify. However, I wish to maintain that even in the face of such necessities in combating social inequities, one needs to be vigilant about what such curricular moves may be assuming. For instance, mirroring-type responses may in fact collapse difference within and between communities. It is not that identifications are not necessary or of no value to questions of community building and for disrupting systems of discrimination, but with regard to education, they alone cannot provide the conditions for ethics, that is, for a nonviolent relationship to the Other where the otherness of the Other is left intact and unharmed. Instead, seeing curriculum as part of a much broader practice of social (and ethical) interaction suggests that focusing on more inclusive representation for the purposes of identification is not sufficient—and not only because such meaning making may go off in unpredictable directions. The implication here is that curriculum needs to be more thoroughly considered as part of the quality of human response between teachers and students, as part of the delicacy of engaging students, rather than as a fixed set of representations.

In terms of the pedagogical contingency of uncertainty, curriculum itself is unstable, for it continually exceeds the bounds of its "content" in terms of textbooks, films, or literature. Instead, understanding that it partakes in a subject's idiosyncratic capacity to symbolize, in a subject's unconscious proclivity to make meaning, curriculum can include a wide range of objects, thoughts, expressions, and affects. Phillips writes:

> From a psychoanalytic point of view, I have my conscious preoccupations and ambitions, and these make me more or less educable. But I also have my unconscious desire and affinities—tropisms and drifts of attention—that can be quite at odds with my conscious ideals. I may go to a lecture on psychology and be fascinated; but I may dream that night about the ear-rings of the woman sitting next to me; which, if I were to associate to this detail in the dream might, like Proust's legendary madeleine, open up vistas of previously unacknowledged personal history.[43]

Thus on another level, curriculum comes from outside the subject but not necessarily via the Other that is the teacher; rather, it also comes via the otherness of the self, the unconscious. The play of uncertainty does not merely lie within the teacher-student relation but within a different kind of relationship to the unconscious, as the preceding discussion on Klein and Dick has revealed. What is significant for curriculum here is how it at once participates in ego formation as well as in the subject's creative capacity for unconscious representation. Curriculum gives form and substance to the delicate relations that mark the process of learning to become.

When reflecting upon the conditions of violence and nonviolence that are present in the pedagogical encounter, the question of what constitutes the possibilities of response may seem easy to ask but far more difficult to answer. Unfortunately, the trauma of wetting oneself in front of the class, or of witnessing such an event, is neither extraordinary nor rare. Yet it does seem to call out for a responsiveness that is at minimum both sensitive and mindful of otherness. Similarly, using texts such as Wiesenthal's with the aim of discussing difficult social justice issues incurs an obligation to be sensitive to the many ways students respond to difference. In exploring here some of the assumptions guiding our teaching practices and in asking educators to consider the uncertainty of meaning and the vulnerabilities that are often displayed in the classroom, I am well aware that teachers and learners are already stretched to capacity in the hectic day to dayness of what it means to teach and to learn. However, if teaching is not going to abandon the ethical significance of its role in "bringing more than I contain," then perhaps the work of an implied ethics resides in teachers being able to live both within and beyond their means, both within and beyond their capacities, simultaneously.

TWO

BEING-FOR OR FEELING-FOR? EMPATHIC DEMANDS AND DISRUPTIONS

EMPATHY IS OFTEN INVOKED in social justice educational discourse and practice as an indispensable emotion for working across differences. As Megan Boler writes: "in the last fifteen years in Western 'multiculturalism,' empathy is promoted as a bridge between differences, the affective reason for engaging in democratic dialogue with the other."[1] The idea is that the more we feel with an other, the better we are able to have a sense of what matters to her and, consequently, come to understand and engage with her better. This indeed is the explicit moral emphasis granted to empathy in social justice education: that empathy leads to a better kind of responsivity and, by extension, responsibility. Within the discourse of ethics, empathy has been identified as having significance for moral sensibility, lending philosophical support to those educational practices. In Kantian terms, for instance, empathy (or fellow-feeling) is understood to be an aid to, if not a sufficient condition for, moral sensibility;[2] in terms of an ethic of care, empathy is seen to be, along with reciprocity and engrossment, one of the emotional qualities that allows for appropriate, caring attention to develop.[3]

Empathy, then, is not simply considered to be one affective response among many, but it is seen to have ethical legitimation in a way that other emotions, such as pity and guilt, do not usually enjoy. In fact, viewed as an explicitly moral emotion, empathy is the very form of attachment seen to be necessary for living responsibly together, and it is this emphasis on what empathy brings to our sense of togetherness that, to my mind, has made it so prevalent within educational projects committed to social justice. In seeking to make students aware of everyday occurrences of inequity and social violence, educators frequently rely on students' capacities for feeling that they can share in another's experience and come to understand better what the nature of that experience might be like.

Consider the following two examples. First, knowing my interest in these issues, an acquaintance once explained to me a classroom exercise in which one of her nieces was expected to participate. For one full day, this class of third graders (from a relatively affluent school in Toronto) was told to refrain from eating any food. The students were to return to school the next day and reflect on their experiences of hunger: what it felt like, how they managed. The apparent aim of the exercise was to encourage children to better understand what Third World hunger was like. Through experiencing and reflecting on their own hunger, presumably they would gain insight into what starving children[4]—whom they have never met or with whom they had never spoken—must be feeling. (It is probably safe to speculate that there was also an insistence to some extent on the degree to which their hunger was so much less dire than that of their Third World peers.)

Second, I asked a colleague who had been instrumental in developing curriculum on the Holocaust for high school students what she had hoped to achieve. Aside from the more obvious goal to promote historical knowledge in order to prevent such events from taking place again, she declared to me that one of her aims had been to "educate empathy" in the students. As I understood it at the time, this was rendered in terms of developing in the students a competence in feeling with others who suffered. Not that they would be asked to experience suffering themselves through some kind of simulation exercise,[5] but that through images, testimony, and texts, the students would be "encouraged" to emotionally attach and connect with the victims through empathic means. This type of connection, it was thought, would then presumably lead to an increased sense of responsibility for those who had suffered, even if they were not directly the cause of that suffering.[6]

While these anecdotes are by no means definitive in terms of the range of curricular and pedagogical demands for empathy, they nonetheless do represent a common tactic to produce a particular emotion within an overall strategy of social justice. That is, pedagogical practices through which empathy is demanded are indeed "tactical"; that is, they focus on the ways in which empathy can be deployed to challenge conventional knowledge and alter students' egos. As de Certeau defines it, a tactic is a "calculated action" that "boldly juxtaposes diverse elements in order suddenly to produce a flash shedding a different light on the language of a place and to strike the hearer."[7] Generally understood as an "art of the weak," that is, of those who do not have power, tactics would not seem at first to fit what it is that teachers do in the class, given their relative power position over students. Yet a tactic nonetheless speaks to the attempt to mobilize a particular affect, namely, empathy, in order to create new ways of being together, and this is done through "calculated actions" and exercises that ostensibly generate the possibility for empathy to emerge.

But the demand for empathy is not simply a demand for an emotion. It also presupposes a certain mode of relationality, a certain interrelationship with the other. To return to the examples above, each tactical demand invokes its own affective dynamics between self and other. In seeking to mobilize students to care for and about distant others, the first creates an experience of hunger that is an attempt to simulate analogous, if not exactly the same, conditions of suffering with those who are starving. The self is asked, as it were, to be in the place of the other. The second tactic brings students face to face with a "representation" (texts, images, live testimony) of one who has suffered, setting up an encounter whereby students are expected to identify by "taking in" the injustice and thereby sharing another's pain. The self here is asked to allow the other to occupy a place within. These two dynamics do not necessarily reflect what *actually* happens when students are subjected to these pedagogical initiatives; rather, these are the emotional and psychic expectations that lie behind them. And what underlies both of these expectations, in turn, is a privileging of a certain idea of togetherness. Each of these pedagogical tactics asserts its own image of what that togetherness should like, and how one ought to relate to the Other in creating that togetherness. It is not that all pedagogical encounters with the Other attempt to encourage empathy to produce forms of togetherness and connection (pedagogies that focus on remembrance are indeed critical of such moves[8]). It is, rather, the other way around: attempts to encourage empathy rely on particular configurations of otherness and togetherness. In short, the demand for empathy belies a larger demand for how we ought to be together.

This idea of being together, of course, is not only important with respect to the *demand* for empathy but also in our *actual feelings* of empathy. For teachers and students do *feel* empathy within pedagogical encounters, and empathic responses do happen, whether we are advocating for them or not. It is, thus, equally important to call attention to what kind of togetherness is being invoked in those feelings. There is, then, a twofold dimension to consider in discussing empathy in relation to ethics and education: empathy as demand and empathy as affective response. For the rest of the chapter I pose and respond to a number of questions with respect to the ethical character of empathy, both as an emotion and as a mode of relationality, on the one hand, and as it appears in the form of a demand, on the other hand. These questions and responses are less about providing a conceptual history of the term and more about exploring the quality of relationality to the Other that informs empathy. For instance, what forms of togetherness and otherness are at work in the demand for empathy and in empathy proper? When we empathize with others, do we engage each one through her difference, through her alterity, or is empathy always already about "overcoming" difference in the hope of finding some common ground? And finally, does empathy allow for learning from the Other as a condition for nonviolence?

TOGETHERNESS: FROM BEING-ASIDE TO BEING-WITH TO BEING-FOR

To think about the ways in which education both demands and embodies certain forms of togetherness (which do not necessarily coincide), it is helpful to consider Zygmunt Bauman's brief typology of forms of togetherness. He identifies six, each marked by distinct patterns of interaction.[9] There is a *mobile* togetherness, such as we find when we are on busy city streets; a *stationary* togetherness we experience when confined in a bus or an airplane with others; a *tempered* togetherness of a workplace, such as an office, which is purposeful and whose encounters are highly structured; a *manifest* togetherness one finds in a sports event or political demonstration where the togetherness *is* the event itself; a *postulated* togetherness that rallies us around signifiers such as nations, races, classes, genders, and so on; and a *meta* or *matrix* togetherness of a bar, party, or populated beach where we are together in ways that anticipate possible encounters.

Education does not easily fit into any single form of togetherness outlined here. One might say it is a stationary togetherness (where teachers and students are often confined within particular spaces for specified periods of time) as well as a tempered togetherness (where structured encounters are the norm, bounded by rules and regulations). Yet whatever form the togetherness might take (and there are a number of metaphors readers might wish to play with here), what is crucial to our understanding of how we are together in education are the modes through which our togetherness is enacted.

Despite their significant differences, Bauman claims that each of these forms of togetherness occurs in three different modalities. First, forms of togetherness are the settings in which people initially are "cast *aside* each other" (50). That is, they inhabit a shared space, yet they are not at the center of it; they have the modality of being-aside.[10] Being together in this sense means that we exist tangentially; each of us occupies space, but we do not interact in any significant way. This being-aside is notable in the ways that students and teachers inhabit classroom spaces, for instance; not all of our time is spent in mutual recognition. At the elementary and secondary levels, much time is spent at desks (or in other specified areas) where interaction is not only kept to a minimum but is strictly regulated. In post-secondary situations, students sit side by side with other students, sometimes listening, at other times daydreaming, and certainly not always interacting.

However, there is also the possibility for interaction while we are together. As soon as one enters an encounter with an other, one "moves into the modality of being-with" (50), the second modality of being together identified by Bauman. Being-with signals that one has relevance for another, but this, Bauman claims, is topical and transient: "No more of the self tends to be deployed in the encounter than the topic-at-hand demands; and no more of the other is highlighted than the topic-at-hand permits. Being-with is a meeting of incomplete beings, of deficient selves" (50). Being-with, therefore, is a mode of communication that is constrained by the parameters of time and place, whereby people may have interesting interactions but are not transformed in any way by them. As a consequence, aspects of the self are engaged in ways that are normative and safe. As Bauman states, such encounters are conventional: "Conventions substitute concern with the rule for the concern for the partner of encounter.... The rule-governed togetherness, the being-with exhausted in the observance of rules, is a colony of hermits, an archipelago of one-resident islands" (56). The risk of "losing oneself," so to speak, through interaction and conversation is simply not possible in the modality of being-with. Moreover, concern for the other fails to develop fully.

In education, teacher-student and student-student interactions are most commonly of this type. Classroom discussions, question-and-answer periods, exchanged whispers—all of these are forms of being-with that do not necessarily entail the type of communication that engages fully one's sensibilities as a subject. In this regard, students and teachers are present for one another in terms of their institutional roles; they exchange information, engage in dialogue about the class, and generally relate to each other by virtue of their positions as teachers and students. One is not expected to reveal personal details or deep emotional commitments in these encounters.

But these two modalities of being together are not what is usually sought after in the *demand* for empathy. The kind of togetherness that is hoped for in many ways is an attempt to transcend the everyday encounter of just being-with each other in class. What is called for is another form of togetherness. In particular, calls for empathy are not just about asking students and teachers to communicate with each other in ways that supersede their prescribed roles, their being-with. The purpose is much larger. Students are, in fact, asked to experience a mode of being together that involves others who usually are not part of the classroom space—however remote or removed those others may be to the actual classroom encounter. That is, it is a demand for togetherness with an other that exceeds the boundaries of the being-with in the class itself, and by staging encounters with others (through images, narratives, actual meetings, or analogous experience), the hope is that empathy will break through the convention of classroom interaction and involve persons in transformative emotional experiences, ones that involve their "whole" selves, their entire being.

For Bauman, our desires for a "more complete" encounter with people indicate that there is another type of encounter that acts as the "imaginary horizon" against which the incompleteness of the being-with experience is measured (51). This horizon is not only imaginary, however, but also serves to depict those moments when people actually break through convention (and people, of course, do). It is a mode of relationality that is not governed by rules; rather, it is an encounter whereby one transcends the limitations of time and place. He writes of the third modality of togetherness:

> Such another way of relating is *being-for*.... Being-for is a leap from isolation to unity; yet not towards a *fusion*, that mystics' dream of shedding the burden of identity, but to an *alloy* whose precious qualities depend fully on the preservation of its ingredients' alterity and identity. Being-for is entered for the sake of safeguarding and defending the uniqueness of the Other; and that guardianship undertaken by the self as its task and responsibility makes the self truly unique, in the sense of being irreplaceable; no matter how numerous the defenders of the Other's unique otherness may be, the self is not absolved of responsibility. Bearing such a task without relief is what makes a unique self out of a cipher. Being-for is the act of transcendence of being-with. (51–52)

The echoes with Levinas resound quite loudly here. Transcending the limitations of being-with demands an attentiveness to alterity, to the "uniqueness" of the Other in a gesture of responsibility. But how is such attentiveness made possible? Can we simply will such a transcendence to occur? Encourage it? Demand it?

For Bauman, such transcendence is (simply) not something that can be planned; being-for emerges unpredictably in the context of the encounter with the Other. "None of the known forms of togetherness privileges the being-for; but none wards off its happening either.... Being-for may only come, so to speak, from behind the back of being-with.... Neither can the self plan, plot, design, calculate the passage from being-with to being-for" (52). In other words, an encounter with the Other erupts through the space of convention without intent or telos. The being-for the Other is a togetherness born out of the immediacy of interaction, a communicative gesture that does not have as its end anything except its own communicativeness, its own response. And it is in this moment of transcendence that convention has no meaning, has no currency within the bounds of the relationship.

Building on Arne Johan Vetlesen's understanding of the person-to-person encounter, Bauman argues that being-for is not about convention but about commitment. Consider his comments in relation to education:

> Eyes stop wandering around and glossing over moving shapes, eyes meet other eyes and stay fixed—and a *commitment* shoots up, apparently from nowhere, certainly not from previous intention, instruction, norm; the emergence of commitment is as much surprising as its presence is commanding. Encounters are pregnant with commitment, and there seems to be no way of controlling this particular pregnancy. (53)

The commitment Bauman writes of here is one born out of the exigency of the face-to-face encounter with the Other.[11] It is a commitment that inevitably arises in open and direct communication, and it is a commitment that one avoids, for instance, when one averts one's eyes away from someone, such as when a teacher asks a question to the class, only to find that all students' eyes are darting to the floor. Thus a committed form of togetherness seems to be more in line with what the demand for empathy is trying to achieve. Even in the case of attempting to create an analogous experience of hunger, where the encounter with the Other is imaginary, the *demand* is not imaginary; it *is* asking for students to feel a responsible commitment for people they do not know. Similarly, in staging encounters with texts, images, or actual survivors of the Holocaust, the demand for empathy is exactly about developing commitment, concern, and moral responsiveness.

It is precisely because it is assumed that empathy has the power to disrupt conventional ways of being together—and to lead to commitment—that it is seen as such an important aim for social justice education. However, if commitment is based on disrupting convention, and if that disruption emerges out of unpredictable forms of communication, then how is it possible to "teach" it? It seems to me that even if we accept that the demand for empathy is a worthy one, we nonetheless cannot ignore how empathic feelings are within no one's sphere of control, neither the one who wishes to encourage empathy in others nor the one who actually feels empathy. Thus the unpredictability and nonintentionality that characterize the experience of being-for turn the demand for empathy into an impossibility. Insofar as a demand has intention and purpose, the demand for empathy ironically becomes a demand for that which cannot be demanded. I do not wish to imply that one ought simply to dismiss empathy as insignificant to moral considerations, but that the demand for it within education must be rethought. In demanding empathy, social justice education seems to remain helplessly committed to the very convention it is seeking to overcome.

But what about *feelings* of empathy themselves, irrespective of demand? Does empathy as an emotion inform a type of communication that transcends the being-with, as is the ofttimes wish of social justice education? What I wish to do in the remainder of the chapter is to inquire into whether feelings of empathy contribute anything to creating moments of nonviolence. I first consider what relations to the Other are implicated in being-for in order to highlight what is particularly *ethical* about this mode of being. I then turn to a more elaborate description of the dynamics inherent in empathy itself in order to flesh out in detail where its ethical limitations and possibilities lie.

ETHICAL ENCOUNTERS: BEING-FOR OR FEELING-FOR THE OTHER?

Empathy has its roots in the notion of fellow-feeling, developed in the eighteenth century by Adam Smith and David Hume, and continued in twentieth century philosophy most markedly by Max Scheler. Fellow-feeling is understood as a capacity for feeling *with* others, and to some degree, this rather broad notion has enjoyed the names of sympathy, empathy, and sometimes pity.[12] With respect to how fellow-feeling is regarded in terms of the relation between self and Other, there is a considerable range of opinion about what such a relation looks like. For instance, Max Scheler insists that empathy is inadequate to moral sensibility as it positions the self's knowledge of itself at the center of the relation with the Other, while fellow-feeling, or sympathy, as long as it is rooted in an "enveloping act of love," is more appropriately suited to developing moral concern for the Other.[13] Edith Stein, on the other hand, views empathy, as opposed to fellow-feeling, as having moral significance, because empathy is a feeling-with rooted fundamentally in the self's knowledge that it is separate from the Other.[14] Diana Tietjens Meyers, for example, makes a distinction between sympathy as sharing in another's feelings and empathy as imaginatively reconstructing another's feelings, and she puts forth the view that empathy is beneficent to moral reflection.[15] Contrast this with Megan Boler's definition of empathy as a "sense of concern" that evokes identical experiences between two people, while sympathy relies on the self's recognition of merely sufficient similarities between them, neither of which lend themselves to ethical interaction between self and Other.[16]

Despite the radical differences between these definitions and perspectives, there is a simple yet basic assumption underlying each position: that our capacity to feel contributes to a mode of living *with* others that has moral significance.[17] It is understood that the ways which we feel in and through a relationship with the Other have a bearing upon how we treat that Other and assume responsibility toward that Other. What I wish to consider here, through a reading of Levinas's portrayal of the encounter between self and Other, is to investigate where ethical possibility lies in terms of our feeling toward the Other. That is, if we are to understand, following Levinas and Bauman, that being-for the Other is somehow a better way of being together than being-with, then what role does empathy play in our encounters of being-for?

Encounters, as we have seen in Bauman's work, usher in different modalities of being together. To reiterate, being-for means that something must break through, disrupt, and interrupt convention, and that this inaugurates commitment through an unplanned and unpredictable encounter with the Other. Moreover, such an encounter effects a responsibility for the singularity and uniqueness of that Other. But what do *feelings* look like in such encounters? Do we feel *with* or *for* the Other as we transcend the being-with? What is particularly ethical about the being-for encounter anyway?

For Levinas, the encounter between self and Other is the time and place of responsibility; it is a profoundly ethical event. What Levinas refers to as an encounter with the Other is what Bauman refers to as a being-for; for Levinas, there simply is no other kind of encounter. As such, it occupies a special position within his ethics. In his depiction of the face-to-face encounter or in his emphasis on the irreducible proximity of the human encounter, Levinas understands an encounter with the Other as constituting a modality of being *responsible* for. This "for" is, as John Llewelyn notes, always rooted in sensibility,[18] in the quality of relationality that lies outside language, outside knowledge. "Knowing, identification which understands or claims this as that, understanding, then does not remain the pure passivity of the sensible."[19] Thus the encounter is that which both transcends being-with while remaining firmly grounded in feeling and sensation. It is what Luce Irigaray refers to, in an apparent paradox, as the "sensible transcendental," that is, a mode of communication where it is through the immediacy of contact with the Other that the self transcends the limits of its own ego.[20] It is precisely this emphasis on sensibility that enables an understanding of how being-for the Other, being responsible for the Other, actually takes on affective overtones and opens up the question of how we *feel* when we are being-for.

Although Levinas does not directly deal with the question of feeling, his understanding of being-for the Other has two distinguishable characteristics that are helpful to this discussion. First is that the encounter with the Other is a relation between two distinct beings. We have seen the importance placed on this diachronic relationship in the previous chapter. As Levinas writes, "the other is in no way another myself, participating with me in a common existence. The relationship with the other is not an idyllic and harmonious relationship of communion, or a sympathy through which we put ourselves in the other's place; we recognize the other as resembling us, but exterior to us; the relationship with the other is a relationship with a Mystery."[21] The mystery here is the radical alterity of the Other, and so the encounter must always refuse reducing the Other to a common ground with the self. "If the relationship with the other involves more than relationships with mystery, it is because one has accosted the other in everyday life where the solitude and fundamental alterity of the other are already veiled by decency. One is for the other what the other is for oneself; there is no exceptional place for the subject. The other is known through sympathy, as another (my)self, as the alter ego."[22] What Levinas articulates here is that while we can have a shared reality with the Other, feelings such as sympathy require renouncing the irreducibility of self and Other. This means, then, that in everyday communication within social situations, such as teaching and learning (the "decency" of civilization, one might say), we of course do commiserate, sympathize, and pity, and these emotional events can connect us in profound ways. Yet they are not constitutive of nonviolence, of ethical interaction. For Levinas, it is not that these everyday feelings are unimportant, it is just that they have little to do with the necessary maintenance of alterity, an alterity that is revealed in the encounter with the face: "The alterity of the Other is in him and is not relative to me; it *reveals* itself."[23] This *revelation* of alterity is a fundamental aspect of an ethical encounter. It is where the Other is not merely heard, seen, or felt with, but where the self is receptive to the revelation of difference and is thereby moved to a level of responsibility. The being-for is, as Levinas says, direct, immediate, and "straightforward": "No fear, no trembling could alter the straightforwardness of this relationship, which preserves the discontinuity of relationship, resists fusion, and where the response does not evade the question."[24] Thus in Levinas's view, sympathy and other forms of feeling-with seem to support a mode of togetherness that is not patently ethical and in fact resembles what Bauman referred to as a "being-with." Feeling with others cannot lead to transcendence, for it blurs the distinction between self and Other that Levinas is so adamant to maintain. What matters for empathy in this view is not whether it bridges the divide of difference (as any feeling-with would) but to what degree it maintains this divide through respecting the Other's alterity.

The second characteristic that is important in the encounter with the Other is the requirement of the self to depose its ego, its intentionality and consciousness, in the service of the Other. Responsibility for the Other, being-for the Other, means that the self is no longer a self-regulating agent but is passively open and exposed. The self becomes commanded by the face of the Other to respond to her *presence*. Although we may respond to what someone is saying, although we may feel with the Other in her articulated pain or pleasure, the ethical relation lies in attending to the approach of the Other in such a way as to limit one's own self-concern. "To give, to-be-for-another, despite oneself, but in interrupting the for-oneself, is to take the bread out of one's own mouth, to nourish the hunger of another with one's own fasting."[25] The importance of sensibility in establishing this passivity and egolessness means that the self feels and senses its way to a response to the Other. That is, passivity is not about being "actionless"—as if giving the bread out of one's mouth ever could be—but about how one is responsive beyond an act, beyond one's own vested interests, beyond one's own best intentions, and beyond one's own ability to reason.[26] Sensibility is important to this in that it grounds such selflessness not in some supreme effort of will but in the capacity to feel: "The signification proper to the sensible has to be described in terms of enjoyment and wounding."[27] Such terms of feeling indicate that the self feels for the Other in such a way as to disrupt its own pleasures, its own ego enjoyments. "It is the passivity of being-for-another, which is possible only in the form of giving the very bread I eat. But for this one has to first enjoy one's bread, not in order to have the merit of giving it, but in order to give it with one's heart, to give oneself in giving it. Enjoyment is an ineluctable moment of sensibility."[28] Counterintuitive to our more commonplace understandings, responsibility is neither ego directed nor consciously chosen.[29] Rather, it emerges out of what Andrew Tallon refers to as a "nonintentional affectivity"; that is, an affectivity that arises spontaneously and conditions responsibility for the Other.[30] With the deposition of the ego as moral agent, the issue for empathy revolves around the degree to which our feelings emerge from within the kind of egoless, nonintentional form of relationality privileged here.

What have we to learn from these two characteristics of the encounter? The first reveals that feeling-with is inadequate in preserving the alterity of the Other. That is, the potential for nonviolence does not emerge from the self's capacity to feel along with an other as this feeling is caught up in erasing difference. To encounter the unknowable mystery of the Other means to be for her. This being-for is, of course, characterized by the second characteristic of the encounter. The egoless passivity that Levinas refers to is entrenched in a sensible orientation to the Other. As such, the self's openness not only conditions a being-for-the-Other, but it also means that it can feel-for the Other. This feeling-for is not a "feeling" in the sense of a cognitive emotion but in the sense of giving oneself across difference through one's pain and enjoyment. When I feel-*for* the Other, I am in a state of exposure, a nakedness Levinas would say, that makes me susceptible to the Other's needs. Thus my feeling-for is a disinterested, nonego-invested feeling that emanates only through the encounter with Other as opposed to being generated from within the subject herself. It is the supreme example of "being moved," "being touched," and "being affected." That is, being becomes inextricably bound to feeling through a passive encounter with difference.

So is empathy a feeling-for? Can it partake in a nonviolent relation to the Other? Can it exhibit an egoless passivity? In response, I turn now to explore the two dynamics of empathy discussed earlier: the putting of oneself into the Other, and the putting of the Other into oneself.

PUTTING YOURSELF IN THE OTHER'S SHOES: A QUESTION OF PROJECTION

Empathy is, perhaps, most commonly depicted by the phrase, "putting ourselves in the other's shoes." It is frequently invoked in everyday encounters with children—how would *you* feel if that were done to you?—in order to motivate moral response. More importantly, however, is how this informs pedagogical and curricular demands for justice at all levels of education. By creating opportunities for students to feel as though they are in the position of an other, it is expected that they will develop a sense of commitment and responsibility, as we saw in the hunger analogy exercise.

Yet Freud warns us that feeling our way into people as a way of *knowing* what the other feels is impossible. It is worth quoting him at length:

> We shall always tend to consider people's distress objectively—that is, to place ourselves, with our own wants and sensibilities, in *their* conditions, and then to examine what occasions we should find in them for experiencing happiness or unhappiness. This method of looking at things, which seems objective because it ignores the variations in subjective sensibility, is, of course, the most subjective possible, since it puts one's own mental states in the place of any others, unknown though they may be. Happiness, however, is something essentially subjective. No matter how much we may shrink with horror from certain situations—of a galley-slave in antiquity, of a peasant during the Thirty

Years' War, of a victim of the Holy Inquisition, of a Jew awaiting a pogrom—it is nevertheless impossible to feel our way into such people—to divine the changes which original obtuseness of mind, a gradual stupefying process, the cessation of expectations, and cruder or more refined methods of narcotization have produced upon their receptivity to sensations of pleasure and unpleasure. Moreover, in the case of the most extreme possibility of suffering, special mental protective devices are brought into operation. It seems to me unprofitable to pursue this aspect of the problem any further.[31]

It is important to note that Freud is not talking explicitly about empathy here; in fact, he views empathy as something quite different than feeling one's way into an other (see my discussion below). What his comments make clear, however, are two illusory aspects of being able to put oneself in another's shoes: first, that the self projects one's own mental states onto an other, and, second, that there is a question of "divining" the intricacies of the other's feelings. In spite of Freud's insistence that these are precisely what make "feeling one's way into an other" an impossibility, I think it is important to explore how projection and imagination structure our general understanding and experience of putting oneself in the place of the other.

In terms of projection, the self casts its own inner life onto that of the other; it is as though it sets the other up to be a reflection of part of the self. In this sense, the other becomes what object relations theorists call an "object." That is, an object is not necessarily a person, but an aspect, a quality, or an attribute of a person, both real and imagined. Generally, the notion of projection within psychoanalytic literature refers only to those fantastical elements of inner life that we cannot tolerate, and we rid ourselves of them by transferring them to others. For Melanie Klein, however, projection involves both good and bad aspects of the ego, and it refers to the way we project "into" and not merely "onto" people. As Hanna Segal notes of Klein's work, good or bad parts may be projected with the aim of controlling an external object.[32] The projected material, however, is not a directly knowable entity; our projections take place unpredictably and without foresight. Thus when I project into the other my "mental states," there is no immediate way of knowing *to what degree* or *what specific content* I am projecting. Yet controlling the external object through projection means that the other can be tolerated by the ego and can even come to be loved and identified with.[33]

This is at the root of a mechanism identified by Klein as "projective identification." Part of what we empathize with in the other derives from our own psychic material and fantasy: we recognize ourselves in the other, we feel like we are that person. Klein writes, "to be genuinely considerate implies that we can put ourselves in the place of other people: we 'identify' ourselves with them."[34] Specifically, projective identification develops in the earliest stages of life when the ego is as yet unintegrated. Instead, the ego "splits itself, its emotion and its internal and external and internal objects. . . . Identification by projection implies a combination of splitting off parts of the self and projecting them onto (or rather into) another person."[35] With projective identification, then, one externalizes one's fantasies into an other and then identifies with that other in turn. In contradistinction to Freud, who sees that placing our feelings onto an other cannot lead to any insight into what that other has experienced, Segal writes, "projective identification, too, has its valuable aspects. To begin with, it is the earliest form of empathy and it is on projective as well as introjective identification that is based the capacity to 'put oneself into another person's shoes.'"[36] Thus while projecting one's mental states onto others leads Freud to conclude that "feeling our way into people" is not a topic worth pursuing, Klein's understanding of projection is, on the other hand, precisely that which eventually leads the subject to empathize and to become "considerate" of the feelings of others.

Furthermore, by introducing the element of fantasy into empathy via projection, we are compelled to ask what it is we do "divine" about the feeling of others. For it seems to me that people *do* claim to put themselves in others' shoes, meaning that we do "divine" or, more appropriately, imagine what it is others feel. And while this may indicate that what one imagines is nothing more than one's own projections (one's own fears, anxieties, pleasures, and desires), cannot such imagination also lead one to act more sensitively and responsibly toward an other? In other words, is there a way in which imagination is useful for coming to feel-for, and not merely with, the Other? That is, even if Freud is right in claiming we cannot *know* the Other's feelings, even if we admit that what we can *know* has been put there by ourselves, can such imaginative projection nonetheless help us *feel-for* an other in such a way so as to be open to the Other's needs? Can constructing analogous experiences of hunger, for example, in fact contribute to an imagining that actually opens a space, not for understanding the Other but for being receptive to the Other?

Diana Tietjens Meyers explores precisely this point in examining the moral significance of empathy as an imaginative reconstruction of another's feelings. She describes empathy as being essential to moral reflection and judgment, and she makes a case against sympathy as a "feel[ing] along with one another" that does not necessarily lead to moral responsibility.[37] Empathy instead is defined by the capacity "to construct in imagination an experience resembling that of the other person" (32). Although Meyers does view the proverbial "putting oneself in the other's shoes as misleading" (33), the trajectory of the imaginative reconstruction of another's experience that she outlines nonetheless lends itself, in my view, to exploring this very dynamic.

Meyers delineates two different types of empathy: incident-specific and broad empathy. Incident-specific empathy is framed by the question "What are you going through now?" It refers to "imaginatively experiencing another person's state of mind within a fairly well demarcated time frame and in relative isolation from other aspects of the individual's psychology" (34). This "most common form of empathy" (34) can occur with acquaintances as well as with those who are most distant. For Meyers, "empathy is accomplished by learning as much as one can about them [strangers] and the situation they face, and then *projecting* as best one can one's own profile of interests, needs, and the like into that constellation of circumstances" (35, emphasis added). Although she views such empathy as "relatively crude and conjectural," in making a correlation between knowing about the Other and projecting onto the Other, Meyers nonetheless implies that one's imaginative reconstruction is a projection that is based on a somewhat transparent understanding of someone else's reality.

Although Meyers grants greater moral weight to the second type of empathy she describes, namely, broad empathy, because it takes into account a more complex view of subjectivity, the same dynamic of projection is at work here as well. Broad empathy asks "What is it to be like you?" and is an attempt "to empathize with another person's subjectivity as a whole." Meyers explains that to "empathize with another's subjectivity is not only to draw on one's past emotional life to conjure up that person's experience in one's own mind, but it is also to grasp the circumstances of that person's life along with the beliefs, desires, abilities, vulnerabilities, and traits of character that give rise to these experiences" (35–36). This focus on *knowing about* the other in great detail would appear to diminish the significance of the role of imagination in empathy. Meyers does suggest, however, that

> broad empathy sets up an interplay between imaginative replication of the other's circumstances and subjective states and analysis of these circumstances and states. . . . The resulting interplay enables intellection to check flights of fancy while imagination presses intellection to break out of habitual analytical categories. Though these constraints are by no means fool-proof, they do guard against crass "empathic" self-cloning. (37)

Meyers's idea of imaginative reconstruction and imaginative replication gestures toward the possibility that one can reconstitute or copy another's experience in one's imagination, but by introducing an imaginary element, empathy then cannot be based entirely on what one can know about an other. Indeed, the projective component must come into play, for how else can one's imagination be made to "fit" the life of an other? It is through the projective aspect of imaginative reconstruction or replication that one inhabits the location of someone else. I project my imagination onto you, and I imagine what your feelings are. Through this, I come to know what you feel, because I have reconstructed for myself what it is to be you. There is created a form of kinship or bonding between the self and the Other where one's feelings are externalized through projection and reinternalized through identification. While I do not wish to suggest that such feelings are insignificant to how we think of ourselves in relation to others, the effect of putting oneself in place of the

Other means that one has, in some profound way, defined that Other in terms of the limits or expansiveness of one's imagination, and in terms of one's own psychical material. In this sense, the Other becomes filtered through a screen of the self's creation; one's response becomes mitigated through one's imaginative reconstruction. Feeling-through-projection (and projective identification) cannot be a feeling-for the Other. That is, feeling-for the Other, as we have seen, is necessarily about an exposure to the Other, an openness to be moved by the Other. Understanding empathy through projective identification means, it seems to me, that it is not so much about getting to know what the Other is feeling but coming to recognize one's own projected material. Thus empathy viewed in this light says more about the self than about the Other with whom the self is empathizing. In this regard, putting oneself in the other's shoes can tell us something about ourselves, and while this may be valuable, as I will discuss below, it seems to fall short of the call to responsibility that the Other commands.

PUTTING THE OTHER INTO YOURSELF: A QUESTION OF IDENTIFICATION

The other affective trajectory to be considered here runs in the opposite direction, so to speak, and suggests that it is through identification with the Other, through bringing the Other "into" the self, that empathy is constituted.[38] It is precisely this dynamic of empathy that informs many pedagogical initiatives that seek to set up possibilities for students to alter themselves by letting another "inside." Elisabeth Young-Bruehl, in reflecting upon the place of empathy in the writing of her biographies on Hannah Arendt and Anna Freud, notes, like Freud before her, that the "clichéd" depiction of empathy as "'putting yourself in another's place' seems to me quite wrong." She contends that

> empathizing involves, rather, putting another in *yourself,* becoming another person's habitat as it were, but without dissolving the person, without digesting the person. You are mentally pregnant, not with a potential life but with a person, indeed, a whole life—a person with her history. So the subject lives on in you, and you can, as it were, hear her in this intimacy. But this, as I said, depends upon your ability to tell the difference between the subject and yourself, which means to appreciate the role that she plays in your psychic life.[39]

Unlike empathy, as that which is constituted through projective identification, grounding empathy in "identification and imitation," as Young-Bruehl and Freud do, suggests that the self's ego boundaries are flexible enough to incorporate another into its reality without having to project anything upon the other.

As Freud writes of empathy: "A path leads from identification by way of imitation to empathy, that is, to the comprehension of the mechanism by means of which we are enabled to take up any attitude at all towards another mental life."⁴⁰ But what does it mean to identify by way of imitation? Annie Reich makes a key contribution in understanding empathy by offering a nuanced reading of its links to imitation and identification. She sees empathy as key to the analyst's role, and her detailing of what is at stake in empathy and identification is important in considering how empathy occurs in classroom situations. The analyst, for Reich, does not merely "interpret" or come to know about the patient through intellectual means alone; rather, the analyst's capacity to empathize with the analysand offers insight into the analytic relation that cannot be obtained in other ways. More particularly, this capacity to empathize grows out of a transitory imitation, and this has to do with being open to the analysand's unconscious affect. It also has to do with the extent to which the analyst is receptive to such material.

Reich asserts that the "suddenness" of the interpretation that often seems to occur to the analyst happens via the analyst's own unconscious: "It is as if a partial and short-lived identification with the patient had taken place."⁴¹ This is what Reich calls, following Wilhelm Fleiss, a "trial identification"; Reich emphasizes the importance of being able to make fine distinctions between what constitutes an identification and what constitutes an imitation or "trial identification." On the part of the analyst, she "identifies" with the patient, psychically imitating the conflicts that are projected onto her by the analysand and "sides" with the patient, giving herself over to the patient's needs. "In a special, transient way, the analyst identifies with the patient and in this way participates in the patient's feelings."⁴² That is, the analyst is "trying something on" in picking up and replicating the feelings of her patient, allowing her patient inside, so to speak. It is at this point that the analyst has fully empathized. Nonetheless, the analyst cannot remain stuck in this position. She must detach in order to recognize that what she has experienced through this trial identification are feelings that need to be brought back to the patient; in fact, she recognizes these feelings as "belonging" to the patient. "Thus, the analyst acquires knowledge about the nature of the patient through an awareness of something that went on in his own self."⁴³ This is the case, as long, of course, as the identification is indeed a "trial" one and not one born out of unresolved conflicts. For Reich, the "trial identification" with the patient is an empathic device geared to the *patient's* end, not something to be acted upon for the purpose of furthering the analyst's own agenda.⁴⁴

Reich is, therefore, emphatic in refusing a definition of empathy as being "based on the fact that the analyst at some time or other also felt like the patient, that the analyst can understand only what he has felt himself at some time."⁴⁵ Instead, through elaborating a notion of trial identification, she accentuates how it is that we can understand another who is unlike oneself. "It is the essence of empathy that something which is not directly inherent in the [*sic*] own experience and history can also be understood."⁴⁶ Moreover, I think her understanding of trial identification speaks to how the analyst not only understands the Other but also feels for the Other. That is, it is through an accidental moment of exposedness that the analyst comes to find herself trying on the feelings of the Other for the sake of the Other. It is a moment of discovery that is contingent upon sensibility. Young-Bruehl remarks, "only the discovering mode, not the forcing mode, seems to me to involve empathy—indeed forcing a person into your likeness is an excellent definition of lack of empathy."[47]

However, the point remains that within these views, there is some aspect of consciousness that needs to go on if one is to take responsibility for one's empathic identifications, and if one is to recognize where the limits and boundaries are between feelings of the self and feelings of the Other. Within Reich's view, for example, it is the *recognition* of empathy rather than empathy itself that gives rise to responsibility. Responsibility thus remains within the purview of consciousness as opposed to sensibility. Further, Young-Bruehl insists that a precondition of empathy itself is rooted in consciousness:

> Any empathy depends, it seems to me, on a certain form and degree of self-consciousness. You have to know—and this is a matter of insight—the role that the subject plays in your wish structure and your ego ideal; you have to make this role conscious to the degree that you can. The reason that this insight is the necessary precondition for empathy is that empathy is feeling the other person's desires in the mode of comparison, and for a comparison you must be able to tell the difference between the subject and yourself.[48]

What Young-Bruehl suggests here is that allowing another to reside within means *recognizing* the Other as being absolutely distinct from one's self in the first place; empathy is possible only as a mode of relationality across difference. Yet in terms of what we might refer to as a nonviolent relation, it is precisely the nonintentionality, the surprising giving over of the self, the affective openness to the Other, and the passivity requisite to being moved where being-for and feeling-for come together. Thus although putting the other into oneself seems to lend itself partially to this quality of togetherness—particularly in Reich's depiction of empathy, where there are analytic moments of openness that are unquestionably a feeling-for the patient—there are aspects of empathy as identification that seek to turn what is essentially an unconscious, indeterminable process into a question, ultimately, of insight rather than sensibility.

EMPATHY AS A LEARNING FROM THE OTHER?

The dynamics of empathy, as we have seen, are replete with complexity, and what it has to offer a consideration of the ethical moments of nonviolence within teaching and learning encounters is equally intricate. As I stated above, the *demand* for empathy (whether putting oneself in the other's place or putting the other into oneself) is an untenable pedagogical aim. But the question remains to be considered: what do feelings of empathy have to offer us as possible ethical disruptions?

My intent in discussing such a question is not just to evaluate the dynamics of empathy against a predefinition of what constitutes the ethical—although this is, admittedly, an important aspect to consider insofar as several markers of that interaction have already provided the groundwork for reading empathy, namely, the connection between being-for and feeling-for; the non-intentional role of affectivity; the irreducibility of self and Other; and the egoless passivity signaling responsibility. However, when we speak of empathy in specifically educational terms, as differentiated from the broader definitions of empathy detailed above, it is important to consider how these broader dynamics of empathy actually work through the event of learning.

Returning to the idea that empathy erupts periodically in educational situations, regardless of whether or not the demand for it is present, suggests that empathy is an inescapable feature of the teaching and learning landscape. As such, the trajectory between self and Other as either a projection or an identification compels us to think about the place of learning in empathy. If we consider projection first, what learning is being effected here between students and teachers, or between students and strangers? And to what degree does that learning contribute at all to the potentiality of nonviolence?

Projection is something, of course, that we all engage in to some degree. We do imagine what it must be like for another person to experience suffering and pain, as well as joys and pleasures. Teachers regularly attempt to feel with their students in order to gain insight into what might be appropriate forms of interaction. To do this, they often project parts of themselves into individual students, claiming to then know what students feel. What smacks of familiarity, of course, is that they unconsciously "recognize" those projected part of themselves in the Other, the commonality a result of projected material. It is not that such projections yield no beneficial consequences. Indeed, projectively imagining what a child living in poverty might be suffering can inform a teacher's decision about how to make life better for that child. Providing food in the classroom, starting a clothing exchange at school, offering time and space at school to do homework, and connecting the family to community supports are some of the direct benefits that can accrue from these feelings. But the issue remains—to what degree are these imaginings at all in synch with what the child feels and needs, and moreover, why is it important to feel what they feel in order to marshal a responsible response in the first place?

Discovering what it is that the Other feels, it seems to me, comes about not through projection but through listening and being receptive to a communicative openness with the Other. In this sense, as a *mode of relationality* across difference, empathy can miss the target completely in terms of respecting that difference. Instead, empathy as projection is unable to open itself fully to the revelation of alterity; its impulse is to overcome difference. Furthermore, to suggest that students ought to "put themselves in the other's shoes" when encountering difference seems to be encouraging a shutting down of the very opportunities for communicative openness and learning from the Other that social justice education works so hard to achieve. For instance, students who may have indeed empathized with starving children in the Third World through experiencing hunger themselves necessarily invest that other with their own qualities, attributes, and affect. And why some qualities, attributes, and affects are chosen over others has to do with the terribly idiosyncratic nature of unconscious projection. Hence, when students do feel such empathy, we cannot assume that this dynamic carries with it *inherent* ethical significance, as though it is automatically a good thing. Rather, what I want to suggest is that students' feelings of empathy are telling us something about how they are learning, about how they are engaging that which is fundamentally external and foreign to them. Feelings of projective empathy signify that the self endows the Other with its own feelings, that it bestows upon the Other its own psychic material, and thereby it enmeshes itself with the Other in a way that elides the Other's alterity. The learning that takes place is one that seeks affectively to sculpt, create definition, and give shape to the Other's unknowability. And since empathy is a psychic event where one's own conflicts, desires, and ambivalences are projected into an other, the movement of learning becomes a relation of self to self, the Other awaiting my creative powers of self-definition.

With identification, empathy becomes a bit more complicated. In fact, the imitative gestures that mark one's entry into identificatory empathy speak to the ways in which the unconscious both passively receives and actively engages with the Other's difference. The learning effected here presents a remarkable receptivity to the experiences and feelings of another. In education, students often imitate certain qualities of their teachers (and I am not referring here to the caricatures they portray), adopting phrases, styles of language, and modes of address. This is particularly evident in graduate education, where trying on new vocabularies, modes of questioning, and writing styles signals a particular attachment to a professor. Such imitative gestures can lead to empathic experiences where students "allow" the Other to enter within, to inhabit them, and at times begin to experience their life work through the Other's eyes. Their feelings for that professor can, of course, be wrapped up in other needs and desires, but the potential of empathic identification is nonetheless very strong, so that students feel they know what and how that professor thinks and feels about certain ideas, books, academic work, and the like. This is, of course, true of teachers as well—and perhaps even more so; we, too, take in what students project upon us. We find ourselves experiencing and empathizing with their fears over exams, their joys at success, and their desires to become academics. On this level, there is a fairly intimate relation at stake.

When we consider, however, the possibilities for empathy arising out of learning encounters with, say, texts, images, or actual testimony of the Holocaust, what kind of learning is taking place here? For example, when empathy occurs with a survivor who has come to speak to the class about her experience, it should not surprise us to find students (and perhaps ourselves) "trying on" what they have seen as a way of feeling toward the Other. That is, students often replicate at some level (however small) what it is they have heard: this can be through a repetition of the narrative (which is, of course, always partial), naming commonalities between themselves and the narrator, or taking on the concerns and issues that the survivor has raised, all to the end of feeling-for the other person. In this sense, students who empathize in this manner reveal themselves to be open to an other in a way that they become subject to that Other. There is thus an implicit receptivity in empathizing through identification, and it occasions a learning that appears at first glance to be a learning from the Other.

Nonetheless, empathy as identification still involves the self in a relation to an other, which may begin in openness but is still rooted in a feeling of sharedness and commonality that troubles the borders between self and Other. In fact, this is why proponents of empathic identification view the need to *consciously recognize* the Other *as* other as being central to any conception of empathy. It is precisely because the movement of unconscious identification does collapse the distinction between self and Other—however brief, however transitory—and that what appears to be an initial feeling-for the Other ultimately folds into a feeling-with. That is, while the ego is open enough to initially receive the Other, it closes down again once empathy itself enters the picture. The very understanding of empathy as putting the Other into the self suggests that although the dynamics at stake are different than putting oneself into the Other, they both achieve (through different means) a parallelism between self and Other that defeats the very difference upon which they are based.

As I alluded to previously, empathy, whether projective or identificatory, can provide an opportunity to learn about ourselves in relation to others, but it is not rooted in a learning from the Other. By this I mean that empathy can tell us something about ourselves—after all, what I feel in the place of the Other is what I and I alone have projected; what I feel in taking in the Other is a result of my identification with the Other, not vice versa. Empathy is thus very much an ego activity that involves unconscious elements, but whose ultimate lessons are derived from and serve the interests of the self. In this sense, while empathy may be constructive to self-reflection, it is not about respecting the singularity and uniqueness of the Other.[49] As both Meyers and Young-Bruehl make clear, it is only our capacity for reflection that disrupts the dangers of empathy itself. However, if the conditions for ethical possibility lie precisely in the approach to the Other prior to understanding, then it seems that empathy, in requiring reflection, thought, and prudence, cannot approximate the spontaneity of commitment and responsibility that arises in the modality of being-for.

Although I think empathy falls short of the mark in providing a condition for ethical possibility, I am not suggesting that we should not empathize, or that empathy ought not to have a place in our emotional lives. This seems to be an equally impossible request as the demand for empathy is. The fact is, we do empathize, and we do so in ways that are already implicated in profoundly ethical relations where the alterity of the Other is at stake. The point is not to see empathy as the starting point for moral concern, or, in Vetlesen's words, as a "precondition of moral performance." As a quality of relationality, it appears that there are better candidates for both the acknowledgment of the Other's suffering and being-for the Other, which are central for learning from and not merely about the Other. Learning through empathy cannot but mask, despite our best intentions, the Other's radically different feelings, experiences, and needs as unique. Empathy necessarily leads to questionable assumptions that the Other is ultimately somewhat like me, that what I feel *is* the same as (or at least approximates) the Other's feelings, whether I project or identify or not. As we have seen, engaging across differences through empathy may provide us with the raw material for *self*-reflection after the fact, but it cannot offer the ethical attentiveness to difference *qua* difference so necessary to projects of social justice. The question is, then, if empathy as perhaps *the* mode of relationality most closely linked to ethical possibility cannot achieve it, where can we turn?

THREE

A RISKY COMMITMENT: THE AMBIGUITY AND AMBIVALENCE OF LOVE

> Communication with the other can be transcendent only as a dangerous life, a fine risk to be run.
> —Levinas, *Otherwise than Being or Beyond Essence*

WHAT DO LOVE and eros[1] have to offer a discussion on the ethical possibilities of education? In considering the work across differences that social justice education engages in, how might that most seemingly private of emotions, love, lend itself to such work? Does eros have anything to do with learning from and not merely about the Other? These questions are by no means easy to answer, for love is a difficult place to begin to think about ethical possibility within the framework of social justice. Indeed, love is difficult to think about, period. It seems to defy adequate description, its depth and texture evoked most powerfully in poetry and literature rather than in philosophy or psychoanalysis.

In terms of social justice education, love takes on a particular difficulty, given that the feeling of love, unlike empathy, is a seemingly rare attachment that the self holds for a unique Other, one that demands something far greater of us in terms of commitment, concern, and responsibility. In addition, love is thought to be reserved for only a few people in our lives, as opposed to empathy, which is presumably more far reaching. In light of this, love would thus seem to be a much too narrow and exclusive feeling to be of any value to education per se. Moreover, to suggest that love might have ethical significance would also bring into focus the place of intimacy and desire between teachers and students themselves, and this would present its own difficulties for thinking through what might be a responsible response to an other, given the institutional constraints of pedagogical practice that frown upon such intimacy. It is for these reasons, in my view, that the focus on issues such as empathy, recognition, and care has eclipsed considerations about what love and eros have to offer to working across differences as an ethical project.[2] For instance, as Kelly Oliver notes, in the struggle for recognition within discourses of multiculturalism, there is a dire absence of love in advocating for ethical *and* political responsibility.[3] Such an absence seems to suggest that there is something dangerous about love, and all its attendant attributes, for it challenges the relative innocence of our institutional relationships. Moreover, to suggest that our responsibility might lie within an apparent rarified sanctity of intimacy troubles our understanding of the explicitly social character of responsibility that social justice education attempts to animate.

Yet one of the most obvious aims in social justice education is to arouse responsibility through "developing" concern for and connection to the lives of "Others," which, like all demands, is by no means innocent. The call to be concerned for an other, often summoned through the pedagogical practice of exposure to another's suffering, seems to me to assume that profound feelings of intimacy are required to mobilize such concern, for the type of concern that social justice strives to achieve is no mere intellectual "interest" or "curiosity," but optimally a *committed* regard for the suffering of an other that has the potential to lead to responsibility and hopefully to responsible action. Indeed, I think implicit in such commitment is a demand for students to become enamored with a cause, an idea, or the condition of a particular person to the point of wanting to do something about the debilitating social conditions that produce such suffering. We often speak of passion as a sign of committed responsibility, and teachers often hope that students will be moved to such a point of intensity. The engrossment and passion attached to such commitment are suggestive of the way eros is mobilized in developing a responsible concern for the Other. While teachers, of course, do not literally demand that students fall in love with the Other, and students rarely identify their responses to the Other directly in terms of such love, I do think that love needs to be more thoroughly analyzed with respect to what it contributes to establishing the solicitude and, ultimately, the responsibility that we are seeking through our pedagogies.

As I discussed in the previous chapter, such responsibility is seen to be grounded in certain configurations of otherness and togetherness that have the capacity to move students out of their supposed complacency and into a mode of being-for the Other that challenges conventional ways of being-with one another. As we have seen, the being-for the Other, through which commitment and, consequently, responsibility emerge, is to be found neither in appeals to nor feelings of empathy, and this, I have argued, is primarily for the reason (although certainly not the only one) that the singularity and difference of the Other is betrayed at the moment empathy is engendered. Yet as Max Scheler proposes, a moral relation to the Other becomes possible through love, because love is a feeling precisely founded on the distinctness of the Other, whose uniqueness is welcomed.[4] Thus my turn to a discussion of love—and its more abstract depiction as eros—is an attempt to consider how the characteristic singularity of love might hold possibilities for an ethical approach to the Other and also to explore the limitations that love has for such an approach within the context of social justice education. It is not my intent here to advocate for love—neither as demand nor feeling; rather, it is to investigate the role love and eros might play in establishing the concern and connection necessary for responsibility.

The *Oxford English Dictionary* defines love as a "state of feeling with regard to a person which ... manifests itself in solicitude for the welfare of the object." As we can see, even within this relatively ordinary definition, love is not simply an emotional state, but it also performs as a mode of relationality to another that carries with it intrinsic moral concern. When we say we love someone, we implicitly mean that we are concerned and do care about the loved one. What I am proposing is that we look at this link between concern and love from the other direction. When we call upon students to act with solicitude and concern for the Other (and indeed for "humanity" or distant others[5]), what kind of dynamics are we invoking? My contention here is that such notions are closely linked to what we understand the consequences of love to be *as a relation*. That is, the *feeling* of love optimally allows for a way of *being together* that seems to confer automatic concern for the Other. When faced with the suffering of others, for instance, does love have any role to play in an ethical response to this suffering? What I explore in this chapter is how the *feeling* of love is always already bound to a *relation* to the Other, and, more specifically, a *communicative* relation to the Other. That is, love is not only a private emotion, but as a mode of relationality, love communicates something to the Other. As such, it participates in a circuit of signification that has repercussions both for learning and for ethicality. Thus this chapter recognizes love and eros as having, as Freud points out, varied manifestations that exist along a continuum, from the most exclusive of sexual relationships to the most far-reaching altruistic attachments.[6]

In exploring love for the quality of relationality it establishes with the Other, and the degree to which it can ultimately allow for learning from the Other, I caution against a romanticized view of it. Following Freud and Levinas, I examine critically the traces of ambivalence and ambiguity of love and eros in order to offer a more complex view of how love participates as a communicative relation between persons. That is, rather than defining love as an unequivocal good that should be pursued in developing moral concern, my intent is to read the communicative effects of love that underlie our attempts at being-for the Other, and to what degree they allow for a learning from the Other. This means turning to the risks embedded in such communication and evaluating the degree to which such risks hold promise for conditions of nonviolence. But first I wish to cast this discussion in terms of what qualities of communication signify the being-for the Other.

AMBIGUITY, EROS, AND THE FINE RISK OF COMMUNICATION

Both Levinas's attention to alterity and the essentially ambiguous nature of communication lead him away from a simple humanism whereby the "inter-human" is a relation between already complete subjects who follow certain rules of engagement in order to be responsible. The Levinasian emphasis on communication instead means that subjectivity and responsibility reveal themselves only in relation to an Other and therefore emerge from a signifying encounter with absolute difference that cannot be predicted beforehand. That is, what counts as ethical in Levinas's thought is not encapsulated within rule-governed behaviors, ethical codes, or moral precepts that can be secured through stable significations. Rather, the ethical lies within the very ambiguity of communication, within that which slips our cognitive grasp and possession. Ambiguity is not so much a question of misunderstanding what is being said (or expressed) as it is a matter of the impossibility of ever knowing the Other through these significations. For Levinas, communication is inherently ambiguous, because it gestures beyond any stable meaning toward the very otherness of the Other that marks her as radically distinct from myself. And it is this relation to the Other as one of unknowability where the ethical promise—and risk—of ambiguity lies.

To return to the quote that opened this chapter, Levinas calls for us to take a fine risk, to place our selves in danger when we communicate. But is eros a *fine* risk? Is love a quality of that transcendent communication Levinas identifies as central to ethicality? And how would such a fine risk, understood as transcendence, be deemed ethically significant in terms of the solicitude sought within the context of social justice education?

The key word for me is "fine." Although Levinas notes that "the word 'fine' has not been thought about enough,"[7] he nonetheless offers some guiding thoughts. For Levinas, a *fine* risk would run the danger of communicative ambiguity, the fineness to be found in the approach to the Other that necessarily lies behind the communication: "Communication is an adventure of a subjectivity, different from that which is dominated by the concern to recover itself... it will involve uncertainty" (120). A *fine* risk is equated with leading a life that ventures forth into an unknown (and unknowable) encounter with an other. What makes a risk fine has to do with a relationship in which the self seeks a radical openness toward the Other, susceptible to being moved by the approach of the Other. Moreover, this encounter strikes another chord of ambiguity with respect to the approach of the Other, for the Other is a person who commands me to respond in communication and at the same time is a being who, in Arne Johan Vetlesen's words, "is utterly defenseless, vulnerable, nude."[8]

The *fineness* of risk intimates that there is a fragility, a delicacy in the openness, as if the relationship were somehow vulnerable to attack and violence and consequently needed to be protected from harm. Levinas writes, "these words [fine risk] take on their strong sense when, instead of *only designating the lack of certainty,* they express the *gratuity of sacrifice.*" (120, emphasis added). Levinas is suggesting here that openness in communication is sacrificial in nature, that the self offers itself for the Other in a spontaneous gesture of generosity that is not self-interested but is for the Other. For Levinas, sacrifice, unlike commonplace definitions, is understood as a responsibility for the approach of the Other, which is not a total abnegation of one's own distinctness. Sacrifice is a relation to the Other that sustains difference; neither does the self feel or believe she is the Other, nor is the self totally erased in the encounter with the Other. Rather, the sacrifice that is a responsible response pertains to the double-edged aspect of the self-Other relation: it answers to the command to respond to the Other, yet it does so with an openness to the Other's vulnerability. Sacrifice, then, is a position of responsibility that accomplishes nothing less than calling the I into being through response, and to accomplish this response, the I learns from the Other, allows the Other to affect it to the point of answering for her. Thus the "being" in being-for is not merely a state of existence or a type of relationality; instead, it signals that one's own being emerges within the communicative encounter that is committed to the Other. Significantly, the subject in communication is *already* a responsible subject. This means that responsibility views communication neither as reciprocal nor dialogic in character, nor is it a form of speech among equal subjects. Rather, responsibility involves a radical openness in communication and an attending to the (unknowable) particularity of the Other that lies behind the words spoken, the deeds committed. In short, responsibility involves transcending what is manifest in speech or gesture. It is in this way that transcendence is ethically significant: "there is in the transcendence involved in language a relationship that is not empirical speech, but responsibility" (120). Since responsibility is a gift born out of the communicative ambiguity between self and other, then running a fine risk means opening oneself up to the very ambiguity that makes us responsible.

But to what degree might we say love participates in this ambiguity required for transcendence, for being-for? Can eros be part of taking a fine risk? For Levinas, the answer is itself ambiguous.[9] In *Time and the Other* from 1947 he claims that eros takes on characteristics of the ethical through the relation to the alterity of the Other, to the transcendent "mystery" of the Other:

> It is only by showing in what way eros differs from possession and power that I can acknowledge a communication in eros. It is neither a struggle, nor a fusion, nor a knowledge. One must recognize its exceptional place

among relationships. It is a relationship with alterity, with mystery—that is to say, with the future, with what (in a world where there is everything) is never there, with what cannot be there, but with the very dimensions of alterity.[10]

As an exceptional relationship, eros is not purely self-interested, nor does it assume a mode of being-with the Other based on grasping, possessing, and knowing, which are synonymous with power.[11] Eros is neither fusional, nor does it seek unity between two. It "consists in an insurmountable duality of beings. It is a relationship with what always slips away."[12]

This slipping away is part of the communication of eros, for love knows not what it seeks. It is not a conscious intention but an anticipation of the future in the present time of love. In this regard, then, given what Levinas expresses as the fineness of risk out of which responsibility is born, such an anticipatory state would seem to suggest that eros is very much a part of an ethical project of transcendence. Indeed, in the final paragraphs of *Time and the Other*, Levinas says as much: "It [temporal transcendence] is the face-to-face without intermediary, and is furnished for us in the eros where, in the other's proximity, distance is integrally maintained, and whose pathos is made of both this proximity and this duality."[13] However, there is a curious turn of events in Levinas's thinking.

Levinas proceeds to turn eros into a type of relation, as opposed to expressing a quality of relationality. He sees, rather, the face-to-face relation (and later proximity) as a special relationship that eros always falls short of. His new formulations depend upon seeing eros as an impulse aimed toward pleasure for the self. Now love has to do with the pleasure the self receives from the Other—which cannot therefore assume ethical relevance. In *Totality and Infinity* (originally published in 1961 and written fourteen years after *Time and the Other*), Levinas writes, "If to love is to love the love the beloved bears me, to love is also to love oneself in love, and thus to return to oneself. Love does not transcend unequivocably—it is complacent."[14] Levinas himself is unequivocal in suggesting that there is little hope here for ethics in the complacent shadow of love.

This is further underscored in Levinas's later thinking, where eros is confined to the metaphorical in order to describe proximity, closeness, and vulnerability. The proximity of one to the other is that which makes signification possible, rooted in a sensible subject who is "of flesh and blood" (77); it is now proximity, and proximity alone, that makes a fine risk possible. Although Levinas is adamant about what we might call the "erotic" character of sensibility, claiming that "as soon as sensibility falls back into contact, it reverts from grasping to being grasped, like in the ambiguity of the kiss" (75), eros itself no longer carries any ethical weight. Proximity, then, is a space/time of communication between two, where the approach of the other signals the beginning of subjectivity and responsibility itself. Here love no longer creates a signifying encounter with difference but relies on signification already in place. Tina Chanter writes: "There can only be non-signification [for eros] because signification already exists, or because the order of meaning is already established. In this sense, eros is always consequent upon ethics."[15]

The shifts in Levinas's own thinking display the ways in which love might be seen as an open-ended communication, that in and of itself may or may not be ethical. Moreover, what becomes apparent is the notion that any *type* of communication in and of itself can ever be ethical to begin with. For it is precisely at the point where Levinas renounces eros as a quality of human relationality, as part of the face-to-face relation with which he begins his ethical journey and turns toward a thematization of eros as a *type* of relation, that eros slips its ethical moorings and becomes something other than transcendent communication. Therefore, rather than simply holding onto one of the views he expresses, I believe the revisions in his thinking are instructive for what they reveal about the complexity of love as a communicative relation.

Read against Levinas's own views of risk and transcendence, I still think that love has an important role to play in the way commitment emerges between self and Other. That is, I do not see that the ethical relation as that which involves a risky openness to the Other in an ambiguous communication needs to shut out eros completely. That is, even if *proximity* is the privileged term in Levinas's later work, it is not clear why love *always* has to be seen as self-interested, and why it cannot be transcendent as his earlier work posits. Lost here is the ambiguity of love itself as a communicative relation. Turning to understanding the communicative aspects of eros means having to attend to how eros signifies in an encounter with difference. Thus I do agree that eros can be self-interested, however, I also think that the difficulties of love lie in being able to see the way love can be more than this.

I turn now to discuss in further detail these difficulties of love in the development of moral concern, and the degree to which ambiguity might help us rethink these difficulties. As intimated above, there is a fundamental problem for social justice education in terms of even viewing love as having the potential to address questions of social and political responsibility. For instance, when the social and political goals of equity are defined in relation to how students ought to "see," recognize, and understand the "Other" through certain *types* of communication that ostensibly promote social connection and solicitude, then the ambiguity embedded within the encounter with the Other can only pose a threat to this responsibility. For it is really the affective, sensible dimensions of that encounter—the passionate commitment, the ardent concern—that escape such codification. That is, *types* of communication are based on empirical speech (rules for speaking, dialogue, consensus building, and resolving conflicts are some examples) and are definite in their attempt to structure responsibility based on knowledge about the Other, about her needs, wants, and experiences; in this sense, they remain tied to a mode of being-with others, whereas ambiguity, and the transcendence that it implies, depicts a being-for that moves beyond the acquisition of knowledge as the purpose of communication. Being-for indicates a committed approach to the Other that transcends the words she speaks. A focus on the being-with can lead to the unambiguous relegation of eros to a separate, private sphere disconnected from promoting responsibility. Thus affixing a notion of responsibility to certain types of communication, as opposed to qualities of communication, undercuts the ambiguity necessary for establishing the kind of responsiveness that an encounter with the Other demands, in all its particularity. What I wish to consider is how might love, read through communicative ambiguity, help us move beyond the impasse raised here? Is love so private that it has nothing to offer to the development of concern and connectedness that is part of a committed response to the Other?

I examine here two views that discuss the ethical dimensions of love: one that contests its place in establishing moral concern for anyone beyond the dyadic self-Other relation, and one that champions its potential for establishing social and political responsibility. What is interesting about both of these views is how they display the difficult problem of love in relation to our moral capacity for concern and connectedness in the face of grave social violence, situating their arguments within contexts such as the Holocaust and slavery. This background is important for my discussion on love, since it is with contexts such as these in mind that social justice education also attempts to create bonds of attachment that inform a committed responsibility.

LOVE'S LIMITS

Arne Johan Vetlesen tackles the difficulties of love in reflecting on moral perception. His work centers on the question of how we come to perceive the lives of others as mattering, as having worth and value. As such, it contributes something significant to my discussion on developing moral concern. Vetlesen takes a critical approach to love as a feeling that can have value in articulating possibilities for moral performance, and he questions, quite rightly, the value of love when considered against the background of post–Holocaust German guilt and the psychic numbing that enabled Nazi perpetrators to commit their crimes. His criticisms touch precisely upon the question of what love as a *feeling* signifies in terms of the *relationality* to the Other. They offer, in my view, an argument that is sensitive to the moral drawbacks posed by love, yet I propose that elements within his argument also serve—contrary to his own view—to elucidate the role love might play in the transcendence and learning implied in being-for the Other.

Vetlesen recognizes that love "is a product of difference" (196), and that when we love, we love precisely the other person as other. "In love, difference is not looked upon as something to be fought and overcome but as a source of mutual enrichment" (198). Love is thus comprised of the extraordinary difference that separates self from Other, and it attends to the singularity and uniqueness of the beloved. Summarizing the foundational position that love occupies in Max Scheler's ethics, Vetlesen writes:

> Love's disclosure of the beloved is perpetual, without a fixed end point, since the qualities love renders accessible to my appreciation are taken to be inexhaustible. Love thus feeds on an everlasting source. Love is spontaneous; it discovers the other as unique and concentrates on the very being of the other, not merely on some specific traits pertaining to the other or (contingently) to his or her situation; in wanting to stimulate the flourishing of that "unique" repertoire in the other, I make full use of the powers of my own unique person as well. The blossoming of love is that of the two persons involved. (208)

This meaning of love therefore suggests that it is not what I know about the Other that is important for establishing connection, but that I simply am for the Other in my feeling for her; I learn from and respond to her difference. The Other as other is therefore related to in all her singularity, and I, too, am singular in feeling love for the Other. Thus drawn out of me is my own uniqueness as a response to the absolute limit the Other imposes. As a consequence, the spontaneity of love establishes a being-for that has specifically ethical dimensions. "In love, commitment and depth are profounder than in compassion; emotionally, more is involved at the giving as well as at the receiving end" (209–210). This suggests that love could be the feeling-for the Other requisite to the kind of commitment that being-for the Other entails. Indeed, if commitment shoots up, as Vetlesen himself says (following Levinas), in the face-to-face encounter with the Other that is nonintentional and ambiguous, then the feeling of love lends itself to that most exemplary of relationships where the Other's singularity is inevitably made the focus.[16] While for Levinas it is in this encounter where responsibility is unconditionally assigned to the self by the Other, Vetlesen remains at a distance from this "bold doctrine" (203). Nonetheless, what I suggest tentatively at this point is that it is precisely the kind of commitment to be found in the being-for, which can appear to us in the relation of love, that serves as a basis of moral concern.

However, Vetlesen carefully goes on to argue why love is inadequate to developing the moral perception that leads to concern for others, and his primary reason is the exact opposite of why I have rejected empathy: that love is *too* engaged with singularity and uniqueness to be of much value. Although he endorses love's focus on uniqueness as contributing something important to morality, Vetlesen nevertheless sees that the ground for moral concern must arise out of something that can be cast much wider than love, which is always "confined to the small-scale setting" (205). Vetlesen marshals in commonplace observations to support his view: "we, to be honest, do not love that many people" (197), and "when love is taken to mean full recognition of the other qua other and therefore of his or her otherness 'in itself,' then we have to confess that, in real life, it takes a lot to love" (197). Measured against this "reality check," love is seen to be lacking the much wider perspective that he claims is necessary for the development of moral perception.

It is his philosophical arguments, though, taken within the context of Nazi crimes, that say something important about the limitation of love in furnishing us with a moral compass point for orienting our moral concern. "Love is not required of us in order that we perceive a cosubject as a moral subject, judge him or her as such, and—optimally—act toward him or her as such. Linked to the felt uniqueness of the other, love is too exclusive, too selective, too narrow, for all that" (213–214). The narrow logic of love works against an understanding of our broader moral obligations. While love might be a sufficient condition for moral concern, it is not a necessary condition.

> In other words, although we treat those whom we love as ends in themselves, we do not love all those whom we treat as ends in themselves; and although it can never become a moral duty to love, not even an imperfect duty, it is morally obligatory to treat all human beings (indeed, all beings capable of suffering, as asserted earlier) not merely as means but as ends in themselves. This is to say that the realm of morality transcends that of love; exploding the range of human love, morality cannot be based on it. (214)

Vetlesen thus comes to the conclusion that "less than love will have to do" (205).

What Vetlesen offers in its place is a view of empathy quite unlike the views expressed in the previous chapter. His notion is not so much based on a specific feeling but on what he calls an "emotional faculty" that is "our basic mode of access to the domain of humanity's emotional experience," and his goal is "to show how the act of judgment we exercise presupposes and rests on an act of perception that logically precedes it" (210). Thus his evaluation of love is measured in terms of how well it serves as the precondition for moral perception, which in turn is a condition of moral judgment and performance. This precondition, then, bears a heavy burden, for it must come to the aid of both perception and judgment. Love, as he says, fails, since it can neither provide the breadth of scope needed to be a *necessary* condition of moral perception nor lead to adequate judgment about persons for whom we may not feel that deep intimacy that is characteristic of love. However, curiously, what becomes overlooked is the place of commitment in this constellation of moral factors. If commitment emerges precisely at the point of a nonintentional response to the Other in an ambiguous communicative encounter, as Vetlesen himself claims, then I am not certain why this encounter does not serve as the precondition through which moral concern might develop. I think, partially at least, it is because Vetlesen favors seeing *conditions* of moral perception as requisite for judgment and responsibility[17] at the expense of *conditions* of commitment. I propose, however, that such conditions are central to thinking about responsibility, for they reveal the ambiguity that lies behind those moments that incite a committed response for the Other, an ambiguity that is at the heart of learning from and being attentive to the Other's suffering. Thus I agree with Vetlesen, that love *as a feeling* is not a necessary condition for commitment, and that it is too narrow to be turned into a moral ideal, as Scheler would have it. On this account, love represents an archē, a stable beginning point from which responsibility automatically flows. But Vetlesen's criticisms end up evading the question of why we need a fixed starting point at all, and why not a theory of the way the ambiguous encounter with difference can produce a commitment that might or might not be supported through *various* feelings and affect. Although Vetlesen is rightly critical of Scheler's naturalistic idealization of love, his grounds for dismissing love completely ironically depend on seeking a fixed starting point elsewhere. That is, seeking to find *the* emotional key to the preconditional lock of moral perception allows him, in effect, to split commitment from responsibility. That is, while Vetlesen recognizes that commitment arises out of the ambiguity of the self-Other encounter and its nonintentional character—a move that makes love sufficient, albeit not necessary, for establishing commitment—he fails to theorize how this commitment—whether established through love or other feelings—is itself a necessary condition of responsibility, and that it might be established through a range of emotional registers. That is, his rendering of love as an unambiguous feeling, as opposed to an ambiguous mode of relationality, forecloses an exploration of love as a dynamic that works its way through the self-Other encounter that can allow for commitment and the responsibility that commitment spawns.

Moreover, implied here is that love is not "social" enough; that is, as a feeling it cannot reach out to the many others about whom we ought to be concerned. However, the being-for that love can establish, according to Vetlesen's own thesis, seems to me to be a social relation that takes place within a social context. That is, as a disruption of convention—which is eminently socially defined—the commitment engendered in the being-for establishes another social relation; the question is whether this new form of relationality can actually lead to responsibility on a broader social level.

I think that it partially can, as long as the ambiguous nature of that encounter is taken into consideration. Put within the context of Vetlesen's discussion of Nazi perpetrators, it is precisely ambiguity that is lacking, where the complete absence of being-for the Other is made possible by a nonopenness and total intolerance of the way persons signify for each other across difference. Not only were victims not perceived as moral subjects in their own right but, more importantly, they could only signify as stable, comprehensible "categories" that obliterated any possibility of ambiguity, and along with it moral concern and commitment. That is, they become objects of knowledge, making any learning from—which would require a capacity to be moved by the Other—an utter impossibility. The psychic numbing Vetlesen discusses is also partially a function of an incapacity to accept, to say nothing of being open to, the ambiguity that accompanies an encounter with another person. Such ambiguity would indeed disrupt the horrific social "conventions" of Nazi violence, for it would mean responding to the Other's vulnerability as sacrifice (a sacrifice, you will recall, that singularizes the self's response and calls the I into being), and it would admit into that self-contained world of human destruction an element of unpredictability and uncertainty that could neither then be accounted for nor thereby controlled. Thus it would install the possibility of disrupting relations to the point where the self would be held in an obligation to the Other that challenged social "convention." Commitment, then, would seem to be a moment for nonviolent possibility.

I certainly do not want to suggest that love is the answer to the question of responsibility, as though love can lead to a remedy of violence on such a scale, and in this I think Vetlesen is right. But neither do I think that privileging any other feeling as being the only key is the answer. The task set before us, it seems to me, is rather to consider how conditions of commitment actually do say something about conditions of responsibility; love cannot be dismissed on the grounds that it is too narrow, if in fact it can contribute to establishing such commitment. Thus the limitations of love must be judged against the ways that love fails its promise of commitment, and the degree to which it does effect the social. Only then can the relationality that love implies begin to bear ethical fruit.

THE PROMISE OF LOVE

A less nuanced reading of love occurs in Kelly Oliver's *Witnessing: Beyond Recognition*.[18] Undertaking a similar stance as I do here, Oliver's work is an attempt to redefine the possibilities of ethicality outside the conventional theories of recognition and within a space where otherness is central to responsibility. Less concerned with detailing love as a feeling, Oliver attempts to locate love as always already implicated in experiences of social and political frames of connectedness. Thus her understanding of the "Other" is, unlike Levinas's or Vetlesen's usage, cast within relations of power. Asking the question, "What is love beyond domination?" (19, 216), Oliver articulates another way of seeing, outside the conventional bounds of recognition that she claims merely reinscribe rather than change oppressive relations of power and control. Concerned with developing a mode of response/responsibility in the face of pain and suffering related to us through narratives of "othered subjectivities," including Holocaust survivors, former slaves, and victims of oppression, Oliver argues for the importance of witnessing with "loving eyes that invite loving response" (19). Unlike Vetlesen, Oliver champions the ethical and, indeed, the political potential of love for such a project. Critical of the absence of love in calls for recognition, she claims, as a radical alternative, that love *is* responsibility:

> Love is an ethics of differences that thrives on the adventure of otherness. This means that love is an ethical and social responsibility to open up personal and public space in which otherness and difference can be articulated. Love requires a commitment to the advent and nurturing of difference. . . . Love is the responsibility to become attuned to our responses to the world and other people, and to the energies that sustain us. Loving eyes are responsive to the circulation of various forms of energy, especially psychic and affective energy, that enable subjectivity and life itself. (20)

Here Oliver establishes quite a weighty claim for love. Claiming not only its importance for responsibility but that it *is* responsibility, Oliver not only makes love into an ethical category but into a political one as well. But how is love responsibility? Does love lead to those conditions of commitment that inform responsibility?

Initially building on Frantz Fanon's understanding of love as having liberatory potential—beyond the Sartrean view of love rooted in conflict and shame—Oliver writes that "Fanon's vision of love opens the way for a love that is not self-centered but other-centered" (42). While acknowledging that Fanon himself has little to say directly on the subject of love (217), Oliver nonetheless emphasizes that his work promotes an affective relation between self and other that is something other than that which is defined by alienation: "affect is a movement toward the other that is born out of love [as opposed to alienation]" (42). The Fanonian logic she describes is thus:

> It becomes clear that for Fanon love is a matter of ethics and ethics is a matter of love—the values of human reality and *wishing for others what you wish for yourself*. And this ethical commitment to love is necessarily part of a politics of liberation. Love restores the agency of the oppressed subject, an agency that is destroyed insofar as she or he is made into an object within the dominant culture. Love restores the oppressed subject to the world of subjectivity and humanity. Affective connection and loving attention can be a liberation from objectification, if only temporarily and incompletely, until everyone is free of oppression and all see and begin to walk through the welcoming, open door of every consciousness. (42–43, emphasis added)

On this account, love creates a mode of relationality where connectedness reigns supreme. The movement toward a deobjectification of the self is brought about through the affective ties of love. To be able to love means to be able to be free; love as an act of reaching out toward another disrupts the convention of oppression and domination through which "otherness" is constituted. Thus triangulating the link between the social construction of subjectivity and the agency needed for altering the terms of domination within this construction is the individual who feels. Love becomes political for

Fanon, since it "can enable a psychic wholeness necessary for social agency" (43). Oliver is aware of the idealization of love in Fanon's work, but she sees it anyway as "the working joint between psychic self-affirmation and social and political transformation" (43). What we see here is that it is connection as opposed to commitment that emerges from the loving encounter: we are ethically committed to love because of its powers of connecting people across differences. This is a substantial reversal of Vetlesen's position. Thus rather than explore love for the ways it establishes ethical commitment through connection, or concern through commitment, for Oliver, it is instantiated as a moral imperative from the beginning. The logic of her argument is that if love is a bond of connection that recognizes difference as being central to each of our subjectivities (which, for Oliver, are always socially and politically constituted), then love ought to be nourished in order to create new possibilities for subjectivity; it therefore becomes a social and political act of responsibility. "Just as an individual cannot develop a sense of agency without loving attention from another and cannot develop a sense of meaning without the loving support of the social, an individual or group cannot develop a sense of social agency or social purpose without a loving social space in which to articulate that agency and meaning" (44). Thus love is not simply a condition for moral concern or solicitude but is central to the robust development of social life itself (a theme to which I return below in my discussion on Freud). What Oliver's take on Fanon suggests here is that being-for the Other not only occurs within a sociopolitical context but conditions the political space in which subjectivities can develop meaning. Moreover, love is the affective point of political and social connectedness in that it binds persons together in ways that explode social circumscriptions of agency.

This broader view of love seems to move us beyond the impasse of love's narrow logic, on the one hand, and forms of social responsibility, on the other hand. Indeed, Oliver is adamant that love both transgresses the circuit of domination that feeds "otherness" and establishes new forms of social relations that recreate subjectivity outside of domination. In this sense, Oliver challenges the distinction made between the public and the private, and the personal and the political. She boldly brings affect right into the sphere of social possibility.

However, her argument is a curious one, on two counts. First, the qualities she attributes to love do not seem to be exclusive to love, and what she means by love becomes enmeshed in ascriptions of moral worth that seem to speak for themselves. For instance, the movement toward the other that she ascribes to love could be equally attributable to other affects, such as compassion or empathy. And, if love is less a feeling and more a mode of relationality, as I think she is implying, then it is still not clear what makes attention, a social space, or a response particularly "loving" rather than caring or compassionate. That is, what is it specifically about love that invokes the Other in a special relationship that leads to new social geographies, where persons and groups of persons can, supposedly, receive love? While I think that viewing love between two people both works as a metaphor for new social relations and operates within and through the social and political realm, I am less certain than Oliver is about its unequivocal ethical value in establishing responsibility. That is, her claim that love *is* responsibility might make sense when we think of what it means when we love someone in particular—in loving you, I am responsible for you in all of your particularity; but is responsibility only achieved through love? The question of *how* love transcends the limitations of the social in such a way as to establish responsibility cannot be achieved through rhetorical fiat. By staking her argument on love as responsibility, since it establishes connection with others that respect differences, Oliver seems to be suggesting that love signifies unambiguously. That is, in the encounter with the Other, love is unequivocally attached to moral response. Moreover, in claiming that in love you want for the Other what you want for yourself, love loses the asymmetry so necessary for assuming responsibility for the Other as a response that is not ego centered. Indeed, love as a response is not about what you want for yourself but about a response to the Other that is for the Other, period. I think this symmetry leads Oliver to overlook the complex dynamics of love in establishing connection to others, in the plural. That is, wanting for others what you want for yourself seems to me to be less about love and more about assuming to know what it is others want. The original problem of how to love others (in the plural) without foreclosing on the singularity that makes the love relation so special is elided rather than remedied. Even as Oliver cautions that "when love or the beloved becomes fixed, stable, recognizable, part of an economy of exchange, then love cannot be maintained" (220)—thereby suggesting that love must remain open ended and equivocal—my point is that what is then being privileged is the openness to ambiguity itself, and not love as such. Thus it is not love in and of itself that allows for responsibility, but that, following Oliver's own argument, it is *only insofar* as love can participate in the conditions of openness and spontaneity that it can perhaps *lead* to responsibility.

Second, and more important, love takes on a surprising intentionality that seems to rub against the grain of the unpredictability and spontaneity that mark love as a unique relation between self and Other. Oliver, following bell hooks, claims that love is a willful decision (220). This means that to love is an act of agency, and it implies that love is elected, turning love into a quasi-rational, voluntary act whereby the self chooses the "Other"—and "others"—to love. Even though Oliver is careful to state that "love is not something we choose once and for all" (221), and that it requires vigilance to maintain it, I think she does not give enough attention to the difficulties of love in transcending the being-with presupposed by conventions of domination. How do we go about intentionally loving an other? By assigning love to the realm of decision making and, therefore, of politics broadly defined, she intimates that we ought to and can reasonably demand that each of us love as a gesture of political responsibility. But what makes this possible for Oliver is not our capacity to love per se but our capacity for reflection. She writes:

> Whether we are talking about intimate love relations or loving one's "enemies," the loving eyes of "self-reflection" are critical. Love must be alive and kicking in order to move us beyond our selves and beyond recognition. Only by continually reinterpreting and elaborating our relations, including self-relations, can we hope to maintain them as loving relations. Love is an openness to otherness. But this openness requires reflection as a turn toward others. It requires the insomnia of a vigilance that recognizes the urgency of opening toward what is beyond recognition. (219–220)

Thus coupled with the openness she deems requisite to response and responsibility is a vigilance that keeps awake that very openness. While I am basically in agreement with this Levinasian turn, and with seeing love as existing on a continuum (from "intimate love relations" to "loving one's enemies"), it still remains unclear to me, though, why love is needed. That is, is it not a question of attentiveness rather than love that is at stake, an attentiveness both to the other and to remain open to the other? And, if so, how does love—particularly an intentional love at that—make possible that openness and vigilance that are the markers of responsibility? Rather than simply claiming that love *is* responsibility, I think the more important question that Oliver's work raises is to what extent love participates in the conditions of responsibility she outlines here, where such radical openness leads to a learning from the Other that lies beyond choice.

Although love may be a condition of connectedness that allows for solicitude, her emphasis on the intentional and cognitive aspects of responsibility seems to place an unreasonable demand on love itself. Can love really be mobilized at will in order to ensure social responsibility? Ought we, as teachers, to assume that we can demand both of our students and of ourselves that we love others because it is our social or political responsibility to do so? I think the tension for Oliver lies in wanting to maintain, quite correctly, love as an unstable movement toward the other while also seeking to erase the effects of this instability—and, indeed, ambiguity—between persons. As a metaphor, love allows us to imagine different forms of relationality across difference, but as responsibility, love becomes dangerously close to becoming an unambiguous ideal. Gone, then, is the dynamical quality of love that breathes life into the flesh-and-blood encounters through which moments of responsibility are created. Thus as soon as love, as both feeling and a mode of relationality, becomes tied to an ought (that is, as soon as it is seen as a necessary condition for responsibility), we turn it into something less risky than I think it is. For as Freud and Levinas demonstrate, along with the poets, love cannot be stable and fixed, because it does reach out toward another in a nonreciprocal movement. In keeping love on the safe side of relationality, we ignore the ways in which love, as it is performed in social spaces between embodied persons, poses great risks to the one who loves. That is, love is that very mode of relationality that calls the ego into question.

I have thus far been proposing that the difficulties of love need to be thoroughly addressed in order to move us beyond the polarization of love as either an idealization of its inherent goodness (Oliver's position) or to its total dismissal in developing moral concern (Vetlesen's position). There are two elements to this. The first is to see conditions of commitment as being essential for responsibility, so that the question then becomes how love contributes to the creation and sustenance of such commitment. The second is to see love itself as ambiguous (and, as we will see with Freud, ambivalent). That is, as opposed to being a singular feeling or relation that means the same thing in all contexts, love itself becomes an unpredictable element in communicative encounters with difference. What Freud's work offers to my inquiry at this point is precisely an understanding of love as a social relation that affectively fuels our concern for others, thereby bridging the gap between the individual and the social world she occupies, on the one hand, and, on the other hand, putting love into a social frame without foreclosing on its uniqueness and singularity for the individual herself.

THE AMBIVALENCE OF LOVE AND EROS

Freud's understanding of the significance of eros as a life drive means that our capacities for connection to others and for developing ties that seek solicitude for others are profoundly intertwined with how social life itself is maintained. While Freud does not directly elucidate how love as a unique bond might contribute to establishing commitment and responsibility, his work carries implications for my discussion on the place of love in being-with and being-for others.[19] In *Civilization and Its Discontents,* Freud attempts to explain and redefine the theory of drives, which impel the subject to pleasure and to seek out community with others.[20] In outlining the place of love and eros in establishing such a longed-for connection, Freud nonetheless continually disrupts any possible romanticization of the erotic potential for communion with the positing of a death drive. Through this ambivalence, he locates how love operates in the social sphere without idealizing or departicularizing it.

The ambivalence of life and death and love and hate makes itself felt on two levels: one is between the individual and society, the other is within the individual herself. In terms of the former, eros is necessary for creating and sustaining communities, and it is that drive for togetherness that impels people to establish strong connective and communicative bonds. Freud has this to say: "Civilization is a process in the service of Eros, whose purpose is to combine single human individuals, and after that families, then races, peoples and nations, into one great unity, the unity of mankind" (122). Society partakes in a libidinal economy that supports a quality of relationality that Freud sees as life affirming, as eros fulfills its purpose of uniting individuals. Yet simply asserting that eros is a necessary condition for social life can neither explain the conflictual aspects of social life nor the ways in which society controls eros.

In terms of control, Freud understands that at the same time society requires firm, libidinal attachments between its members, it also puts forth laws, rules, and customs that circumscribe their flourishing. Love is the necessary social bond between individuals, while social institutions work to restrict the conditions under which this bond is allowed to take place. "On the one hand love comes into opposition to the interests of civilization; on the other, civilization threatens love with substantial restrictions" (103). This embedded contradiction is an unavoidable consequence of the attempt by society to mitigate against pure self-interest while still allowing enough love to flourish in order to sustain significant relations to others. Social mores and regulations exert pressures that cut off or transform loving attachments into "appropriate" forms of behavior, into forms of being-with. Thus conflict between individual drives for attachment and social formations that restrict, redefine, and limit such attachment with others is an intrinsic feature of social life.

We may view these social formations in terms of domination, as Oliver does, but I think there is something more complicated implied here. As we have seen in chapter 1, the demands that social institutions, such as schools, place on us are both necessary and excessive, and thus imposing restrictions on love is an inevitable feature of social life, even outside the terms of social domination of which Oliver writes. If we turn to education, for example, teachers' and students' institutional roles and the interpersonal forms of communication they seek are not just incompatible at times, but their very tension is part of the structure of how modes of relationality are fashioned. That is, social pressures configure types of relationality that permit certain social bonds to flourish while prohibiting others *in the name of social cohesion*. Consider a pedagogical exercise in which students are asked to befriend and help out a homeless person. Teachers would be demanding of students to take up a commitment with some passion and, indeed, intimacy, but they would not be encouraging them to "love" that person in a romantic sense. However, for Freud, the differences in such expressions of affect are less about an individual's capacities for love and more about the social conventions through which such capacities can be channeled. Our drive for being together, then, is routed through circuits of affect that at once promote and enable relations in which individuals come to feel connected to others, while at times frustrating the very desire for connectedness. The question is, however, how much social control is necessary for the continuance of bonds that will create opportunities for ethical modes of relationality, for establishing concern and connectedness, and how much is merely excessive?

Part of the answer to this lies in Freud's worry over the way conflict develops within the social arena. That is, if eros sustains social life—as Oliver also suggests—then how does one account for our seeming incapacity to live well together? This is an especially important educational question, it seems to me, if we wish to develop a moral concern for others that counteracts such conflict. Oliver's position is that we need to love more in order to alter existing forms of subjectivity within the terms of domination. Vetlesen has argued that love is too narrow to bear such a heavy burden. However, for Freud, it is the conflict within the individual as it gets played out in the social sphere that offers some insight into why the drive for togetherness is so easily disrupted. Thus unlike Oliver and Vetlesen, Freud sees that the problem lies in the difficulties of love itself.

As he writes, "the development of the individual seems to us to be a product of the interaction between two urges, the urge towards happiness, which we usually call 'egoistic,' and the urge towards union with others in the community, which we call 'altruistic'" (140). This dividing up of urges, or drives, into that which serves the ego and that which serves the other suggests a play of tensions that continually and inevitably occupies the subject. Ego-instincts are invested with the capacity to "provide the ego with the satisfaction of its vital needs and with control over nature" (121), while object-instincts strive after others through love. Through this dualism, Freud begins to see that a portion of the drives that seek ego satisfaction is aggressively directed toward the outside, and that the drive for satisfaction itself is an indication that the ego wishes to return to a state of non-desire. Such a state for Freud is the drive toward death, which is only mitigated by the outwardly seeking love attachment to others. Thus to satisfy a narcissistic desire for satiation, the ego will exhibit destructive (i.e., deathlike) tendencies; the ego begins to take over the purpose of eros in order to satisfy its own ends. As in sadism, the ego derives erotic pleasure from the mastery it exerts over another. "In this way the instinct itself could be pressed into the service of Eros, in that the organism was destroying some other thing, whether animate or inanimate, instead of destroying its own self" (119).

What Freud makes clear, however, is that this sadistic tendency is only an extreme indication of a struggle that occupies each of us—that between life and death. Eros, for him, is not something that can be easily separated from the death drive; in fact, it is the "mutually opposing actions of these two instincts" that explain the "phenomenon of life" (119). Further, Freud stresses that these two drives "seldom—perhaps never—appear in isolation from each other, but are alloyed with each other in varying and very different proportions and so become unrecognizable to our judgement" (119). This statement is particularly radical, for it leads us to understand that eros is as much hidden from view as is the death drive. Although Freud insists, "it must be confessed that we have much greater difficulty in grasping that [death] instinct; we can only suspect it, as it were" (121), in being alloyed with eros, we are compelled to ask a similar question of eros; how do we know whether our relations to the Other are purely altruistic, purely for the Other, or whether they are always tinged with self-serving interest?

Whether or not one accepts Freud's drive theory, or his biological basis for it, there is nonetheless something to be gleaned from positing a concept of eros that is fundamentally entwined with a drive for death, desirelessness, and destruction. It means having to analyze the degree to which love participates both in moments of commitment that would factor into possibilities of response *and* the degree to which such love is sought purely because it fulfills the ego's own interests. Actively *pursuing* love for love's sake, or willfully choosing to love an other, becomes untenable in this view, precisely because the ambivalent drives that fuel our loving relationships prevent turning love into a moral ideal. Love, in Freud's view, is not merely always a good thing. However, neither does the alternative lie in rejecting love as being totally inadequate, since it is the fuel that drives the possibility that we can—and do, sometimes—live well together. Rather, the point becomes how to think through the possibility of what eros might offer to the transcendence of the self in the eruptive and unpredictable character of its emergence. It is in relation to this that Freud is helpful in a second way.

Freud cues us into how eros as that life-affirming, affective bond that brings people together performs a type of altruism. This suggests that eros can indeed surmount the self in approaching the Other; love seeks out the Other in a communicative capacity where the ego's interests do not occupy the primary place in the relationship. And this, it seems to me, might occur in ways that disrupt the being-with of convention. That is, altruism, as so defined, is an unpredictable and sometimes a socially unamenable quality of eros, insofar as it displaces self-interest in an encounter with difference. It cannot, then, guarantee safety or predictable forms of relationships. Indeed, the risk implied is that altruism can lead to the very disruption of social convention in ways that are open to the unpredictability of the Other; thus unlike Oliver's position, love in the form of altruism does not presume to know that the Other wants what you do. Indeed, lying as it does in excess of self-interest, altruism signals precisely our capacity for being-for the Other. So despite Freud's insistence on the unifying nature of eros, which would suggest a relation to the Other that returns to the self, I think that understanding this particular love attachment can actually be reread as that which facilitates a connection to the Other that exceeds the limits of the ego. Through love, the Other disrupts the stability of the ego, insofar as the ego becomes extended, its identity challenged and called into question in the very connection it establishes with the Other. In this sense, love lends itself to the conditions of commitment, whereby the drive for connection involves a certain capacity for openness that surpasses the ego itself. Hence, the ethical potential of eros lies in the way in which it paradoxically works its way through the ambivalent structure of the death drive and simultaneously supersedes the controls of the ego. For this reason, the altruism based on love is not simply the result of acts of projection or identification (such as we have seen with empathy) but exhibits a drive to exteriority, away from any narcissistic devouring of the Other. Altruism itself is not simply a drive for unity or sameness but touches upon, in my view, the very quality of relationality necessary for ethical interaction: maintaining the alterity and unknowability of the Other.

Freudian ambivalence is therefore important in understanding that solicitude and concern are no easy feats of pedagogical practice, and that the moments of commitment that present themselves in the being-for the Other are eminently linked to the ways in which institutions, such as schools, both permit and control certain manifestations of eros. That is, how we judge whether or not love participates in the being-for that exceeds the being-with must be rooted in an attention to social context. In this way, love as a mode of relationality is social, not only between self and Other but between self, Other, and the larger context of social prohibitions. Although institutions have the important function of circumscribing types of relations conducive to social well-being, such circumscription has manifested precisely a drive to destroy the bonds of affect that often bring students and teachers and students and others together. For instance, in the rigid restrictions imposed on touch in schools, what we are witnessing is an overly exercised attention to what teachers, seemingly by virtue of their institutional roles and positions, should and should not do, to the point of absurdity. What is worrisome here is the way in which the very capacity for loving human communication has become self-serving from the perspective of the institution; that is, seeking to destroy certain manifestations of love is itself a way of sustaining the very control of the institution. Under such strictures, what matters is that the roles and functions of teachers and students are codified to minimize spontaneity, to reduce risk. If risk, however, is implicit in acting responsibly toward an other, then what kinds of institutions are being created when opportunities for risk are depleted, and when the development of necessary social bonds is so severely policed? More significantly, within the context of the aims of social justice education to develop concern and solicitude for others who have been oppressed by such social scripts, how might it be possible to acknowledge love as participating in some necessary risks (e.g., the risk of altruism) without glorifying it?

At the level of the individual, of course, there is a question about what is being served in any loving attachment between self and Other within this social context. The ambivalence of the driving forces of life and death structures these attachments in educational encounters in a complicated manner. Freud's ideas help us navigate them, in two ways. First, his work cautions against a sentimental view of eros's potential. In coupling eros with the death drive, Freud facilitates a concern for viewing love as potentially being in the interests of the ego, just as much as they may be in the interests of the Other. In this sense, we must remain cautious about claiming love for any ideal, for our very desires for attachment might actually be doing the Other harm; that is, our seeking solicitude might be based on forming attachments that are not about sustaining communicative openness or commitment but about putting the Other in the service of our own needs. And insofar as the ego uses the Other to sustain its own boundaries, its own repetitious self-same, learning from the Other is a foreclosed possibility. Yet even though eros may be alloyed with the death drive on many occasions, Freud's work, I think, helps us understand eros itself as a drive that nonetheless serves the *relationship* or connection between self and Other. Indeed, insofar as solicitude is invoked in, say, confronting the suffering of another, there is a quality of altruism, a relation to exteriority, that emanates from relations of love. Thus precisely because it is part of an ambivalent structure of affect, we cannot turn love into a fixed relation (neither idealize it for moral purposes nor reject it on the basis of its singularity); consequently, our vigilance must be directed toward how well love establishes the quality of relationality to the Other outside of pure self-interest, for it is in such a relation that commitment for the Other is to be found.

COMMITMENT AND LOVE

As we have seen, there are two tensions at work in discussing the potential relevance of love in ethical relations, particularly in the context of educational projects concerned with social justice. First is the apparent impasse between developing concern that takes into account the many others for whom we are responsible and the intimate setting of the love relationship. As a response to this impasse, we witness the second tension: that love can become idealized as the mode of relationality that promotes responsibility, or it can be dismissed as being inadequate for the task of developing concern on a larger scale. My point here has been not so much to erase these tensions as to put forth an alternative that helps us reflect on love as a mode of relationality and I believe that viewing love in terms of relationality offers us a different starting point for considering its place in creating moments of nonviolence across difference. For I do think that seeing love's ambivalence, on the one hand, and seeing it as an ambiguous mode of relationality, on the other hand, will help us reconsider what the specifically ethical import of love might be. My approach has been to show that the real questions at stake must be framed in terms of how love creates and sustains commitment for the Other, and how love itself signifies ambiguously and ambivalently in our communicative encounters.

As a mode of relationality that brings us together with another whose experience we do not share, love is precisely that which can condition a responsivity where the Other's difference is cherished. However, placing love under the signs of ambiguity and ambivalence means refraining from turning it into an ethical or a pedagogical ideal. Instead I am suggesting that we examine love through a double paradox: first, while the ethical potential of love lies in its capacity to attend to the uniqueness of the Other in a way that exceeds the self's own interests—in what Freud has termed *altruism*, and what Levinas has termed *sacrifice*—its dangers lie in the way love functions to sustain self-interest and pleasure at the expense of the Other. Second, while being-for requires an unknowable, unpredictable element in response to the uniqueness of the Other—Levinas's fine risk—love as a relation is also channeled, as Freud makes clear, through social prohibitions and conventions. This paradoxical situation requires, then, a careful consideration of how love emerges as a relation across difference, particularly since staging these encounters through curriculum, as well as engaging in actual classroom exchanges with students, is part of the practice of animating responsibility within social justice education.

Given these paradoxes, we can see that for teachers to demand love (following Oliver's advice) in order to develop moral concern holds little promise, since the commitment essential for concern and responsibility is incited in the spontaneous openness to the Other that is the essence of a fine risk. In addition, to demand that students love as a *type* of relationality is already conceiving of love in the mode of being-with, where risk and the possibility for response to alterity become an impossibility. That is, we cannot create a simple list of expected behaviors and have them function in the modality of being-for where commitment emerges. We cannot tell students that this kind of love is what you ought to feel, and if you feel otherwise, you are somehow morally impaired. Nor can we demand that students simply repress feelings of love, and the mode of relationality that love implies. For we do recognize that the passions driving the altruistic gesture to act without self-interest and for the Other themselves are implicated in love. Thus we need to look outside of our own demands to explore how the passion, desire, and tenderness framing students' development of concern and commitment factor into establishing nonviolent relations. Unlike empathy, then, where the feeling itself involves a mode of relationality that ultimately consumes the Other, love does carry with it, as we have seen, certain possibilities. It would be naive to think that students are not mobilizing love in some form when they become overwhelmed, taken with, or passionate about a particular Other in an educational encounter, and consequently become equally desirous and passionate about responding responsibly. Thus through the framework of an implied ethics, it is the way love is expressed in our classrooms that must be read for the way it contributes to establishing commitment for each of our students.

In teaching, the vigilance that Oliver writes of is not so much about demanding or encouraging love but about attending spontaneously to student spontaneity, outside of institutional frames of reference. In this sense, no expression of love is judged as *automatically* being moral or immoral. I would venture to suggest that erotic (and even sexual) expressions of love between teachers and students (i.e., between consenting adults) can be something other than what institutions codify them as being (e.g., deviant, aberrant, or irresponsible); they are forms of communication that may or may not in and of themselves enhance the quality of human life of the particular persons involved, thus they might not be definitively violent.[21] That is, the risk that is the condition of commitment can erupt in indeterminable ways. The point is to keep open the question to what degree such affects might be performing an ethical nonviolence that disrupts convention in ways that are responsible. So claiming that love is ambiguous means actually having to find ways of reading its place within specific social contexts and in relation to specific people.

In one of my classes, a graduate student who is a teacher told us that she brought in some of her son's winter clothes for a student in her class because his family did not have enough money to buy the necessary jacket, mittens, and boots. She claimed that she felt a profound responsibility for him, felt protective and loving toward him as she does toward her own child, and had established a deep bond of affection with him over the few months that she was his teacher. The school she worked in frowned upon such personal giving and preferred to give clothes to children through a central system in the office; however, they did not have everything the child needed at the time. She said she was concerned about his welfare and simply could not act otherwise; she felt she had to do something.

On the face of it, we might be inclined to read this story as an admirable tale of a concerned teacher who took it upon herself, out of her deep affection and love for a student, to make his life a little more comfortable despite the prohibitions from the institution. But the story also reveals many other possibilities: how she gave these clothes to him and his family; whether she saw herself as "rescuing" or "saving" this child; how her response was guided by the child's own interests; or why the clothes were not donated through the office are all significant elements to consider in exploring how love participated in the commitment that led to this particular act. None of these considerations is to deny that what she did had some ultimate benefit in keeping the child in some physical comfort against the cold and perhaps alleviated some harsh treatment from his peers in being singled out. My point is that the teacher's passionate commitment to, and her declared love for, the student cannot be read unambiguously from the start. Being a recipient myself as a child to some similar acts of charity, I know all too well the doubleness that can accompany what appears on the surface to be an altruistic gesture, but which can lead instead to humiliation, shame, and confusion, and to the expectation that one will be grateful in return; a form of gratitude, moreover, that is supposed to conform to a specific social script. Yet I also know how altruism can perform in graceful ways that are indeed inspired by love and an attentiveness to the sensitivity of personal circumstances that do not require reciprocation, and that resist rules laid out by institutions that do not always guarantee each individual's well-being. It is these moments that do disrupt the heaviness of social life in ways that allow each of us to live with some dignity. This is why I am emphasizing that it is the openness and risk to attend to ambiguity, to admit that we cannot "know" beforehand what it is the Other wants, to be vulnerable to the consequences and effects that our response has on the Other, and to be continually receptive to the Other's unforeseeable needs that ground love's ethical potential. Love alone cannot always accomplish this. Thus I am not suggesting that one refrain from action until one gets all the angles figured out, because the point is we can never figure it out completely; we cannot calculate, in some algorithmic fashion, the end result in order to keep our actions safe and ourselves intact. Rather, what I am suggesting is that the ethical dimension of such actions is not guaranteed through the love itself (because I love you, I will always act ethically toward you) but through the way love sustains a mode of relationality where the self comes into being through response to the Other (my love for you enables me to be for you, insofar as I can be open to you through my love). In this sense, our commitment to our students involves our capacity to be altered, to become someone different than we were before; and, likewise, our students' commitment to social causes through their interactions with actual people equally consists in their capacity to be receptive to the Other to the point of transformation. In large measure, then, it is the recipients of our altruistic attachments who keep love from becoming morally complacent to the degree that they challenge us to remain responsive to their vulnerability. In this sense, the Other teaches us something about the difficulties of love and commitment, something about the risk needed for responsibility. What matters, then, in terms of the example above, is the extent to which the teacher's love enabled her to learn from the student in the moment of her response, a response that puts at risk the teacher's own self-assurance.

A passionate commitment that leads to a responsible response can emerge precisely through that loving bond that gives itself over to the other in a gesture of communicative openness. Responsibility would then come to have meaning in ensuring that such openness is maintained, and it would require an attentiveness that critically reads our interactions through the very ambiguity and ambivalence I have discussed here. It is precisely when eros is about a selfless approach toward the other, or to put it in more Freudian terms, a drive for connection with exteriority, that it erupts into an ethical interaction. Viewing love in this way, then, means attending to expressions of it with an openness that exceeds what is institutionally defined. It requires us to listen carefully to the passion, ardor, and tenderness with which our students speak about their concern, a listening that enacts its own committed regard. In other words, it is not about demanding the impossible: that each of us love the Other. It is about recognizing that affective bonds of love can shape those passions so necessary for moral commitment. It is about listening with attention and presence to such affect. And it is about listening for the riskiness of love with risk. To reiterate, it is not that all love leads to ethical possibility; our potentialities for aggression and control, our desire to satisfy ourselves through the Other, interrupt such ethical potentiality. The riskiness of love lies in the self's unwitting capacity to be moved to excess by the Other, and the fine risk inherent to commitment lies in the self's capacity to respond with sacrifice to the uncertainty that this movement entails. Thus love is not *necessarily* a fine risk, but I think it can be.

FOUR

STRANGELY INNOCENT? GUILT, SUFFERING, AND RESPONSIBILITY

IN CLASSROOMS DEALING with traumatic histories of injustice or with the troubling violence and inequities that continue to mark everyday life in this new millennium, guilt often surfaces, persistently and indelibly, as a relation between the stories of suffering being retold and those who listen to their retelling. The fact that guilt is so commonplace in accounts of classroom encounters dealing with social justice issues (e.g., the Holocaust, racial injustices, and homelessness) raises numerous questions regarding how students and teachers understand guilt as a relation between one's sense of moral responsibility and the suffering experienced by others. Indeed, a primary question for me concerns the ways in which teachers—like myself—who bring such stories (e.g., newspaper articles on homelessness, accounts of institutional racism, biographical material on the Holocaust) into the classroom for their "pedagogical" value are doing so in order to influence students' attitudes in a particular direction, optimally seeking to shape a more complex understanding of social responsibility. Because of the presence of such a desire—indeed, demand—to touch and shape another's life in this way, these pedagogical strategies and the responses they incite require a careful consideration not only of what it is we hope to do but what the actual effects of our educational encounters produce. Admittedly, the responses to stories of suffering can be as varied as the students who listen to them; however, I wish to focus on guilt here, because it is the one kind of response whose frequency is met with apprehension and even hostility on the part of educators. Unlike empathy, or even love, guilt is a kind of response that is seen to represent a pedagogical failure of sorts, for guilt is not generally held to be morally or politically productive, and certainly it is not viewed as having much educational value. Yet the significance of guilt it seems to me lies in its tacit acknowledgment that some harm has been committed against another, for which one feels some kind of obligation, whether or not one has been directly involved in such harm.[1]

What I am particularly interested in exploring here are two questions that open up a possibility for considering guilt as having pedagogical and ethical significance. First, what makes us susceptible to guilt in listening to stories of suffering in the first place? That is, why is guilt such a common response to being exposed to another's suffering? Second, how might we think about responsibility—both teachers' and students'—in light of such susceptibility and guilt? For instance, to what degree do students' guilty responses provoke a sense of responsibility toward people who suffer, and what responsibilities do educators have in the context of these student expressions of guilt? In response, I offer a close reading of two views of guilt, both of which speak directly to its ethical significance in the context of how each of us engages with suffering that is not our own. Melanie Klein focuses on the role that our earliest feelings of love and aggression play in guilt, and she views guilt as a necessary feature of the moral work of making reparation. Klein's work reminds us that this moral work is a psychical event, rooted in a particular set of relations from one's empirical past that has an impact on how we encounter suffering in our classrooms in the present. Emmanuel Levinas's writing concerns itself less with an empirical past and more with considering how our "pre-originary" openness to the Other gestures ethically toward an unknowable future. In doing so, Levinas draws attention to the metaphysical aspects of guilt and susceptibility, and how these give rise to an inevitable responsibility. Levinas's work allows us to read our classroom encounters with suffering as formative to responsibility. As in all the chapters, there is a definite theoretical incommensurability between the two views under study. Yet I am reading them here in tension with each other to frame our attention to guilt as a complex ethical formation that involves the subject inescapably in both a psychical history and a metaphysical dimension. Together, these dual aspects of guilt highlight why it is that guilt needs to be attended to.

GUILT AS A PEDAGOGICAL PROBLEM

There are many ways in which guilt structures students' response to what Levinas refers to as the "uselessness" of suffering, that is, the absolutely unnecessary nature of another's suffering.[2] When students confront such suffering, they frequently invoke various types of guilty responses. At the risk of oversimplifying what is a complex phenomenon, I wish to draw attention to three different, although not fully discrete, types of response to illustrate how guilt often plays itself out in the classroom. These types have not only appeared with some regularity in published accounts of teaching but in my own experience as well. They are presented here less as a typology than as a set of discursive constructs that frequently overlap and are often expressed by the same person. The methodological risk, of course, is that the complexity of guilt as a phenomenon is reduced to these types. Using these three types heuristically, however, allows us to consider the multivalent nature of guilt itself, to identify what might be ethically significant about claiming guilt, and to examine how pedagogies of social justice produce the very dynamics they often rail against.

First, it is not uncommon to hear students proclaim their guilt *and* their feelings of responsibility for deeds they have not directly committed. When discussing the issue of urban homelessness, for example, students frequently tell me, "I feel so guilty because I don't know what to do to help." These students generally feel weighed down by the inadequacy of their position in the face of suffering they are witness to, and they express a sense of being overwhelmed by the enormity of it all, struggling to maintain a sense of hope when all they feel is despair. These students inhabit a place in which recognition of the suffering of an other brings with it a commensurate (if not an equal) suffering to them. That is, their guilt is a kind of punishment directed toward themselves, for they feel they cannot act—or have not acted—in such a way as to prevent or ameliorate such harm. They often reprimand themselves for not being able "to do enough," and they struggle to articulate what it is that can in fact be done. What is often obvious in these situations is the sense of remorse that sets in in the face of another's pain, not because one actually has been *directly* involved in causing that pain, but because the self is nonetheless called into account in confronting it.[3]

A slight variant of this is the second response offered by students who also feel overwhelmed by stories of injustice, yet whose focus is less on what can be done for an other and more on trying to come to terms with one's own privilege. Awakening to the harshness of others' experiences of the world, they feel guilty because they have not "suffered enough." A hierarchy of oppression and suffering emerges in their understanding of an other. This position does not concentrate on what can or ought to have been done to prevent or remedy the injustice. Rather, it centers the ego—if one may call the ego that cumulative set of experiences that emerges out of the conflict between the social and psychical—as the site of the problem. In some ways various pedagogies encourage the taking up of this position, for the reason that it is precisely in the act of undoing or *unlearning* one's privilege that one is supposedly then able to assume responsibility. The focus on one's own lack of suffering (for that is how privilege is defined in such declarations) reflects a type of survivor guilt, whereby one's ego is called into question for having been spared the indignities (and, in confronting stories of genocide, perhaps even death) to which an other has been subjected.

Lastly, it is, perhaps, equally common for students to proclaim their innocence and their anger at "being made to feel guilty" by the very pedagogy that is supposed to make them "more enlightened" and "feel better" about themselves. These students attempt to negate the overwhelming effects of guilt by proclaiming that they cannot be held responsible for actions that they have not themselves committed. Moreover, part of this negation is that it produces its flip side: an assertion of one's innocence, which is often accompanied by equally strong statements of criticism against the teacher or other students. (I am not speaking of those students who espouse hateful speech or who see people who suffer as being blameworthy; instead, my focus is on the students who appear to struggle with what their involvement is in the suffering of an other when they have not been "directly" involved.) Here, then, there is no sense of remorse present, nor is there a centering of the ego's privilege and lack of suffering; instead, there is a powerful attempt to squirm out, seemingly unscathed, from underneath the oppressive weight of their new knowledge of someone else's suffering. The focus is on how they are not responsible for past injustices and that they personally have done nothing wrong and therefore have nothing to atone for—and it is assumed (often quite rightly) that this is indeed what the teacher is demanding. Their declarations of guilt and innocence appear less like guilt and more like externalized anger—the trajectory of which often effectively disrupts the teacher's pedagogical intentions. In its repetition of innocence, such a position may be seen to be a form of resistance to hearing about another's suffering. However, what remains more interesting for my purposes here is the curious way in which these students, by proclaiming their guilt (and apparent innocence), also affirm that some wrong has been committed. That is, their act of speech betrays that which they cannot directly speak: another's pain. In identifying guilt as significant in listening to stories of suffering, these students' speech, like the ones above, also recognizes that something wrongful has occurred, even as they underscore their own personal distance from it. For it is precisely because they do see the need to declare their distance that indicates to me that there is a far deeper, if tacit, realization that there is something from which they need to distance themselves. Naturally this does not only mean that they recognize harm has been committed, but that this harm involves them to such an extent that they feel compelled to make certain they and others know that they have had nothing to do with it.

In each of these accounts what is put into sharp relief is the preeminence of guilt as a pedagogical force to be reckoned with, where learning about someone else's pain becomes refracted through one's declared sense of responsibility (or lack thereof). What such responses suggest about guilt is that it signals to the self that one is implicated in a wrong committed against an other. Unlike shame, which focuses on how the self is perceived *by* the self in relation to an event that might not even involve the suffering of an other (e.g., one can feel shame for behaving or thinking in a certain manner, even when no other person was the object of those actions or thoughts), guilt, on the other hand, assumes a social responsibility, where the Other's well-being is always at risk.[4] Thus arises the need to self-declare that one is or is not responsible, often either to comfort the self that one is as good as one thinks, or to persuade others of the same; and this responsibility is invoked because it is precisely responsibility that is at stake in guilt. Guilt connects the self to the external world, to the realm of the social, while shame remains confined within the self's parameters of self-idealization. Guilt, in this sense, although obviously concerned with how the self is perceived, is more closely tied to how the self is perceived in terms of the *quality* of relationships with others. If one were simply to feel shame (and I do not mean to imply that shame is ever that simple), then it is not clear that one would feel some responsibility for an other; it would merely indicate that one holds oneself in severe disregard, and it often involves something that one cannot bring oneself to articulate to another person.

Given this, could it be that what these students are describing are actually feelings of shame—particularly in the first and second instances—and that their statements are merely misrecognitions of guilt? My response can only be that it is not so much whether students have identified their feelings "accurately" or "correctly" according to some prior and stable definition of guilt; instead, it is the very *movement of self-identifying* as a guilty subject and how this movement is such a commonplace response to stories of suffering that calls for some unpacking. In this regard, I am interested in why guilt gets identified so readily, how these self-declarations actually do speak to a guilt that arises out of a susceptibility to the Other, and how this carries profound ethical significance. More importantly, it seems to me, is to ask ourselves how educators handle these movements of self-identification, these utterances of guilt and the acts of uttering them, given that it is our very pedagogies that make possible such declarations in the first place. In turning to a close reading of the work of Klein and Levinas, I hope to offer some navigational tools by which we might consider guilt as being fundamental to the process of making reparation and to the formation of responsibility; as well, I hope to offer some observations as to how and why this is at all significant for education.

THE GUILTY SUBJECT OF EDUCATION

The phenomenon of guilt in education has been a subject of commentary (and numerous parenthetical remarks), if not full-fledged inquiry. There have been many ways of approaching the meaning of guilt in these educational contexts, some authors asserting that what lies behind such evocations is self-pity or a form of defensiveness, others claiming that such responses are simply inadequate, and may even be improper, in the face of the pain experienced by others.[5] Nevertheless, what unites many of these responses is a view of guilt as a manifestation of "liberal" sensibilities. The subtext is that "liberal guilt" is an individualistic response that detracts from marshaling the energy needed to recognize the larger, systemic factors that promote violence and maleficence toward others. Moreover, such guilt, it is charged, leads to paralysis with respect to taking social or political action to repair the harm committed. Guilt *qua* liberal guilt, then, is thus held to be problematic, and it is alleged to be responsible, at least in part, for a kind of moral catatonia at worst and political indifference at best.

While the term *liberal guilt* may be familiar to most of us, there is, on the one hand, a troubling lack of precision about what counts as liberal guilt, while, on the other, there is a broad-based assumption regarding its value or worth within progressive circles. What appears to count as liberal guilt often boils down to expressing one's guilty feelings over another's condition of pain, misery, or suffering.[6] That is, any and all guilt that results from coming face to face with individual or group suffering has the potential to become liberal guilt. Liberal guilt appears to be less about a specific type of guilt (such as Oedipal guilt or survivor guilt) and more about grouping guilty feelings together under a rubric that is understood to have certain political connotations and valuations.

With respect to such valuations, Julie Ellison, in her history of liberal guilt, points out a number of characteristics.[7] Liberal guilt has become a notion of disparagement, a futile exercise in self-absorption, making it an abject condition for progressives. Liberal guilt is of the rank of the petty, its logic redolent with sentimentalism and embarrassment rather than with a sense of political or social purpose. Ellison writes, for example, that "the embarrassments of liberal guilt arise from the authenticity of a more absolute pain discovered by the white intellectual in the gaze of the racial Other."[8] That is, in comparison to the suffering endured by others, any guilt experienced by one who is privileged seems downright petty. Consequently, the words we use to attach liberal guilt to actual persons cast their own moralistic shadow: one can be "accused" of liberal guilt, one "suffers" from liberal guilt, and one can "wallow" in liberal guilt. Read under the moralizing rubric of liberal guilt, guilt itself becomes a moral failure of sorts, where the pettiness of self-doubt and uncertainty that guilt bestows on us is a debilitating condition seen to be in need of a remedy.

For example, at one point in her book *Feeling Power*, Megan Boler quotes a student's perceptions of her own guilt: "The collective guilt that overpowers many of us should not be the reason for examining the Holocaust. We need to explore the origin of the cruelty of it."[9] Here we see that guilt "overpowers," it stands as an obstacle to exploring roots and "origins," and it ought not to be the "reason" for seeking out answers (to what are, perhaps, ultimately unanswerable questions). Such a reading of guilt suggests that guilt prevents us from counteracting the misery that we continually witness and rewitness through literature, film, or face-to-face encounters in the streets and in our classrooms. As Ellison remarks, "in the throes of liberal guilt, all action becomes gesture, expressive of a desire to effect change or offer help that is never sufficient to the scale of the problem."[10] The pedagogical task, it would seem, then, is to overcome the obstacle—guilt—that stands in the way of making adequate and effective social change.

As it is named, labeled, and categorized as liberal, it is *all* guilt that becomes that obscure object of denial and repudiation in progressive pedagogies. Through metonymical displacement, liberal guilt stands in for, and thereby conceals, the traces and layers of pain, struggle, and "ontological shock"[11] that are frequently found in what Shoshana Felman calls the "event of teaching": a teaching that "strive[s] to produce, and to enable, *change*."[12] Guilt is seen as an unruly force that threatens our capacity for making "real" or "authentic" social change, and, as Ellison points out, guilt is the "embarrassed position which nobody wants to occupy."[13] Both as a threat and source of embarrassment, guilt, it appears, needs to be disciplined and held at bay. Conceiving of guilt as liberal guilt in effect tames, as it denounces, the potentially disruptive flow of sorrow, anger, and embarrassment that often accompanies expressions of guilt in the classroom. Liberal guilt at once recognizes the strength of such affect, yet it also functions simultaneously to control such affect by its illocutionary dismissiveness. Thus liberal guilt, I would argue, acts like a sentry, barring us from probing too deeply into the significance of guilt within progressive education; and, as Freud claimed of the function of the superego, liberal guilt also acts like a "garrison in a conquered city."[14] That is, guilt *qua* liberal guilt guards and protects us from inquiring too deeply into whether guilt can have moral or political value, since our very understanding of morality and politics has already censured guilt in the form of a prohibition. If we grant guilt any moral status, we often run the risk of being charged either with appealing to crass sentimentalism or with a failure to recognize the political futility of guilt.

More importantly, perhaps, the term *liberal guilt* also serves to defend us against thoroughly analyzing how we might be placing unreasonable demands upon students to bear burdens for deeds not directly committed by them. That is, if our pedagogical strategies create the conditions for guilty subjects to emerge, then how responsible (and responsive) are we when we dismiss guilt as yet another moral failure? If guilt is such a relatively common response to others' suffering, pain, and discrimination, are we really doing it justice when we simply denigrate it or condemn it as being petty and sentimental under the rubric of liberal guilt? Can we recover an understanding of guilt that seeks not to deny or repudiate its affective power but instead considers the significance of such affect for moral action? Might we, as teachers, resist the urge to denounce our own and others' guilt in order to think carefully about how guilt is implicated in making reparation and in assuming responsibility for deeds that we may not have committed ourselves?

REFRAMING GUILT: AWARENESS AND SUSCEPTIBILITY

One of the major factors, it seems to me, contributing to the appearance of guilt in the classroom is the psychical bridge it builds between the listening and telling of stories of pain. Patricia Williams tells of a student who, after attending Williams's class on poverty and the law, declares with some anger that she is being made to feel guilty about poverty, about her uncle who is a "slumlord," and about her family's privileged status in general, thus declaring her innocence in the process. Williams comments that "the class discussion had threatened the deeply vested ordering of her world."[15] Guilt and innocence emerge precisely at the point of new awareness, where the stories of suffering (in this case due to poverty) become too difficult to hear, to bear, and to integrate into one's sense of self and one's worldview. Yet even more significantly is the way guilt and innocence operate together here as a concerted response to this threat. Shoshana Felman remarks:

> If innocence is an illusion, guilt is not a *state* opposed to innocence, it is a *process* of coming to awareness: a process of *awakening* which, as a process, is not theory, but as Camus here [in his book *The Fall*] puts it, an actual *practice:* a practice, or a process, of a constantly renewed wrenching apart.[16]

As a process of awakening and wrenching apart, guilt involves the subject in an often painful recognition of another's pain. Stories of suffering call upon us; they involve us in a response to an other, they hail us and demand, in the moment of their telling—or, more precisely, in the moment of our listening—that we say, do, or feel something in return. That it is not always easy for us to respond is evident in Williams's example above. Yet the demand to respond to stories of suffering does not tell us why guilt, rather than, say, shame or envy, is so prevalent and persistent. As I have stated above, guilt explicitly involves social responsibility; yet why is this so? What is it about guilt that binds itself to an intrinsic sense of another's suffering?

One possibility is that guilt is a constitutive feature of subjectivity itself, characterizing an *anticipatory* state, a *susceptibility* to becoming a subject in relation to another person. Judith Butler has discussed this susceptibility with regard to Althusser's work.[17] In peeling back a critical layer from Althusser's illustrative example of interpellation, Butler problematizes how it is that guilt and subjectivization come to be seen synonymously. Althusser's paradigmatic case posits a subject who, while walking down the street, is hailed by a police officer with a "Hey you!" The subject turns toward this figure of authority who has called out and thereby accepts the terms of the law by which he or she is hailed. Reminiscent of the Freudian Oedipal drama, whereby a subject comes into being by internalizing, through identification with the father, the laws and mores that govern social relationships,[18] Althusser's theory of interpellation posits guilt as the end result of being subject to such inevitable laws. That is, as the subject turns to the abstract and impersonal hailing ("hey you!"), he or she tacitly assumes his or her guilt before the law. However, Butler searingly asks, "why does subject formation appear to take place only upon the *acceptance* of guilt?" (107, emphasis added), highlighting the fact that guilt comes to the subject from the outside. Her response to this question is not a castigation of Althusser, or of interpellation per se, but rather an inquiry into the dynamics of guilt for subject formation read in reverse (106).

Rereading this paradigmatic story leads Butler to consider how the turning toward the hailer is already profoundly suggestive of another anticipatory state of being: "Although there would be no turning around without first having been hailed, neither would there be a turning around without some *readiness* to turn" (107, emphasis added). For Althusser, it is *after* turning toward the hailer that the subject assumes a position of guilt, a position that enables its birth into language, into the law that confers identity upon the subject. For Butler, it is the *susceptibility* to the other's call that enables the subject to turn, and where the subject's guilt is to be found. She quite rightly notes that Althusser's whole schema rests upon an inversion of guilt and innocence, whereby the subject, in its readiness to turn, exhibits a guilt that both proceeds as though the subject had already broken the law and yet is oddly guiltless. In this sense, Butler is suggesting something quite different about guilt here—and I think more Kleinian. According to Butler, the subject turns because she is already prepared to subject herself to the Other; she is already responding as a guilty yet innocent subject. Butler writes:

> prior to any possibility of a critical understanding of the law [Who is hailing me? Why should I turn around?] is an openness or vulnerability to the law . . . in the anticipation of culling an identity through identifying with the one who has broken the law. Indeed, the law is broken prior to any possibility of having access to the law, and so "guilt" is prior to knowledge of the law and is, in this sense, always strangely innocent. (108)

Strangely innocent. Guilt is not about knowing beforehand what is right or wrong in the realm of social relations; rather, guilt emerges because one is susceptible to the call of the Other, to the call of the social relation itself. Indeed, as Freud theorized (and Klein following him), guilt initially has less to do with understanding good and bad as moral terms and more with a vulnerability that revolves around fear of the loss of love.[19] Thus guilt's strange innocence not only has to do with the double play of innocence and guilt that Felman speaks of in coming to an awareness of another's pain but also with one's own affective connection to other human beings prior to the establishment of moral authority.

This notion of "strange innocence" is helpful in understanding how guilt plays itself out in students' responses to stories of suffering. Taking Butler's consideration of susceptibility into account enables us to see how students are at once both hailed by and susceptible to stories of suffering. That is, on the one hand, these stories address or hail students through the pedagogical act in a way that demands an acknowledgment that there has been harm committed; here the figure of the teacher acts as the authority who hails the subject, with the assumption that the student has yet to receive the "law," the "correct" attitude or moral position. Students respond to the hailing as though they had already done something wrong, as though they were already guilty before the law for causing another's suffering. On the other hand, it is the very susceptibility to that suffering in the first place, that readiness to accept and "receive from the Other beyond the capacity of the I,"[20] that sets guilt into motion. It is precisely because what is at stake is a sense of relationality to the Other, where that Other can threaten to annihilate one's sense of self, or at least threaten to alter it, to leave it loveless and deprived, that students can experience such intense guilty feelings.

What I am arguing here is that understanding guilt as "strangely innocent"—as characteristic of an initial susceptibility to another's presence—is compelling for moving us out of discourses of liberal guilt, as well as for theorizing what might be at work for students in staking out a guilty position. Rendering guilt in terms of such susceptibility may help explain why it is that guilt so often emerges at the point when the suffering of another is exposed and brought into one's sphere of awareness. It is important to underscore here that one's response cannot sufficiently be explained by claiming that one merely has been exposed to another's suffering; rather, it can only be understood as a *vulnerability* to that exposure. Indeed, it may be argued that the entire enterprise of education is founded on a belief in the susceptibility of the subject to be open to what it is teachers have to teach. But why are we so susceptible to others' stories, to the point of producing such strong reactions of guilt? Why does the suffering of others matter to us in this way? And to what degree is this significant for moral responsibility?

A MORAL ORIENTATION: "LOVE, GUILT, AND REPARATION"

Suggesting that guilt is involved in an awareness of another's suffering and in one's susceptibility to that suffering means understanding guilt as a moral orientation rather than as a moral obstacle. It is the confluence of love and guilt that Klein identifies as part of the work of making reparation, and it is the vulnerability and susceptibility *to* the Other that Levinas views as significant for being responsible *for* the Other. Read through these moral categories (reparation and responsibility), guilt emerges as a pressing concern for grappling with the moral demands of responding to the injustice of another's suffering.

According to Klein, making reparation, or making good the wrongs done to an other, stems from one's own sense of guilt about one's potential to do harm to other people. Klein notes in particular that it is not so much the deeds we actually commit that make us experience guilt, but rather that guilt emerges in conjunction with our *fantasies* of aggression. What happens when we experience guilt is not so much an awareness of what we have actually done but a nascent recognition that we have the imaginary capacity to cause harm. Although Klein (and Kleinian analysis in general) accentuates the importance of these early aggressive impulses, coupled with this is an attentiveness to the love that is also required in order for us to feel guilty in the first place. It is this emphasis on love—and its connection to guilt and aggression—that may help us reconsider what dynamics are at play in caring about another's suffering.

In her key work on guilt, "Love, Guilt, and Reparation," from 1937, Klein offers a developmental account of the emergence of guilt from infancy onward. Despite its rather literal emphasis on family stereotypes, this text works to articulate the ways in which early infantile and childhood experiences profoundly affect the emotional and psychical landscape of the adult. In this rather lengthy and convoluted essay, Klein begins with the significance of aggression in constituting guilty feelings, but she is fundamentally concerned "to give a picture of the equally powerful force of love and the drive to reparation."[21] Thus what we have from the start is a text that seeks to detail the ambivalence at the heart of what Zygmunt Bauman refers to as the "moral impulse,"[22] and what Klein here calls a "drive to reparation."

Klein's schema relies upon her work with children in analysis,[23] work that has led her to posit that early formations of subjectivity are inherently violent as much as they are inherently innocent and full of love. According to Klein, an infant lives through this ambivalence by directing toward the one she is most bound to in love various physical acts of rejection (e.g., biting, kicking, and pushing away). More importantly for Klein, however, are the early fantasy formations that occur alongside both the aggression and love that the infant has for the caregiver (i.e., the mother), to the point that aggressive fantasies themselves (not the actual acts of aggression) give rise to intense feelings of anxiety. (As we have seen in chapter 1, it is this early capacity for fantasy that both causes anxiety and eventually paves the way for symbolization as a way of dealing with this anxiety.) According to Klein, "A most important feature of these destructive phantasies, which are tantamount to death wishes, is that the baby feels that what he desires in his phantasies has really taken place; that is to say he feels that he *has really destroyed* the object of his destructive impulses" (308). Moreover, in providing a figure of subjectivity that is tied to one's early relations with others, Klein suggests that guilt is itself an inevitable and important part of one's development. More surprisingly perhaps—and this is key, I believe, to Klein's understanding of reparation—is her assertion that guilt is also involved in the subject's capacity for love. She writes:

> My psychoanalytic work has convinced me that when in the baby's mind the conflicts between love and hate arise, and the fears of losing the loved one become active, a very important step is made in development. These feelings of guilt and distress now enter as a new element into the emotion of love. They *become an inherent part of love,* and influence it profoundly both in quality and quantity. (311, emphasis added)

What Klein is suggesting here is that guilt, even as it is an expression of the death drive, is part of the very landscape of love, and that consequently such love bears traces of the death and destruction wrought by fantastical representations of the loved one. (And as we have seen in the previous chapter, love, too, is itself ambivalent.) Guilt and love, although emotionally distinct, are nonetheless inextricably linked through the complicated and ambivalent ties that bind us to other people and the fears we have about losing them. Indeed, it is, according to Klein (who follows Freud here), the fear of losing love that initially arouses guilt and the subsequent (albeit, nascent) awareness that one loves the Other; consequently, the subject must protect the injured Other from the violence of the self. It is in this sense, then, that guilt begins to participate in feelings of love, insofar as this love carries with it an insecurity borne out of an impulse to destroy.

Hence, rather than view guilt as simply debilitating, on Klein's account, guilt, alloyed with love, provokes a desire to repair the damage thought to be suffered by the loved one. That is, the subject seeks to make amends, to restore and repair the injured party through yet another layer of fantasy. But does this occur in order to remain loved (in order to master the fear of loss of love), or is it to keep one's love of the Other intact (because one finds doing harm to the loved one intolerable)? What exactly leads to such reparative and restorative impulses?

There are no simple answers to this for Klein. At times, Klein asserts that love for the mother gives rise to guilt and the reparative impulse, yet we have seen that she also declares that guilt is a fundamental part of love itself, suggesting that love is already tinged with guilty affect. On other occasions, it is the sheer fear of loss of love and the fear of one's own aggression in contributing to this loss that are highlighted. At other times, she announces that reparation is central to love relations, rather than the other way around, seeming to indicate that reparation lies in a prior relation to love ("This making reparation is, in my view, a fundamental element in love and in all human relationships" [312].) At yet other times, Klein asserts that reparation is of the order of a "drive," which in psychoanalytic terms signifies an impulse whose existence lies internally within the subject (akin to the life and death drives discussed in chapter 3).[24] Thus this lack of clarity over the specific dynamics involved in reparation speaks not only to a confusion on Klein's part, but it is also, I think, symptomatic of the tenacity with which reparation is held onto by Klein as the only possibility for theorizing our moral impulses.

As Jacqueline Rose points out, it appears as though the notion of reparation within Klein's work enacts its own reparation.[25] It acts as a redemptive textual strategy for the brutality that marks the Kleinian subject. Rhetorically speaking, reparation seems to be marshaled in as a defense against the positing of our potential to do harm to an other. Reparation as a concept (loosely defined as such) itself becomes a form of restoration and repair in order to make good the horrible truth of subjectivity Klein is postulating. It is as though the despairing recognition of our potential to commit violence—even in fantasy—necessitates the ushering in of some degree of theoretical hope.

Klein herself suggests that hope is important to maintain: "Normally, the drive to make reparation can keep at bay the despair arising out of feelings of guilt, and then hope will prevail" (342).

Thus there is a double sense of reparation within Klein's account of guilt—both in the actual *content* of the account and in the textual *strategies* employed in the account—that speaks directly to this need for hope. For what Klein is struggling with here theoretically is a shift away from viewing guilt as emerging through the internalization of the law, the identification with the father who represents the social order—an identification that marks the resolution of the Freudian Oedipal complex. Instead, she shifts toward a meaning of guilt as something that emerges alongside one's early love feelings for the mother, for the one who provides love and nourishment. Her textual strategies, then, suggest a deeper conceptual struggle with the psychoanalytic establishment. Klein's push toward the maternal marks a distinct achievement in the theorization of guilt as a very early factor in the development of the child. Her hopeful appeal to reparation, therefore, is crucial in understanding how one copes with the guilt one experiences when one has imagined another's suffering, particularly since it is rooted in imagining the *loved one's* suffering.

The problem for Klein is how love can be maintained and sustained in the face of fantasies of destruction from a very early stage. Put another way, if these early fantasies occur in the first love relation of one's life, then how can love ever survive their power? It is certainly not clear how the infant could ever move into an Oedipal situation which, in Freudian terms, demands holding intact the purity of that first love relation. Admittedly, while Freud also is adamant that one fears the loss of love in feeling guilty,[26] this is ultimately an incentive for identifying with the authority that represents the social order at a much later stage of development. In contrast, Klein sees that the early love relation with the mother is far more complex in involving early aggressive fantasies (and actions), and that the fear of loss of her love, as well as the love the infant begins to feel for her, is present from the very beginning of one's life. Thus in order for the Kleinian subject to move beyond the despair of destruction—which needs to happen if any development at all is possible—Klein is compelled to reconsider how guilt and love together structure the very possibility for human relationality. That is, she needs to show how one can work through the ambivalence that cuts through one's first relationship, and she does so by claiming that guilt surfaces long before there is any knowledge of—or identification with—an authority figure.

Ironically, perhaps, given the Kleinian emphasis on the power of aggressive fantasies and the dreadful account of the capacity for destruction humans have, guilt nonetheless occupies a position that is, as Butler would say, "strangely innocent." That is, it is characteristic of an initial susceptibility to the Other's presence, and it lies in a prior relation to any assumption of the law, or language, or identity. The subject's capacity for guilt, according to Klein, occurs in a pre-Oedipal moment (to use Freudian terminology), where it is the nascent awareness of another's suffering and the part one plays in it—rather than knowledge of right and wrong—that is firmly at issue here. What Klein's work implicitly traces is how one comes to care about the suffering of the Other, and how this leads to a development of one's moral sensibilities. It is because we feel love and cause pain simultaneously that we experience guilt. Despite the confusion over the precise sequencing of love, guilt, and reparation, Klein's text continually iterates that it is the presence of both love *and* guilt that is necessary for forming moral relationships with others. Although we can only perhaps feel guilt if we are capable of love, so, too, can we only make good the harm that is done to someone else if we are capable of guilt—and capable of bearing that guilt.

Unlike liberal guilt, then, viewing guilt as a moral orientation toward reparation recognizes the ambivalent emotions that lie behind our attitudes to another's suffering. Guilt has the potential to incite moral action,[27] but it does so as the result of profound vicissitudes of affect, where aggression and kindness, love and hate, reside in a contradictory and ambivalent space. It is precisely because a notion of reparation recognizes the strength of this affect that it can, in my view, speak directly to the rage, embarrassment, and genuine passion through which students express their guilt and innocence in becoming aware of the suffering of others. Moreover, Klein's emphasis on fantasy is helpful for assuming a much more complex position vis-à-vis the emergence of specific dynamics of guilt in the classroom.

Fantasies of aggression as well as love can be seen to be at work in students' declarations of guilt—even for deeds they have not committed. How one imagines another's suffering—and how one imagines oneself in relation to that suffering—permeates and frames such declarations. Like the notion of broad empathy discussed in chapter 2, such reconstruction of another's suffering is given life through our imaginative investments. In considering the three articulations of guilt mentioned above, one can see that in each case students reveal where they imagine themselves to be situated in relation to the harm they have witnessed and thus speak to the way they perceive themselves as both potential injurers and potential repairers. Each position reveals several possible reversals of meaning, where the absent presence of the utterance, or what remains unspoken, lies in the twinning of love and aggression that marks the students' entry into guilt.

The first position regarding the despair of not being able to do enough about an injustice (e.g., homelessness) reveals two implicit messages. On the one hand, in voicing worry and concern that one has not done enough to alleviate suffering, the idea is simultaneously conveyed: "If I don't do enough, I am harming the Other." Here we see how one's own concern about the Other's suffering implicates the self in causing harm and rests on one's imagined presumption that one has indeed caused harm to another. This is not to say that there is no external truth to this statement; certainly the failure to take action definitely can lead to causing or furthering actual harm. Nonetheless, what remains important is that one's imagined role in the life of another's suffering also is connected to one's imaginative reconstructions of the capacity to cause harm, in spite of any external factors. On the other hand, there is also an opposite trajectory at play in one's concerns over doing enough, for implied here is yet another meaning: "If I *do* do something, I can ameliorate the Other's suffering." Thus there is an imagined reparative tendency embedded within the very concern with the Other's pain or misery. In this respect, to claim that one may not have done enough may also be opening up the possibility for recognizing that there is something to do.

As for the second example, the claim focuses on one's own lack of suffering in the face of another's pain. Here we see a similar though different kind of pattern. Students read their own privilege as the very marker of someone else's injury: thus "my privilege has caused someone else hardship." Here, too, the statement contains an imaginary element that one has caused suffering, this time through one's relative difference to the Other. There is a tacit recognition of aggression here, insofar as one's privilege is the basis of pain for someone else. However, the tendency to reparation is not so straightforward as in the first example, and it often takes one of two directions: either one can "unlearn" one's privilege in order to relieve the suffering that that privilege has caused or, in an attempt to reverse the equation "lack of suffering = harm to another," one could seek to suffer equally alongside the Other.[28] Thus in this position it is essentially the centering of the ego as a privileged site that suggests that the *reparative* response needs to be seen in terms of "undoing" privilege rather than "obtaining" equal suffering.

The third type of utterance, you will recall, concerns the need to distance oneself from the suffering of the Other altogether. Here, too, we see the capacity for aggression and reparation internal to such statements. Aside from the anger embedded within such a response, this utterance reflects a concern with one's own implication in the suffering of another person. While the direction of the aggression is significantly different from the other two types of declarations of guilt, insofar as anger is often directed against the teacher or fellow students, the statement nonetheless reveals similar fantasy constructions. Read quite literally, the insistence on distance can also be understood as an admission of aggression toward the one who has suffered. That is, one of the meanings underlying this distance is: "If I don't distance myself, I am the oppressor." Guilt in this scenario carries with it the devastating idea that one has the potential to harm others without intention, and that this idea is itself too painful to bear. As for its reparative tendencies, distancing oneself (and declaring one's innocence) not only means that one has attempted to wash one's hands of the suffering (thereby effectively negating any involvement in that pain), but it also signals another meaning: "By distancing myself, I am not harming you anymore." For unlike statements of outright hate for a group, or of blaming people for their own suffering, this kind of declaration of guilt underscores the profound ambivalence about one's own ambivalent relation to the Other. That is, it is precisely in the moment of becoming aware of the Other's suffering that one encounters one's own aggression and love from which one has to distance oneself. In this sense, the distancing is not just about creating a space between self and Other but about effectively distancing the self from itself, from its own affective response.

The hope that Kleinian reparation offers is constructive for escaping the straitjacket view of guilt that claims it is either morally insignificant or politically noxious. In explaining the psychical dynamics of how guilt incites moral action, Klein's work is especially fertile. She enables us to reflect on the dynamics at stake in various positions of guilt, and on the kind of fantasies of aggression and reparation that subtend them. As Klein suggests, such capacities for aggression and reparation stem from an initial alloying of guilt with love in our early relationships. And growing out of this initial love attachment to the mother, Klein postulates that we transfer onto others our "interest and love," and hence, our capacity for "making reparation . . . widens in scope" (342). Thus for Klein, as for psychoanalysis in general, the psychical past cuts into the present, giving the subject a history that continually shapes our relations to others. It is a history, moreover, without which we are, I believe, theoretically impoverished when it comes to considering the delicacy and complexity of human relationality across difference, and the difficulties that arise as a result.

However, the notion of reparation still cannot fully explain the state of responsibility in responding to stories of suffering. By this I mean to suggest that while fantasy plays a pivotal role in theorizing the psychical investments in self-identifying as feeling guilty (especially those feelings for deeds we have not committed), what it cannot accomplish fully on its own is the constitution of responsibility. That is, the drive or impulse to "make good" the harm done to another is accounted for through an empirical set of concerns over how we may come to develop a moral impulse. What it cannot sustain is asking questions of responsibility outside of this empirical frame, questions that are important to ask if there is to be some understanding of the Other as unknowable, or more accurately, not subject to empirical analysis. Thus, reparation is always already constituted within the given frames of reference of the Other as a psychical subject, understood through psychoanalytic discourse. And while this subject may not "be like me" in its idiosyncratic detail, how we understand it is nonetheless subjected to a thematization that applies to both of us, that, as it were, catches us both in the same ontological net.[29] As discussed in the introduction to this book, it is a thematization that is not only unavoidable but indeed indispensable; yet it also means that we already come to the Other with the presumption of a knowledge that belongs to us alone.

Levinas's view of responsibility, while certainly tied to its own philosophical tradition, nonetheless attempts to put into question the very nature of the subject and theorizes responsibility not as something that lies "within" the subject but as something that comes to the subject from the Other. That is, responsibility avoids the thematization of the subject that reparation necessarily relies upon. While reparation speaks to the moral capacity of the individual as an empirical subject, responsibility, as we have seen, refers to the inevitable ethical condition that makes each of us subjects in the first place. It is in Levinas's work where subjectivity itself is radically constituted as responsibility. As Alphonso Lingis succinctly puts it: "Responsibility is in fact a relationship with the other, in his very alterity. Then a relationship with alterity as such is constitutive of subjectivity."[30] What this means for guilt, as we shall see, is that not only is it a psychical response to the specificity of another's suffering but also a condition of the susceptibility to the Other that constitutes subjectivity itself as a suffering. The point I wish to address below through dwelling on Levinas's work on responsibility, guilt, and susceptibility is not just about how we might feel a sense of reparation in light of the dynamics of aggression and love that plague us, but how it is that *I am* and do not merely *feel* responsible for an other in light of my guilt. In other words, how are students' utterances of guilt speaking about their own suffering?

RESPONSIBILITY, SUSCEPTIBILITY, AND SUFFERING

In *Otherwise than Being*, Levinas argues unequivocally that we *are* responsible for the Other—inevitably and without question. This is so because we are susceptible to the Other, to the alterity that marks the Other's life as infinitely unknowable. When we consider what this means in terms of the suffering of another, and in terms of the significance of guilt as a moral orientation, then it is important to consider Levinas's conception of responsibility insofar as it does not reside in the full knowledge we can have of the Other's pain—although we may know *about* such pain; instead, it resides in the susceptibility we exhibit toward this suffering. Part of the dense landscape of responsibility in Levinas's work involves the subject being susceptible to the Other to the point of guilt, and it is this connection that I wish to explore here.

As we have discussed, Butler's articulation of the importance of susceptibility for theorizing how it is one becomes a subject (i.e., the readiness to turn and be vulnerable to the law) is crucial in understanding the emergence of guilt as coming before our apprehension of the law, as being strangely innocent. Levinas goes quite a bit further in suggesting that such susceptibility is "pre-originary" (122), originating not in some empirical past (that would give the subject a psychical or developmental history, for instance) nor in some stable point in the past (such as Althusser's interpellation story that seeks to fix the origins of identity) but in a past that is wholly unrepresentable and "immemorial."[31] Guilt, in this view, lies in a strange relationship to time, for it continually emerges out of this unrepresentable and nonthematizable relation with the Other and yet simultaneously always gestures to the openness of the future. Levinas attempts to articulate the inarticulable conditions of subjectivity without relying on a master discourse or overarching theory to do so.

Instead, his project is concerned with the traces of susceptibility that are to be found in the qualities of relationships that we have to other people, and in our capacity for response to them. Even more importantly, Levinas pushes our thinking on susceptibility a step further when he claims that such susceptibility is a "passivity prior to all receptivity, it is transcendent" (122). This statement may seem to confuse the issue of susceptibility more than it explains it; yet it is this transcendent passivity that holds the first key to understanding the links between susceptibility, responsibility, and guilt.

The idea of transcendence signifies in Levinas's work a specifically transcendent relation to the Other.[32] Located in the immediacy of the relation between self and Other, transcendence is about a form of relationality that moves beyond fixed identities or essences toward an attention to alterity. To be transcendent, then, is to be fully open to the Other in a way that one's ego (one's conscious ego) is not at stake in the relation, where such an openness is prior to all thought. Passivity, then, insofar as Levinas identifies its transcendental quality, is that mode through which the self approaches the Other beyond essences, and it is that irrevocably naked position that the self occupies in the face of the Other. As a radical openness that is not seeking to "understand" or "know" the other, passivity is "the way opposed to the imperialism of consciousness open upon the world" (92). It is not that passivity is merely inactive in its nonconsciousness, but it indicates instead an "exposure" to the other that lies prior to consciousness. In this sense, passivity is a kind of radical susceptibility. The subject's passivity does not mean that one ought not to act, or that one's actions in the world are unimportant; it is, rather, that even to consider action is already presupposing a profound exposure to the world. And it is precisely this presupposition, this necessary condition of exposure (and exposedness), that constitutes subjectivity—and responsibility. Levinas writes:

> Responsibility for the other ... is a passivity more passive than all passivity, an exposure to the other without this exposure being assumed, an exposure without holding back, exposure of exposedness, expression, saying. This exposure is the frankness, sincerity, veracity of saying. Not saying dissimulating itself and protecting itself in the said, just giving out words in the face of the other, but saying uncovering itself, that is, denuding itself of its skin, sensibility on the surface of the skin, at the edge of the nerves, offering itself even in suffering—and thus wholly sign, signifying itself.[33]

There is a double movement—or effect—of susceptibility at work here. On the one hand, it is because one is susceptible to the Other that one is launched into subjectivity; that is, subjectivity is not an act created *ex nihilo* but is dependent upon a relationality with the Other, whereby the subject is assigned through the encounter with the Other. On the other hand, it is susceptibility that gives rise to responsibility, insofar as the condition of passivity initiates a relation in which the I is *subjected* to the Other; the self is always responsible for the Other because it is in a relation of subjection—a relation, Levinas writes, of destitution, persecution, and accusation. Levinas's depiction here is clear: the other commands the subject into being and in so doing inaugurates responsibility. Responsibility for the other is the very structure of subjectivity.

But how does Levinas arrive at the necessity of responsibility for the subject? And how does being persecuted by an other feed a sense of guilt? Part of one's susceptibility to an other is an openness to the Other's command, to that fine risk of communication; thus not only is susceptibility to the Other a one-sided affair, whereby I, and I alone, am commanded, but so, too, is responsibility. It is the self's susceptibility to the other that makes the self *solely* responsible: "The knot of subjectivity consists in going to the other without concerning oneself with his movement toward me" (84). How the other is for the self does not play a factor in the self's responsibility for her. This is the case because responsibility is not located *within* a subject. Instead, involved in the initial susceptibility I have *to the other*, responsibility *comes from the other* and emerges out of the difference that structures the human relation—a relation that does not presuppose that self and Other are the same. There is always only a self and an other, not two selves or two others that are interchangeable, for this would imply a knowledge, a thematization, an understanding that "we" are all the same. In seeing difference as central to human relationality, Levinas endeavors to posit this difference at the center of responsibility, and thus he emphasizes the uniqueness of the self's responsibility and its nonreciprocal nature. For Levinas, responsibility can only ever be attributed to the self, the singular subject. Even as Levinas writes in the plural, it is the I, the self, the unique subject that is at stake in responsibility: "In the responsibility *we* have for one another, *I* have always one response more to give, *I* have to answer for his very responsibility" (84, emphasis added).

In construing subjectivity as inevitably responsible, and construing this responsibility as coming from the Other, Levinas's portrait of the self's encounter with the Other takes on drastic and grave overtones. Insofar as "I am obliged without this obligation having begun in me" (13), the self is bound to the Other in a relation of guilt in which the self bears the burden of the Other's subjectivity, the Other's freedom, and the Other's mortality. What responsibility and what guilt! How could one possibly avoid the stain of guilt in bearing this burden? Surely the self must be inadequate in the face of this monumental command.

Although references to guilt abound in his work, guilt is generally a complicated and little-articulated notion for Levinas. Fond of quoting from Dostoevsky's *The Brothers Karamazov*, Levinas insists that "'Each of us is guilty before everyone for everyone, and I more than the others'" (146).[34] Consistent with his emphasis, then, on the singular and unique nature of responsibility, Levinas invokes this quote repeatedly to indicate the enormous *weight* of responsibility. Yet how does responsibility come to be seen as guilt? Or rather, why does Levinas appeal to guilt as a marker of responsibility?

It is not always made thoroughly clear, and the continual quoting from Dostoevsky acts in some ways as a substitute for a more elaborate account of guilt. However, there are a number of key characteristics associated with guilt in Levinas's work that are important for reflecting on declarations made in the classroom. First, guilt emerges because it is almost as though responsibility—indeed subjectivity—*demands too much of the self.* The self is always in a state of subjection to the Other, and therefore it is always caught in the demand for the Other's freedom. The self alone is guilty before the Other, because it can never fully provide for that freedom, since the Other always faces a mortality that the self cannot reverse. By this I mean that it is precisely because the self alone can only *bear* the Other, rather than take over her, identify with her, consume her, or console her, that the self is left inadequate to the task of responsibility commanded by the Other: "A face is . . . given over to my responsibility, but to which I am wanting and faulty. It is as though I were responsible for his mortality, and guilty for surviving" (91).

Yet another, second, characteristic Levinas draws for us is the *belatedness of response* to this command from the Other:

> The neighbor assigns me before I designate him. This is a modality not of a knowing, but of an obsession, a shuddering of the human quite different from cognition. . . . In an approach I am first a servant of a neighbor, already late and guilty for being late. I am as it were ordered from the outside, traumatically commanded, without interiorizing by representation and concepts the authority that commands me. (87)

Thus the "traumatic commandment" that always comes from the Other cannot be assumed, understood, or foreseen beforehand, nor can the command be theorized in terms of internalizing the authority that the Other represents (as both Freud and Althusser postulate). It is not a command that emerges from some authoritative position the Other occupies. Instead, the command is prior to the law, it comes from the Other in an anticipatory state. The self's encounter with the Other is of the nature of a surprise—unplanned, unthematized—thereby making all responses to the Other belated, after the fact, and post-traumatic. In not being capable of the response that would fulfill the command, one can only be found guilty. As for Klein, guilt here emerges prior to any law or authority, and it is installed through the very susceptibility to another's presence.

But more importantly still is how guilt is invoked in Levinas's work in terms of the effect of this presence, this commandment from the Other. The trauma of encountering the Other *devolves into a persecution and a suffering,* and this marks the third characteristic of guilt.[35] We are guilty because we are being accused by the Other, are susceptible to this accusation, and suffer for it. The Other's command (to which the only response for Levinas can be responsibility) is traumatic insofar as it calls me into question, and it does so through my own suffering.[36] For Levinas, to be guilty even in the face of such persecution—perhaps especially in the face of such persecution, where the suffering of the Other and the possible death of the Other pursue one fully and absolutely—is part of assuming responsibility not for one's own suffering but because of it. Our susceptibility to others means that we *are* guilty for deeds we have not committed, for guilt is not about deed or action, or about the content of the suffering of the Other, but is a response to the trauma incurred through the Other's *telling* or *saying* of such suffering. In this way, one is persecuted by the speech act itself; in speaking her suffering, in addressing the self, the Other inflicts a wound upon the self. A saying demands to be heard and requires a response.

Within this world of responsibility, guilt is seen as a responsible response. The three elements of guilt discussed above—the inadequacy of the self in responsibility, the belated response to the other, and the redoubling of suffering through the persecutory call of the other—all gesture toward the moral significance of guilt and the complex formations it takes with regard to one's exposure and susceptibility to another's pain. For this reason, Levinas's conception of guilt enables us to look beyond the self's motivations (both conscious and unconscious) in order to uncover—or posit—what it is that first must be in place in order for the subject to be responsive. Guilt does not ask "What then is it to me? Where does he get his [the Other's] right to command? What have I done to be from the start in debt?" (87). These questions reveal the ways in which the self reduces the Other to the same, reduces the Other to *effects* of the self, as though the only thing that mattered was how the Other pertained to *me*. Alternatively, in decentering the self and in centering alterity, what Levinas emphasizes is how guilt comes from the Other. What guilt asks then is: What can I learn from the Other? How might I respond to the Other's command? How can I be for the Other?

In learning from Levinas's own allusions to guilt, it may be that we are better able to navigate our way through the self-identifications of guilt that students make when confronted with the knowledge *about* another's suffering. What Levinas theorizes must be at stake in the susceptibility to the Other is that one's response is formed in relation to the command of the Other, not to the content of what another says. In this regard, student declarations of guilt say something about how they have responded to the Other, how they have learned *from* and not merely *about* the Other—no matter what the teacher's intentions have been. That is, self-identifying as guilty subjects, they inhabit positions that speak to all three conditions of guilt mentioned above, revealing a nakedness and an exposure in claiming their relation to the Other. Moreover, in thinking about how the Other persecutes the subject, declarations of guilt also speak to the very suffering that constitutes subjectivity. That is, self-identifying as guilty signifies the suffering associated with listening to the Other, the inescapable involvement students experience as they listen to stories of pain. Moreover, each of the positions described at the beginning of this chapter illustrates how listening brings with it its own traumatic repercussions.[37]

What is evident in all three responses, for instance, is the very feeling of inadequacy in the face of another person's suffering. Whether one declares such inadequacy outright ("I cannot do enough"), or whether one declares inadequacy as not having suffered enough, each articulates a sense of responsibility that is struggling to figure out how one bears the weight of someone else's pain. Even in seeking to distance oneself from the Other's pain (in the third instance), there is a tacit acknowledgment of the inadequacy of one's disposition in the face of such pain. That is, there is an inadequacy to the task of responding to the harm that has been done, and so one must retreat to a position of innocence.[38] However, such declarations of guilt can be more or less tied to responsibility, depending on whether or not self-identifying as guilty brings with it the capacity to ask, how might I respond? At times, this type of distancing is precisely a struggle with this question. How *does* one respond when one both is guilty and yet has not "done" anything wrong, when one is "strangely innocent"? At other times, it functions more (although not exclusively) to ward off any involvement of self with the Other. It seems to me that this, then, is the pedagogical task set before us with regard to this kind of declaration. How do we engage students who struggle with their own place in engaging with difference?

All three positions reveal a structure of guilt in which students are awakening to the burden placed on them, and to the necessity of shouldering that burden responsibly. What we see here are variations within an approach: the movement to self-identify as guilty may be read as a tentative movement from an initial susceptibility to the Other toward assuming responsibility for the Other. Yet what must be emphasized here is that the links between susceptibility, guilt, and responsibility cannot (and should not) be turned into a developmental process, one that follows a simple sequence of events (i.e., one is susceptible to the Other, one self-identifies as guilty, and then one is on the royal road to responsibility). Instead, what I am suggesting here, following Levinas, is that one's approach to the Other is just that, a *movement* toward the Other. Being able to theorize susceptibility, guilt, and responsibility as movement, helps us think through what it is students may be saying in their declarations—declarations that do not always follow the heuristic types sketched above (human responses are, of course, rarely so neat). What Levinas's work leads to is a consideration of the way in which movement toward an other is fundamentally a learning *from* the Other. That is, our susceptibility to another's pain, our ability to suffer and be persecuted by the Other, means that one has exposed oneself to the Other, that the Other has entered us and pierced the membrane of self-identity. That the Other can transform us, can affect us from the outside, indicates to me that guilt is a response to learning itself.

CONCLUDING THOUGHTS

Rendering guilt as a possible moral orientation means inquiring into how encounters with suffering build on our initial susceptibility to an other. Considering guilt as having ethical weight offers possibilities for thinking through what it is we are attempting to do in introducing stories of suffering into our classrooms. I cannot stress enough that I do not view all expressions of guilt as occupying a privileged ethical site; yet I do think we need to concern ourselves with attending to articulations of struggle that students produce through their guilty self-identifications. Educators who deal with social justice issues often do so out of the conviction that conscious awareness about another's suffering can have a positive effect upon the way people develop concern for others in a gesture of being-for the Other—a conviction that is largely premised on the subject's capacity to be moved by such suffering. If our intent is to create possibilities for students to be moved by listening to stories of injustice, then we need to reflect carefully upon what such an encounter entails and to begin to understand where our responsibilities as educators lie. That is, when we count on students to be susceptible to those stories, then we need also to consider how such susceptibility is itself a condition of guilt and responsibility.

As we have seen, the subject's susceptibility to the Other comes *prior* to knowing *about* the Other. It is this that makes guilt possible and that makes educators' efforts to teach about suffering fraught with (necessary and inevitable) tensions. That is, while educators may desire that knowledge of suffering will inform moral action, such desire is often frustrated. Defensively mustering the discourse of liberal guilt speaks less about the place of guilt in developing moral concern and more about our profound discomfort with inciting such guilty affect, especially since such affect is frequently read as a failure of students to learn. Moreover, simply to dismiss guilt as a moral failing is, therefore, a grossly inadequate response, for guilt may be reflective of a kind of moral suffering on the part of students. However, if we understand that our initial susceptibility to an Other provides us with the hope to work against injustices, then we also need to understand how this very susceptibility places all of us in a fragile learning community. For being susceptible to an other means attending to the work of learning as emotional labor, a labor that involves all of us—students and teachers—in new awarenesses. That guilt should emerge as part of this work is a sign of our emotional vulnerability. Reframing guilt as a tentative encounter with the suffering of others is not a mark of the failure to learn but one of the symptoms of emotional struggle to learn across differences.

What I do not want to suggest is that educators simply stop teaching sensitive material. Indeed, exposing students to portrayals of suffering seems an inevitable part of any educational project concerned with social justice. Nonetheless, two issues need mention. The first is an ethical question concerning how such material is given time in the class. Talking about reports of homeless people dying, for instance, can push some students to (almost) unbearable limits. Thus in thinking carefully about how to grapple with declarations of guilt in the classroom, there is first a need, I believe, to allow students opportunities for articulating their own complex responses (which can, of course, cut across a range of emotions, such as empathy and outrage, as well as guilt). Whether this is done through various forms of discussion, essay writing, or poetic expression, the point is to encourage students to see that their responses inevitably implicate another. That is, no matter what the content of the response might be, it is the act of responding that places students in a potentially ethical relation with the people who are represented through stories of suffering. It is not that students ought to engage in endless navel gazing, but that their responses of guilt, for instance, are seen as morally significant for how one comes to take up a position of responsibility.

Second, the task for educators, it seems to me, is to think carefully about declarations of guilt in the classroom since there is a way in which guilty utterances produce their own "saying," their own command to which teachers respond, in the same way that students respond to stories of injustice. Thus teachers themselves are susceptible to the sufferings expressed through students' declarations of guilt. But to what, exactly, are teachers responding?

Klein's work makes it possible for us to consider such declarations as bound to a love that enables one both to feel badly for another's suffering and to reach out in a reparative gesture that seeks to ameliorate harm. In this way, the question for teachers becomes, how might I respond to guilt in a way that encourages students to think about its complexity, that is, to see individual guilt as a relation that the self has to the Other? How might an educator's response incorporate a sense of guilt that neither negates its possible moral significance nor the vicissitudes of affect that students bring to such declarations? On the other hand, Levinas's work allows for an understanding of guilt as a responsible response toward another's suffering—a response that creates suffering for the one who cannot help but be guilty. Teachers, then, are compelled to ask, how can my response to my students' suffering, refracted through their declarations of guilt, be itself responsible? To this end, there is a need to be open to and nonjudgmental about the guilt expressed by students. Such openness means attending to the saying of student declarations in such a way as to encourage a more open dialogue about the place of affect in one's moral life.

What guilt so readily unveils is the difficulties of working across differences: that between students and stories of injustice and that between teachers and students. This interminable work across differences, across the sufferings that wound us and bind us together in a guilty embrace, is what makes guilt so strange, so seemingly out of place in what we think ought to happen in the classroom. All too often we focus on what may be "appropriate" content for teaching across differences, forgetting at times that we inhabit a space where differences are embodied, a space that can be both wonderful and threatening, full of love and aggression. But what Levinas and Klein have taught us is that there is hope in learning from the Other and, moreover, that guilt can participate in such learning. Perhaps we need to refocus on what it is we think we do when we introduce stories of injustice in our classrooms, and how it is we think we respond to students' guilty declarations. For if our students are suffering under the burden of an awakening responsibility for the Other, struggling to work through their own love and aggression with regard to another's pain, then guilt needs to be heard—and, indeed, listened to.

FIVE

LISTENING AS AN ATTENTIVENESS TO "DENSE PLOTS"

"SOMETIMES I FORGET I have a face." The quote comes from Maggie Cogan, the title subject of Michel Negroponte's documentary film *Jupiter's Wife*.[1] The film chronicles the filmmaker's relationship with Maggie, a homeless woman living in Central Park, over the course of two years. It is a powerful portrayal of the nature of listening in responding to the Other—a relation of intrigue, confusion, and responsibility, whereby Maggie summons Negroponte to attend to what he calls the "dense plots" of her life story. More importantly, it displays the way listening as a mode of relationality creates the possibility for learning from the Other, and it gives us a ground from which we might consider the specifically ethical potential of listening.

As we have seen, both the relationship to the Other that is the teacher and the relationship to the stories of injustice introduced in classrooms elicit a variety of complex responses from students. Such responses reveal some of the ways in which students "receive" the Other and become hosts, as it were, to the Other's narrative presence. Underlying each of these responses is a certain quality of attentiveness in the listening brought to those stories, and it is this quality that seems to me to be important for considering ethical relations across difference. Someone who might deeply empathize with an other who may be suffering (e.g., a victim of racial or sexual violence) may not be listening and attending fully to the difference that marks the Other's experience as unique and distinct from one's own. Thus in thinking about the ethical significance of encountering the Other in education, it is important to explore the quality of listening that goes on in these encounters. What is it that we listen to when we listen? What effects does listening have on the one who listens? How does listening contribute to establishing a specifically ethical attentiveness to difference? Equally central to this is what kinds of responsivity on the part of teachers themselves promote moments of nonviolence in the face of students' response? While I have thus far gestured to the importance of listening to students' empathy, love, and guilt for the way they potentially open up a communicative openness with the Other, we need to consider what it means to listen in more elaborate detail.

There are three dimensions to listening I explore in this respect. First, building on the work of philosopher and psychoanalyst Gemma Corradi Fiumara, I discuss the general problems and potentialities of listening in relation to narrative. Listening is viewed here as an intrinsic, as opposed to an incidental, aspect of speech and language. Second, I draw upon Cornelius Castoriadis's idea that speech is a creative and unconscious process of making meaning. Listening, in this view, requires an attentiveness to how the irruptive and errant plays within language bear significance for the Other, a significance that lies beyond the listener's comprehension. To extend this idea further, read across Levinas's understanding of listening as not only central to conversation but as central to ethical response and responsibility, means viewing listening as an attending to the alterity of the Other that is not recuperable through language. Taking all three aspects together, what I argue for in this chapter is a notion of listening that does not merely respect the Other's alterity but indeed *attends* to it. That is, I seek to show through the example of *Jupiter's Wife*, how listening not only contributes to an ethical response to suffering, but—through its very capacity for attentiveness—how listening can itself be an ethical response.

My tack here is methodologically different from the other chapters in that I begin with the relations of ethicality outside of a conventional educational point of reference. Yet in working with the film *Jupiter's Wife*, it is precisely the moments of learning through listening that interest me here. More precisely, by exposing and being exposed to what is perhaps still one of the most blatant examples of social difference that exists in North America, namely, a homeless woman, the film pointedly uncovers what is involved in "paying heed"[2] to another's speech, to another's narrative presence.

LISTENING TO AND IN *JUPITER'S WIFE*

Jupiter's Wife opens with a shot of Central Park that would make even Woody Allen proud, and as viewers, we are led into a film whose story will take a dramatic twist. Panning its landscape, Negroponte captures its bucolic lushness and begins a narration about his family and the park in the first-person present, showing us a childhood photograph of himself and his brother dressed as cowboys presumably posing in the park. The film, he tells us, originally was to be a documentary about the park itself. He lapses into a fantasy about what the park might have looked like 100 years ago, and we are presented with a series of archival stills that captures its illustrious past. Hence, from the very beginning of the film, Negroponte is deeply implicated in his subject matter; his is no detached perspective. However, his fantasy is suddenly interrupted, he says, by his fascination with a woman with a team of dogs. The camera then picks up a shot of Maggie, and we are positioned as Negroponte is: a voyeur looking at a strange woman. We are told by Negroponte that upon meeting him at this time, Maggie said she had been expecting him for days.

This mysterious interruption marks the beginning of Negroponte's listening adventure, as well as ours. Suddenly the film begins to enfold as a narrative about two people becoming enmeshed in each other's lives. The filmmaker's response does not only retell this voyage from his point of view but, through its elaborate attention to the words Maggie uses to speak about her life, summons viewers to listen and respond to Maggie herself. Throughout the film we witness the filmmaker's struggle, which borders on the obsessional, to make sense of Maggie and her self-narrative. His listening and questioning draw out of Maggie a panoply of surprises, and we ourselves become immersed in the strange tales that Maggie has to tell.

Compelled by her initial address to him, Negroponte returns to the same spot the next day and waits for her. Even though the film takes two years to shoot, he narrates it in the continuous present, as one would document in a journal the day's activities and one's feelings and thoughts about them. Through this strategy he conveys a sense of eagerness, expectancy, and immediacy. Negroponte's emotional investments in Maggie are startling and become increasingly pronounced as the film progresses. In fact, we are invited to share along with him his sense of discovery, his wonderment, and his puzzlement as he engages with Maggie throughout the course of the film. His encounters with Maggie appear in sequence, with no perceivable disruption of time (with the exception of one flashback and a couple of shots of her from twenty years ago, but these are all part of Negroponte's narrative, not Maggie's). In this sense, the film both reads like Negroponte's diary and, in effect, diarizes the viewer's own encounter with Maggie. While his narration is about his relationship with Maggie (and about piecing together Maggie's history), Maggie's narration—the one we, like Negroponte, encounter—is a perplexing collection of assertions about her present, her past, and her future.

Maggie's story begins in two places in the film. The first occurs with the visual image of Maggie with her family of dogs, representing the initial encounter with Negroponte. She says nothing to the camera; we only hear Negroponte telling us about her expectation of him. The second occurs with her first statement to the camera: as she is rubbing her hands over her face to wash herself, she declares "sometimes I forget I have a face." This statement sets the whole tone for what follows; the film, in part, becomes a quest to seek out what Maggie can no longer say in the language of the everyday, can no longer appear to fully remember. Taken as a metaphor, the face she forgets is the mask of her former life, the history of trauma, loss, and psychical conflict long suffered and continually present. But what becomes clear throughout the course of the film is that it is not so much that she forgets the past, but rather she articulates it otherwise, through a series of significations that gesture beyond the commonplace. Just as hysterics have a bodily language for articulating psychical conflict, Maggie resorts to the language of the cosmos to represent and reveal herself.

As we proceed through the first half of the film, Maggie tells Negroponte that she is Hera, sister of Zeus, and that Jupiter was her husband, who now "controls the radiowaves" and communicates to her via radio messages. She claims that her father was Hollywood actor Robert Ryan, that she has a son Michael, born in 1969, and quintuplets who were born sometime later. Maggie says that she was a horse-and-carriage driver, was brought up on Long Island by parents not her own, and was kidnapped at birth by a man/God named "Hemera." We also learn that she is part of what she calls the "Class of '86"—the year she ended up living on the street with her dogs. She speaks of her survival, and how she has "evolved to a certain level" where she relies on a support system of friends, dives only in Upper East Side dumpsters, and no longer goes to soup kitchens nor feels, in her words, "beleaguered and lost and angry anymore." All of these rich and baffling details of her life narrative constitute what Negroponte refers to as her "dense plots."

Negroponte reads her story as a set of clues that will give him some indication of who Maggie is beyond being a homeless woman in Central Park. At one point in her conversation with him, she suddenly blurts out that they are in the "shadow of the living room." On other occasions, she says she has seen her children or Hemera in Central Park. Negroponte is continually wondering aloud what these strange phrases mean: "Who is Hemera?" "What living room?" Of course this strategy of asking questions sometimes reinforces the main narrative of the film, for we do find out from Maggie what some of these enigmatic statements refer to. However, not all of them are resolved, and Negroponte's openness to her story, to listen for the otherness of Maggie and to repeat questions that he knows have no answers, creates moments in the film that exceed the bounds of understanding—both Negroponte's and our own. It is at points such as these that the film presents Maggie's story as something other than Negroponte's portrayal of it. Negroponte, even at the moment of inserting himself into the discourse of the film through the posing of questions, still leaves space for us to witness Maggie's self-representation, in the sense that her creative capacity to signify and to freely associate outside the rules of sociality and grammar reveal that she cannot be contained within his narrative structure of the present. And, Negroponte, rather than cutting sections that do not easily fit the filmic or narrative order, merely muses about his own perplexity. Thus it is not so much in spite of but precisely because Negroponte's musings do not work to filmic or narrative advantage that there is a split between the filmic Maggie and Maggie the person. The viewer gets the impression that she is not only watching Negroponte's construction of Maggie but Maggie's construction of Maggie, with her signifying the face that she has not really forgotten after all.

By indexing time in the present, both in word and in picture, Negroponte attempts to "straighten out," as it were, Maggie's "queer" temporal ordering of words as well as her allusions to Greek deities, ESP, and Hollywood stars long dead. This reordering of her cosmic language for himself reveals something profound about the way we often approach listening to others, about the way we attempt to make meaning of another's life story by translating it into something we can grasp and understand.

What makes this film so compelling, however, is how it also displays a refusal of understanding itself as the only basis for response. Rather than render Maggie's seemingly nonsensical delusions as purely symptomatic of mental illness, or as a romantic refusal of civilization's demands, Negroponte listens and responds to that narrative in a way that acknowledges its own incompleteness. The real achievement of the film lies in those moments where Negroponte does not seek comprehension but simply listens to Maggie in her own words. He listens in such a way that he hears more than what is being said, knowing that what he can know about Maggie in terms of facts (he does attempt on a number of occasions to find out whether her curious words have any foundation in "reality") cannot capture who Maggie *is* in any systematic way. The film itself is a response born out of a certain quality of listening, a quality that allows Negroponte to see how Maggie herself is working through the complications of her own life, in her own way. In other words, in the face of the suffering and loss that is often evident, and in the face of the nonconventional logic Maggie's speech lapses into, Negroponte offers a curiosity that not only facilitates Maggie's modes of expression but alters how he perceives himself. In fact, he begins to recall the stories from mythology his Greek mother used to tell him as a boy, reflecting on the meaning they carried for him, and he integrates Maggie's language of the Gods into his own voice-over. Although Negroponte also offers her alternatives (e.g., he helps her find an apartment at one point), what is remarkable is how listening, as opposed to understanding, ultimately grounds his orientation to her.

As viewers, we are challenged to listen attentively to both Maggie and Negroponte. The film, by containing a double narration, allows us room to question what it is we hear, and how it is we hear it. The film does not, then, seek closure, and we are left, as Negroponte claims at the end, with confronting the mystery that lies in his relationship to Maggie. Her "dense plots" are there for the listening, and they are not only treated as raw material in need of deciphering. As opposed to engaging solely in the type of dialogic relation with Maggie that demands that each reciprocate equally in a verbal exchange for mutual benefit and understanding, Negroponte's listening, as well as his representation of that listening, suggests that attentiveness demands more of us than understanding words spoken by others.

The film deals with the complexity involved in listening, displaying an attendance to three facets of signification that are important for my discussion. First is the speech that emerges out of, and because of, an immediate, concrete relation. The spontaneity of Maggie's speech becomes ever evident as Negroponte's listening creates a context in which she can be heard, questioned, and responded to. Second is the structure of meaning that is implied, but not fully recoverable, in Maggie's elusive narrative. That is, Maggie's speech bears significance for her in a way that is neither entirely comprehensible to Negroponte nor to us as listeners. Third is the person who is revealed through speech but who nonetheless exceeds what is being said. Maggie is not simply a social category, a "homeless woman" with a history of mental illness, nor can she be summarily wrapped up through an interpretation of her speech. The listening that Negroponte displays reveals an acknowledgment that Maggie exists as a mystery who cannot be fully apprehended through a decoding of the dense plots she has to tell.

This documentary portrays learning itself as something that is deeply bound to listening. It introduces possibilities for thinking about the multidimensional nature of communication and the role listening plays therein, in ways that move beyond the regular dialogic task of "getting to know the other."[3] That is, it is Negroponte's learning from Maggie and his response to her not only *in* the film but *as* a film that tell us something about the contingent nature of our response, a response that takes shape around the utterance that the Other offers us, to the point of becoming an act of generosity, a gesture of openness that risks our own suffering. When he refrains from trying to place Maggie into a comprehensible framework, Negroponte *gives* his listening to Maggie and struggles with the consequences of this gift.

THE LANGUAGE OF LISTENING, LISTENING TO LANGUAGE

Focusing on listening and on the contingent aspects of listening means reconsidering how listening participates in forms of communication that do not conform to a simplified version of dialogue. The notion of dialogue is no stranger to education, and, in particular, social justice education is concerned with the dialogic possibilities for creating meaningful interaction across differences. Classroom strategies often invoke the notion of a "safe" space in which to speak, where everyone can participate equally. This frequently has been seen as an issue of bringing marginalized people to "voice," of giving them space and time to articulate their own desires, needs, and perspectives. And although there is a tacit agreement that it is important to hear what this voice has to say, dialogue very often implies that the ethical point of listening is to come to understand so we may speak better in return. What often gets left out of a conventional rendering of dialogue is the immanent risk of speaking (a risk that too often is consoled with appeals to safety), as well as the specific place of the listener as someone distinct and unique in relation to the speaker. As Gemma Corradi Fiumara points out, this is not simply a misdefinition of dialogue but of speech and language itself. As the "other side of language," listening functions as a necessary but forgotten component. "Listening belongs to the very 'essence' of language."[4]

As such, listening, for Corradi Fiumara, is integral to the unfolding of any communication between subjects and to the construction of stories we tell about ourselves: "No narratives would exist without some disposition to listen.... A narrative propensity may be a necessity for regaining a sense of our own history and the continuity of life; in fact our own history may be ultimately construed as being as ancient as life itself.... Yet no narratives could be conceivable in the absence of some listening disposition."[5] Corradi Fiumara renders language and our use of language (which for her are inseparable) as themselves being contingent upon our capacity to listen as much as on our capacity for expression. Even when we consider the expression of dreams, for example, that is, even when we move from the most private of worlds to a communicative mode of relationality, the articulation into language of another kind of symbolism is made possible in light of someone who attends to that articulation. "The dream is unknown to us; it is accessible only through the account of the waking hours. However, an account is possible only if there is someone who *can* heed, even if this were the same person who originated the dream. Dream-life and listening are vitally interwoven and cannot be detached."[6] Looked at from this point of view, listening provides a context through which thoughts and images can be organized and given structure and meaning. For Corradi Fiumara, it is not speech in and of itself that gives birth to ordered means of communication; listening is the precondition necessary for that order to emerge. The narratives of others are, by virtue of their being linguistic expressions, always already participant in the function of listening, and so the kind of listening we bring to speech situations is crucial for the way in which speech evolves.

This seems to suggest that the stories of suffering we introduce via curriculum, or via other students in the class, have already "found" listeners in the very moment of articulation. These narratives can only be understood in relation to the listening that conditions their receptivity. Similarly, for *Jupiter's Wife*, Maggie's increasingly intricate self-narrative is linked to Negroponte's reception of her tale; he is instantiated as audience as soon as Maggie speaks to him. Speaking narratives thereby "command" an audience, but the question is how that audience participates in listening and takes on that command, and what forms of attentiveness are embedded in the speaker-listener communication. Within the context of the film, it is Negroponte's taking up of Maggie's initial address ("I have been expecting you for days") as a command that leads him not only to alter the very subject of his documentary but to become involved in a relationship with another person to the point of altering himself.

Hence, listening is not merely a structural condition of language, but, to state the obvious perhaps, it is also a practice humans engage in among themselves. Certain kinds of listening can awaken certain kinds of articulatory practices, and Corradi Fiumara's advocacy for "maieutic listening" suggests that the role of the listener is that of a midwife who facilitates for the speaker the birth of linguistic expression. This view may seem at first to suggest an uncomplicated model of speaker-listener interaction, where the speaker is expressing something from the "inside" that is already known and merely needs to recover this knowledge through speech with the proper "guidance" from the listener. However, Corradi Fiumara's view is far more elaborate than this, insofar as it grants currency to the difficulties embedded within intersubjective communication that have to do with the place of the listener in relation to the speaker. Putting aside, then, for a moment her midwife model, I consider here three aspects of listening that Corradi Fiumara raises with respect to the relation between self and Other, which is where the specific contours of attentiveness, in my view, begin to take shape.[7]

First, Corradi Fiumara considers the ways in which the listener "enters" the other's speech. The listener fully participates in the speech of the other but remains somewhat distant and outside of that speech. This double-valent position is described as follows: "The message from the other will not attain its expressive potential except in the context of a relationship through which the listening interlocutor actually becomes a participant in the nascent thought of the person who is talking. But a listener can only 'enter' in a way which is at once paradoxical and committing: 'by taking leave,' by standing aside and making room."[8] This so-called entering involves the listener in an interaction that seeks not to take over the other's discourse or project oneself into the other; rather, entering is a symbolic function that enables the listener herself to become fully immersed, as it were, in the other's speech. Moreover, it means that the listener provides opportunities for further speech, for further elaboration to occur, where what matters is not the listener per se but the speaker being able to speak. For Corradi Fiumara, listening is thereby an "attentiveness" to the "incipient thought of the other" (145).

Second, and in direct relation to this, arises the following issue: to what degree can we be selfless in facilitating a listening environment conducive to attending to the other? That is, how do we attend in order to cultivate further communication? "The point at issue is whether it is possible to suspend or surpass the most surreptitious or deep-seated automatic responses of approval or recrimination" (152). While Corradi Fiumara has no immediate answers to this, she draws out the significance of renunciation both for the speaker and for the one who attends to her. That is, there is always a riskiness implicit in the act of speaking and listening, where the one who speaks loses an old mode of thought in the process of communicating a new one: "any new attitude must take on the semblance of a loss of the previous mode of seeing things and of evaluating them" (152). Similarly, the listener also goes through "an unavoidable process of mourning" (152), whereby one's thought shifts as one listens, one is compelled to alter one's position, and one suffers the loss of previous certainty. That is, as I listen to you and attend to your speech, I realize that what you are saying cannot be mapped on to what I have known before;

"we can be confronted with so much difficulty in reaching for language that we may even foresee the risk of having to 'transform' the whole of our vocabulary" (154). In this regard, listening is as risky a proposition as speaking is. What Corradi Fiumara taps directly into here is the structure of learning, where it is only through a position of ignorance, misunderstanding, and being challenged that one can learn. As Corradi Fiumara expresses it, only listening to what is obvious and easy is not really listening (158).

Third is the idea that listening implies a sense of trust on the part of the listener. It is a trust that is born of the uncertainty of the communication (and one might say the ambiguity of communication), where the vicissitudes of language yield unpredictable and unqualifiable narratives. In her discussion of how to reawaken an "inner listening," Corradi Fiumara writes: "The assumption that we can approach the optimal use of even the most rudimentary communications and that there is a desire to represent and express oneself is deeply interwoven with this trust. A trust that our interlocutor may convey what is yet unknown, unexpected or even what might actually be necessary for our own constant renovation" (162). Engaging in a speaker-listener encounter creates a potential space of hope for both the listener and the speaker. This is a hope that signals trust in new forms of knowledge and new forms of relationality. Tied to this is how the listener engages with the creative and idiosyncratic means of expression manifested by the speaker. We need to trust in ourselves and in what the other says in order to create the conditions under which learning itself takes place.

These three points raise fundamental questions about the ethical possibilities of listening, particularly insofar as they speak to the ways in which we not only listen as though we were merely engaging in the surface of the spoken words but as though we were fully committed to them in the moment of communication. Corradi Fiumara's insistence on listening as a structural condition for speech, and indeed for language, is an important place to begin to think about our inevitable responsibility as listeners at the moment someone speaks. Her pointed insights reveal something of the paradoxical nature of listening. In the first instance, she identifies an inherent tension within the listener as someone who both participates and yet remains removed from the spoken exchange between persons. In the second, she astutely renders the problem of selflessness in terms of how the very point of listening puts the self into risk through the difficulties that the words of another impose. Finally, placing hope in the trust that the listener must have that a communication will open up possibilities for new thoughts and new relationships means that the listener will have to hang on in spite of her own discomfort. For these reasons, Corradi Fiumara's work is of central concern for thinking through how attentiveness structures any communicative relation. However, alone, her work can easily be rendered into a series of applicable "skills" or "attitudes" or "how-tos" that not only structure the condition for speech but would then structure the actual relation between persons in ways that would seem to be not open—or responsible—to the play and vicissitudes of the other. In other words, it would turn listening into a type of relationality. In this sense, her work does not go far enough in discussing how listening is an attentiveness not only to speech but also to the Other that speaks, to the Other that exceeds the spoken words. That is, while I agree that attentiveness to the words spoken is absolutely crucial to communication, I wish to suggest that responsibility can only emerge as an attentiveness to the trace of the embodied presence who signifies, even when the speaker may be an "absent presence," such as may be the case for viewers of video testimony, readers of newspaper interviews, and audiences of *Jupiter's Wife*.

What I explore further, following Castoriadis and Levinas, is that speaking not only signifies a signified, but at the same time it "reveals" an other beyond comprehension of the words themselves. Robert Gibbs puts it this way: "The one who speaks the words is intrinsic to the meaning of those words. . . . The speaker appears across the words spoken. . . . She shows herself by not speaking about herself, but by 'proposing the world,' . . . she accompanies the sign."[9] Moreover, speech reveals the otherness of the Other in two ways. First, as Castoriadis points out, speech reveals the unconscious dimensions of meaning making. That is, the unconscious processes of meaning unfold through discourse; it is not that *the* unconscious as an entity or thing is exposed, but its dynamic capacity for representation is revealed. Second, as Levinas writes, "The alterity of the Other is in him and is not relative to me; it *reveals* itself."[10] This revelation, which exceeds the signified, becomes important for our entry into the sphere of responsibility. This alterity is not about a difference in meaning but is that which lies beyond meaning itself. Collectively, both of these views suggest that listening requires an attending to the revelations of the Other in speech in order to be responsible.

LISTENING AS ATTENDING TO THE OTHER'S MEANING

Any notion of attentiveness, it seems to me, also has to account for the meaning the speaking subject makes of her own speech. In hearing Maggie's dense plots, for instance, it is clear that her words are impregnated with sense. They are not entirely random, nor are they simply an array of accumulated sounds. Even Negroponte feels they are not "arbitrary." Through their persistent repetition, they betray a creative logic that bears some meaning for Maggie, even if we and Negroponte can never know what that is. Psychoanalysis, of course, as a discourse and practice seeks a way of making insight out of the meaning that speech has for the subject who speaks. Given a psychoanalytic reading, Maggie's delusional speech, by not participating in a recognizably logical form that can be shared between interlocutors, might be considered to occur in the time of psychosis and therefore lie beyond the curative or interpretative potential psychoanalysis has to offer.[11] What I am concerned with here, however, is not with the goal of psychoanalysis—that is, how insight is made from an interpretation of the unconscious—but how attentiveness to the creative capacity for making meaning becomes part of the ethical project of listening, an act that lies prior to any understanding. As Castoriadis writes:

> But we should also point out that psychoanalysis never encounters this Unconscious, so to speak, "in person"; at most, psychoanalysis catches a fleeting glimpse of a few of its effects with the aid of a dream, a verbal slip, an abortive act. Psychoanalysis always encounters a flesh and blood human who speaks—and who speaks not a tongue in general but in each case a quite particular tongue—who has or does not have a profession, a family situation, ideas, behaviors, orientations, and disorientations.[12]

It is precisely this idea that speech cannot be abstracted from the one who speaks that is so important for considering our attentiveness in listening, for do we not still have an ethical obligation to listen to and learn from persons, even when understanding their speech is no longer possible?

As a psychoanalyst himself, Castoriadis does, of course, place importance on the insight that might be gleaned from the speech of another person, and he details how psychotic communications may be analyzed and ultimately understood; however, what he also has to offer is a way of understanding how those dissembled communications hold meaning for the Other, regardless of whether "we" come to understand them or not. Castoriadis's work places little emphasis on the specific act of listening itself, yet in its assertion that meaning sticks even to the most slippery of narrative surfaces, it has implications for listening in terms of what, and particularly who, needs to be attended to.

Maggie's dense plots, involving Jupiter, Hemera, and the radiowaves, emerge out of an idiosyncratic capacity to put signs together that are not strictly part of any recognizable social reality, although each sign in and of itself is comprehendible. In Castoriadis's words: "We are speaking here, of course, of the radical imagination: not the capacity to have 'images' (or to be seen) in a 'mirror' but the capacity to posit that which is not, to see in something that which is not there. . . . For the human psychism, there is unlimited and unmasterable representational flux, a representational spontaneity that is not enslaved to an ascribable end, a rupture of the rigid correspondence between image and X or a break in the fixed succession of images."[13]

For Castoriadis, this radical capacity to create is what underlies our ability to change the world we live in, to imagine it otherwise. It is precisely that which eschews the very social significations given to us. However, this radical capacity to create takes on a special significance when language is used as the symbolic form through which such creativity is revealed. "To speak is a sublimated activity, first of all because this activity procures no organ pleasure; second and above all, because it is instrumented in and through an extrapsychic creation that goes beyond what the singular psyche is capable of doing by itself: that is, the institution of language; finally, because speaking always potentially implies that one is addressing other participants, *real* ones, situated in society."[14] Speech thus holds social and communicative functions through which our psychic representations find order and structure. Moreover, the very use of language implies that one is in a relation of exteriority. Speech brings the subject out of the immanence of the psyche as it is oriented both to a socially given symbolic system as well as toward another who can listen. Presumably, when we speak through the instituted logic of language, those representations make sense for others. However, in Maggie's case, her speech is aberrant; it disobeys conventional rules and structures, and it challenges the listener precisely because it does not conform to expected trajectories of presence and absence, past and future. Thus it is not only the content of what Maggie says that disturbs, but it is the way language is used to collapse time and space that is so confounding. Yet Castoriadis asserts that language in and of itself does not grant meaning to the one who signifies (although it is necessary for establishing meaning with another). Aberrant speech fundamentally remains tied to the subject's impulse to create meaning for herself, to the radical imagination to which the listener does not have access.

> In the human being, pleasure is essentially the pleasure of representation, it is a defunctionalized sort of pleasure. However, even such pleasure in representation gives way before the imperative need to *make sense*—even when at the price of immense psychical (and somatic) displeasure. This is, in extreme form, what we witness in psychosis. Such "meaning making" [*faire sens*] is henceforth to be understood as the instauration of a certain sort of representational coherency, even when to the detriment of the organic, to the detriment of pleasure (even representational pleasure), and to the detriment—in psychosis—of coherency with respect to others' representations, their social significations.[15]

So even if, for the sake of argument, psychoanalysis can categorize the condition that gives rise to the tangled webs of Maggie's speech as psychosis, the point remains that even when speech "fails" in proposing a world *in common*, it nonetheless does not fail to propose a world. Our attentiveness would then seem to be directed to how we, as listeners, receive that world we cannot share. After all, the speaking subject speaks *her* attachments, speaks *her* representational arrangements, speaks *her* world. Thus even in its incapacity to signify coherently (and what counts as coherency, as Castoriadis reminds us, is a socially instituted logic), speech reveals a profound uniqueness that cannot be rendered—or dismissed—solely as a breakdown in common meaning. Rather, it is that the very uniqueness of meaning reveals itself in this breakdown. What remains remarkably other to a listener is the speaking subject's own peculiar ways of signifying. In this regard, sense and nonsense for the listener are only markers of how close a speaker's speech approximates a given system of signification and cannot refer to the speaker's own relation to herself. Castoriadis states that "all this boils down to characterizing psychosis in terms of the creation—starting from an initial 'non-sense' for the subject—of something meaningful [*un sens*] *for* this subject that is non-sense for others."[16]

With respect to the three points of listening that Corradi Fiumara addresses—entering, selflessness, and trust—Castoriadis draws our attention to the complexity of what is revealed in the speech of another. Entering the speech of another is distinguished here from entering the one who speaks. Castoriadis emphatically states: "We do not enter into the living being. We can bang on it, shock it in some way, but in any event we do not enter into it: whatever we might do, it will react *after its own fashion*. The analogy with the psychoanalytic situation—and with every human relationship in general—is direct. One does not enter into someone as one pleases; one does not even enter in at all. An interpretation—or a period of silence—is heard by someone."[17] The one who speaks is ultimately separate from the one who listens, and thus listening requires a certain respect not only for what is being spoken but—because it is *being* spoken in the full sense of that verb—for the person who is speaking. Thus the paradoxical nature of entering the speech of another—of partaking in yet remaining removed from speech—takes on the added burden of respecting the boundaries imposed by the person who is revealed through speech.

In this sense, the selflessness and the riskiness inherent to listening become further pronounced, since what the listener risks in listening to the speech of another is nothing short of entering a relationship with another meaning maker. By construing the speaking subject as a locus of meaning, however incommunicable that meaning may be, Castoriadis suggests that listening requires an initial suspension of a socially prescribed logic. What we hear is not a transparent representation of an unconscious entity but a movement of signs through which a subject makes meaning for herself. As such, the risk implied involves a renunciation of certainty, for the speech of the Other always implicates the listener in something beyond what can be anticipated.

Embedded in this, of course, is a certain trust in the subject as a meaning maker. That is, the hope that surfaces when one "hangs on" to speech is no longer just about the possibility for new thoughts to emerge within a shared system of communication but an acknowledgment that the failure of speech to be understood, grasped, and transparently apprehended is also a time of meaning for the one who speaks. Thus tearing meaning away from commonality means that trust is an approach to the radical difference and uniqueness of new thoughts or images that are *already* present. What matters is not only the anticipation that we might make new thoughts for ourselves when we listen, but that what we listen to is always already an imaginary constellation that is different from our own, and that who we listen to is always accompanied by an unconscious, dynamic play of signs.

Attentiveness to another's meaning, then, is a demand of learning from difference. Taking the extreme case of communicative breakdown witnessed in

Jupiter's Wife helps, I think, to put into relief how difference emerges *as* (and not simply in) a communicative encounter. Difference is thus not something that is communicated through language but by virtue of listening to an *other* who speaks, difference is manifest in that communication itself. Attending to this difference in meaning is part of the work of learning—that is, it is a quality of relationality that marks our receptiveness and openness to the Other. Learning from this difference, learning from the meaning of the Other, is not an act of interpretation or decoding but a holding open of disruptive possibilities where self-transformation is implicitly at stake. And this learning risks causing discomfort and suffering to the learner because the stakes are so high. That significations signify differently for the one who speaks than they do for the one who listens is an unbridgeable gap that sets the terms of nonviolent relationality, terms that are essential to respect if the alterity of the Other is to be preserved.

LISTENING AS ATTENDING TO THE ECHO OF THE OTHERWISE

The third aspect of signification has to do with considering alterity as lying outside the bounds of meaning itself. Thus it is not only difference in meaning that is important for listening but also the irrecuperability of difference through meaning and language that marks the ethical approach to the Other, and indeed marks, following Levinas, the ethical dimension of learning. We have seen in previous chapters that Levinas's project concerns itself with the constitution of the ethical subject. The dynamics inherent to this constitution are by now familiar: the asymmetry of the self-Other relation, the irreducible nature of self and Other, and the infinite unknowability of the Other. Within this context, then, is situated the listener, the one who, in an encounter with the Other, does not merely "pay attention to" what is said but *attends to* the Other, or, more appropriately, the otherness of the Other. The distinction for me is one of emphasis on the initially nonconscious aspect of subjectivity, where attentiveness is engendered through a mode of nonviolent passivity. Thus what is ethical about listening for Levinas emerges not out of an easily adopted attitude or position but out of the very immediacy and unpredictable nature of the communicative relation. In this regard, what Levinas's work offers to an account of listening is the significance of that which lies beyond language, meaning, and comprehension, namely, the *approach* to the Other found in direct, face-to-face contact:

> Our relation with the other (*autrui*) certainly consists in wanting to comprehend him, but this relation overflows comprehension. Not only because knowledge of the other (*autrui*) requires outside of all curiosity, also sympathy or love, ways of being distinct from impassible contemplation, but because in our relation with the other (*autrui*), he does not affect us in terms of a concept. He is a being (*étant*) and counts as such.[18]

Attending to being outside of the parameters of comprehension occasions the birth of responsibility. Gibbs, in partial response to his own question "why listen?," states with reference to Levinas: "My first responsibility arises in listening to an other person, not in speaking to her"; "I listen to the other as my teacher."[19] Listening is, perhaps, the learning event par excellence. Although Levinas does not address listening in any systematic way, his rendering of how responsibility is born of a welcoming of the Other, of how the Other calls me into question, and of how a communicative openness to the Other might be sustained gives us entry points for marking out the ethical terms of listening as learning. Revisiting the terms of attentiveness discussed previously—entering, selflessness, and trust—from Levinas's point of view gives us a specifically ethical understanding of listening—and, consequently, of learning.

First, the tension between participating in yet remaining removed from the speech of the Other indicates an inherent asymmetry between listener and speaker. That is, there is a different and unequal relation, whereby the Other's speech takes primacy in the relation, a primacy that commands the listener to attend. For Levinas, the speaker is marked by "height," an elevation that renders the speaker as absolutely other to the listener. Summoned by this height, by the mastery of the Other, the listener is capable of receiving something new, of being taught. "The height from which language comes we designate with the term teaching. . . . The first teaching teaches this very height . . . the ethical."[20] Moreover, listening, insofar as it is a receiving of alterity, is fundamentally a learning from the Other, is a response to the otherness that reveals itself in the face of the speaker. "The face, preeminently expression, formulates the first word: the signifier arising at the thrust of his sign, as eyes that look at you."[21] The face, as expression, then, is not merely the vehicle through which words are spoken but signifies itself as signifier, as bearing significance beyond the words spoken. Thus the attentiveness of the listener (who is also a learner) is a response to something more than speech. That is, as a response to the alterity of the Other, listening becomes a responsibility in its attentiveness to the face that signifies. This is not accomplished through "understanding," "assimilating," or "grasping" the Other (which would put listener and speaker on the same plane) but through an attending to difference "in order to learn what I cannot make my own."[22]

It is precisely this incommensurability that is stressed in Negroponte's relation to Maggie. At times vacillating between seeking out the "truth" behind her statements (to make them his own) and being open to what he cannot make his own, Negroponte reveals the struggle inherent in facing radical difference. It is those moments in which he simply faces Maggie, allows her story to emerge without interpretation, where he displays a submission to Maggie's command. At these points he listens for no "reason," and allows the words to wash over him—and over us as viewers. As a listener, Negroponte is removed from the speech of Maggie to the degree that he responds through his attentiveness to Maggie's command.

In light of this, Corradi Fiumara's second point takes on an even greater significance, for how can we put ourselves aside as we are exposed to the risks attendant to listening, that is, to the command of the Other? You will recall that Corradi Fiumara understands these risks in terms of how the listener must listen to that which is not easy and which has the potential of disrupting a sense of self. Levinas takes this a step further. It is precisely at the moment when the speaker calls the listener into question, when the listener is put at risk to the point of suffering, that responsibility is itself inaugurated. He writes, "in discourse I expose myself to the questioning of the Other, and this urgency of the response—acuteness of the present—engenders me for responsibility."[23] The time of risk, therefore, is the time of birth for the ethical subject. Responding (or listening) takes place in the immediacy of the communicative encounter; the other person's questioning of me presents an exigent demand to respond. The speaker, moreover, accomplishes this not through the content of what she says (that is, she does not literally question the listener) but through the very revelation of alterity that she signifies for the listener. "The calling in question of the I, coextensive with the manifestation of the Other in the face, we call language."[24] What Levinas flags here is not only the significance of listening in language (as Corradi Fiumara does), or the significance of listening to another's meaning proposed in language (following Castoriadis); rather, he signals listening as an *ethical* condition *of* language. The surprising ways, then, that the listener is called into question, the unpredictable risks in listening, become the ethical enactment of language itself; it is an enactment that is beyond the exclusive reach of consciousness. Levinas states: "Being attentive signifies a surplus of consciousness, and presupposes the call of the other. To be attentive is to recognize the mastery of the other, to receive his command, or more exactly, to receive from him the command to command."[25] In one way, we can read Negroponte's shifting of the topic of his film as a response to this very command. Once chosen by Maggie, he can no longer escape the command given to him: the entire project of the film shifts its focus and becomes something other than it was before meeting her. His reception of Maggie has the effect of transforming the very grounds of his own self-understanding and his own signifying in terms of the film. More precisely, it is his attentiveness to Maggie's presence as command that allows for Maggie's otherness to be revealed outside the confines of comprehension.

Levinas posits that attentiveness to alterity is an ethical reception, a conscience that "welcomes the other person as remaining other."[26] For example, it is this welcoming that summons me to speak not as a speaker "in turn," such as we might find in a typical dialogical relation, but as a listener who always holds herself open to the question and command of the other person. In this way, then, it is not so much that the listener is selfless, but that the listener's response, her attentiveness, must incorporate the conditions of her own self-questioning, her own difficult subversion.

Third, the trust and hope that Corradi Fiumara identifies as being central to the attitude of listening take on added importance within this ethical framework. The trust required to remain open, to hang on to the words of the Other, even through difficulty and pain, means that listening must be a continuous, ongoing process. It is a continual opening up toward future possibilities. It is not as though once I have listened, I have learned from the Other and then do not have to listen again. There is a strange interminability to listening insofar as it is a response to another that is never quite finished or complete. For Levinas, this interminable attentiveness to the Other is given the term *saying* and becomes the hallmark of a responsible response. What matters for sustained trust and hope in communication does not occur through the content of what one speaks (what Levinas refers to as the *said*) but through the nearness, closeness, and orientation we bring to the other: the saying is "the proximity of one to the other, the commitment of an approach, the one for the other, the very signifyingness of signification."[27] The saying signifies something beyond the said, and thus our communication always occurs as a double event: the said that signifies being (the words that "propose a world"), and the saying that signifies otherwise than being, as the alterity that is not recuperable through language. As Gibbs puts it, the saying is a "deepening of listening. . . . The attention of listening now becomes a drawing near to another person, which signifies as welcoming the other person."[28] Although it may first appear paradoxical, listening becomes a kind of saying in this regard. One can see how *Jupiter's Wife* can be construed as a saying; that is, the film *qua* film is a response that, insofar as it is possible for any film to refuse a definitive stance, acts as a mode of signification that welcomes the Other in its own incompleteness. However, there is more to listening and saying when we consider what they mean between actual persons as opposed to representations of persons. Listening as saying is an acute attentiveness to the otherness of the Other, to what Levinas refers to as the "echo of the otherwise."[29] This echo resounds through signification, but it cannot be heard in any conventional sense. To attend to it, then, means to approach it. This approach is an ethical movement, where in receiving the gift of the Other, the listener gives of herself, risking her own suffering. "In saying suffering signifies in the form of giving, even if the price of signification is that the subject run the risk of suffering without reason. If the subject did not run this risk, pain would lose its very painfulness."[30] What one gives in this ethical gesture is not what is superfluous but what one needs; it is the very "bread taken from one's mouth."[31]

Trust here becomes a kind of faith in the "fine risk" of communication,[32] where the exposure to suffering leads to the possibility for ethical relationality, for a way to respond to the Other that does not violate that which is unknowable about her. This means that one listens not in order to acquire knowledge about the Other but in order to learn from her—continually. For Levinas, then, hope resides in the possibility of a suffering that is opened up not through cruelty or hatred but through a profound exposure to the Other that constantly risks the rupture of one's being. For it is only through this rupture that the listener—at this very moment—can give of herself fully.

Rereading the three aspects of attentiveness in Corradi Fiumara's work through these Levinasian terms has the danger of making listening into some masochistic or self-annihilating gesture where the Other's commandment leaves no room for one's own interest or pleasure (criticisms that are often levied against Levinas's work). However, I do not think that this is what is implied. Rather, what Levinas proposes, in my view, is not a normative discourse for our actions; rather, he provokes a way of understanding what may be ethical about listening. It is not that when we listen we void ourselves of consciousness, but that the ethical consists in attending to the Other in ways that exceed the bounds of thought. This is not an Arendtian "thoughtlessness" that leads to unethical action—or evil—but a quality of relationality that refuses to see communication as having comprehension as its only goal. The passivity required to be moved, to be touched, to be affected means that listening lies in a necessarily prior relation to thought itself. So if thoughtfulness is to matter at all with respect to learning, then it is the very passivity of attentiveness that needs to be thoroughly heeded. The difficulty, of course, lies in thinking about such a nonintentional response as a condition for learning in education. How can I be "awakened to an attending to my attending"[33] in a way that does not merely revert back to thought in becoming an adopted position or attitude, or in becoming an instantiation of how-tos or prescriptions for practice?

LEARNING, TEACHING, AND THE TIME OF LISTENING

Listening, as I have been discussing, involves qualities of attentiveness that occur in three facets of signification—the implicit role listening has in language, the meaning the Other makes through her own speech, and the otherness of the speaker that lies beyond meaning. What I wish to detail here, following from my discussion above, is how these qualities actually give rise to a view of listening that can be construed as a modality of time through which we learn. Thus listening is not about occupying a position or taking on an attitude but about a *quality* of relationality that occurs as part of the time of signification, a time when we meet the Other.

Read in terms of time, listening transpires in the here and now of communication, in the immediacy of a signifying encounter with difference. But what is also opened up in the encounter, as we have seen, is a play of significations that resounds with the past and anticipates an unknowable future. Listening as a relation to the Other that cuts across this time of signification—what it holds, reveals, and gestures toward—cannot be seen as synchronic. The time of listening is fractured. So the question of awakening to an attending of my attending is not about assuming a fixed position but about an approach to the multiple time of listening, an approach that cannot be fully identified before one comes into contact with another person.

When narratives are listened to, more than words are at stake. There is the embodied presence of the one who speaks. Listening means attending not only to what is transparent in communication, what it is we can share (a common language, a proposed world in common) in the moment someone speaks, but also to what is unshareable (the Other's meaning, the command of the alterity of the Other). It is not that these unshareable moments are incidental to speech or are simply a failure of mutual understanding. Rather, they accompany all speaking situations by virtue of the fact that *someone* speaks. These unshareable moments are an inevitable part of the immediacy of communication; what one speaks both reveals a creative representation of the past in the present and a future that is opened in the anticipated response commanded by the Other. When I listen, I surrender myself to the Other's dense plots, to the profound idiosyncracies that mark her speech as bearing her own historical relevance without knowing how or why, and I yield to her appeal to me to respond and welcome her. When I listen, I face difference, pay heed to it, and attend directly to its presence. Listening, in this view, does not have as its aim understanding difference ("getting to know the other"); this would fix difference in time, turning it into a constant against which all my responses could be measured ("once I know you, I will know how to respond"). Instead, listening always already occurs because of the presence of difference, and it lies prior to any understanding that we can make of the Other's speech. That is, difference reveals itself in the moment that someone speaks, and listening is implicated in the very revelation of difference that speech engenders.

The time of listening, then, is an event, an occasion, if you will, of the difference that emerges *as* a communicative relation. It is a passive occasion, where we are immersed in an undefinable difference, where we become implicated in an encounter beyond our own ways of making sense, beyond our own comprehension. When meaning breaks down, for instance, listening still remains the condition that enables a quality of meeting between persons that calls forth further communication. In this sense, the passivity of listening is not about "taking leave" or abandoning the subject who speaks but about an engagement with her that is, in the simplest terms, a response to her speech. It is an approach that takes responsibility for itself. Listening is an occasion where the I, in the act of welcoming, "says" something to the Other; it signifies an approach to the Other in time: I am here, I am present, I hear you. Listening, then, is a passive orientation to the person who speaks that declares its presence only through its enactment; it is eminently a being-for the Other. This presence is declared not when I *literally* tell the other "I am here, I am present, I hear you," which reduces "listening" to a series of routine utterances and practical skills—what I would call a *type* of relationality—but through the very quality of relationality that I perform in excess of the content of my speech, a presence that meets the Other as other. The quality of relationality that is listening is a time of proximity, of closeness.

But this closeness is never easy and, as we have seen, listening as an exposure to the Other brings with it a profound disturbance to the self. Moreover, it occasions, through our capacity to be moved and touched by another's life story, a painfulness that we simply cannot escape, a painfulness that is part of what is required to learn from, and not merely about, the Other. In effect, to listen and to bear this pain also says to the other "I can change." As both Castoriadis and Levinas discuss, albeit through radically different perspectives, time is unthinkable without change, without the transformation, alteration, or motion that disrupts sameness. Change is necessarily implicated in a before and an after, a past and a future, a that-which-was and a that-which-is-not-yet. Listening transpires in the interval between these terms. We listen to stories others tell as having meaning for them, carrying vestiges of experience, loss, trauma, and exaltation that we cannot know but can be profoundly affected by. We also listen to those stories as an exposure to another human being that is absolutely not me. Hence, my relation to the Other through listening is first and foremost a quality of relationality to difference that opens me up for change. Hearing the words of others *only* to confirm what I know (or what I think I know) can be seen as a violation of the difference that emerges as communication. Listening as a saying, as an approach to the Other that signifies "I can change," is a responsible mode of relationality in that it is a nonviolent and unpredictable response to alterity, even when my passivity results in my own discomfort. The one who listens risks nothing less than an alteration of self in responding to another's speech, and it is within this context of risk and alteration that listening is required for learning to take place. As discussed in chapter 1, such alteration of the self, this "learning to become," occurs as an inevitably violent demand made upon the learner; yet the hope for nonviolent possibilities seems to me to lie precisely in the capacity for response that emerges in those moments that exceed the demand. That is, learning is also nonviolent insofar as it represents a time of response to the Other, a time marked by our attentiveness to another's narrative presence.

But there are two important things to discuss here, for if learning occurs in the time of listening, then how might students' responses be read in this time? And how might teachers attend to students' responses? What I propose is that if listening is eminently a learning from the Other, then our responses are conditional upon our ignorance and our own capacities to participate in the risks of communication. For me, the *quality* of listening that permits the self to encounter the Other's difference does not lie in adherence to rules about what constitutes "good" listening. Thus to listen to a homeless woman speak her life does not mean to perform, or to expect students to perform, certain conventional scripts or roles; it does not involve practices such as tilting or nodding one's head, repeating back what the speaker says, or leaning forward to indicate attentiveness. Instead, attentiveness involves a sensitivity that cannot be reduced to a set of skills; it becomes a question, rather, of the extent to which one remains open to the difference instantiated in a communicative relation. As we have seen in previous chapters, such openness is requisite to commitment and responsibility, and certain affects contribute more or less to sustaining such openness and the difference that makes a communicative relation possible. It is not that listening can be divorced from empathy, love, or guilt. Listening is very much a part of one's affective response, and we can say that the degree to which any feeling occurs in the time of listening, it participates profoundly in our capacity to learn from the Other.

How students listen to difference, and how teachers listen to students' responses to difference, become part of the ongoing pedagogical task set before us. If we consider that stories of suffering invoke certain affective responses, then our responsibility as teachers turns upon our capacity to listen to those responses in ways that are for the Other, in ways that display our ignorance, that communicate to students "tell me, for I do not know." Teaching with ignorance implies a humility where each student's struggle is met as her own, as revelatory of her own meaning and history and of her own uniqueness that remain inaccessible to our systems of meaning, theories, and knowledge. It requires a trust in that what students say has meaning for them and acknowledges that their significations might signify differently for them than they do for us as listeners. Listening as a response to students' speech invokes a commitment to hear and "hang on" to their words as they struggle to articulate through language complex responses to difference that can be laced with powerful affect. Of course, students say things that provoke our own defenses, our own tastes and judgments, and perhaps even our own desires for what we want our pedagogies to accomplish; we do interpret, explain, and theorize about those responses, and, moreover, we do find ourselves disappointed, delighted, and even bored by what they have to say, just as they can be toward our utterances. Such recognizable and customary reactions indicate all too clearly the difficult demands of encountering difference, and I do not mean to imply that these can be dispelled with a simple appeal to listen better. My contention throughout this book has been to identify those points of hope where nonviolent relations to the Other appear as possibilities already within our educational encounters. Those moments when we give our listening in time, when we are susceptible to change, when we can be surprised and challenged, offer precisely such hope. That is, I am not suggesting that we can listen in time all of the time. What I am underlining, however, is that learning occurs through such listening, and as such we need to attend to when it happens, to embrace its unpredictability as part of what it means to teach and learn across difference. Listening in time requires an attentiveness that we cannot plan for; attending to particularity demands something new of us each time we listen. I cannot know before an encounter with another person how that person will affect me; I might be altered in ways I could not even have imagined, and my listening as a response to the

Other who speaks might occasion further uncertainties. The risks implicit in listening to stories of suffering, in particular, are therefore great, and there is no way to diminish or make safer such risks through appeals to knowledge. Deborah Britzman reflects on the difficulties thus: "The paradox is that because learning from another's pain requires noticing what one has not experienced and the capacity to be touched by what one has not noticed, identifying with pain requires a self capable of wounding her or his own ego boundaries, the very boundaries that serve as a defense against pain."[34]

When I listen to students struggle with their guilt, for instance, I am immediately implicated as both teacher and listener. My response as a teacher can only operate within the given context of my responsibility as a listener; thus to hear, for example, a student's expression of guilt as merely reflective of a moral failure is already to assume to know a great deal about the meaning guilt has for that student and to reduce the unique experiences of the student to a category where listening becomes a foreclosed possibility. Moreover, as Britzman suggests, such foreclosure seems to sustain a defense against the pain of our own possible pedagogical failure. That is, if we can interpret students' affect as aberrant, rather than as a point of pedagogical and ethical possibility, then we cannot be affected in ways that sustain a learning from the Other through which our own pedagogies might be put into question. Our capacity for attentiveness, then, bumps up against our capacity for tolerating the pain, distress, and discomfort that listening brings. In this sense, to attend to our attending, to nourish and develop the attentiveness in our listening, we need to be alert to the ways our limitations factor into ethical possibilities. Thus it is not that we can do away with our limitations, but that the specifically ethical orientation to the Other is an act of exceeding ourselves; it is a generosity that spontaneously gives attention to the Other by being present and responsive in the here and now.

Awakening to an attending to our attending means reminding ourselves as teachers of our own ignorance in the face of difference that emerges as a communicative relation. It is neither a posture of ignorance nor a guise of attentiveness I am speaking of here, as though when students speak, I am going to effect surprise or earnestness in the hope of drawing them out further. Rather, to become awakened and alert means to be moved to a sensitivity that can only come via a relation with the student, as opposed to our own conscious intention to act in a specific manner *before* we meet her. Of course, *reminding* ourselves of our own ignorance in the communicative encounter with difference does involve reflection and thoughtfulness; yet the point I wish to stress is that such thoughtfulness does not emanate from the ruminations of an autonomous ego prior to an encounter with difference but is instead conditioned by our susceptibility to be stirred by the presence of the Other to respond. That is, awakening to an attending to my attending occurs because of the immediacy of the communicative moment with the Other in which *we are already positioned as having to answer for the one who speaks*. Taking this answerability, this responsibility, as our point of departure, as opposed to autonomous self-reflection, we are able to more clearly see how thoughtfulness about our attentiveness surfaces from within our obligation to receive the Other rather than obligation surfacing from our thoughtfulness. To claim that teaching must embrace ignorance as a condition of listening in time is not to demand that teachers can simply start the day by saying to themselves, "I will void myself of thought so I will be able to listen to each one of my students today." One can see the absurdity of such a situation. Rather, teaching with ignorance performs as a gentle and subtle reminder that the conditions of ethical possibility lie in the degree to which I am capable of transforming myself without knowing whom I will become.

As Negroponte says about his film, there is no perfect ending. What we learn from *Jupiter's Wife* is that our listening is incomplete, unfinished, and always disruptive of the contingencies of our own lives. Teaching and learning across difference similarly have no such end; our responses to stories of suffering obligate us in a continual challenge to sustain and build upon the ethical possibilities that spring forth in surprising ways from our everyday contact with others.

POSTSCRIPT

WHERE ARE ETHICAL POSSIBILITIES?

THIS BOOK HAS BEEN a consideration of ethical possibilities as they exist as modes of relationality across difference in education. In my discussions of empathy, love, guilt, and listening, I have argued for an understanding of ethics that refuses to locate responsibility within a rational, autonomous subject but in the very forms of relationality that structure our encounters with other people, ones that are frequently infused with powerful feelings and emotions. In this regard, what counts as conditions of responsibility are therefore based in the quality of relations we have to others as opposed to adhering to predefined principles that we then apply to the particular situations in which we find ourselves. However, such an understanding of responsibility (or, more appropriately, of its conditions) poses some difficulties for teachers, for it does not seem to offer the security that codes or principles of ethics might. Moreover, it implicates all responses, including students' responses to curriculum, in an unavoidable obligation that we may choose to disregard, but from which we cannot escape. Each of us, then, is therefore burdened with a responsibility for the Other that is not of our own making.

Taking pedagogies of social justice as the point of my departure, my task has been to rethink the ethical basis of such responsibility through the complex ways we engage difference in the classroom. In arguing for seeing ethical relations as those that emerge out of a response to alterity, I claim here that we need to explore how certain affective attachments to difference create or disrupt nonviolent relations to the Other. My argument, therefore, has been that responsibility is not a singular position, behavior, skill, or attitude that one takes up in relation to a principle but is an approach to the Other born out of the uncertainty that a relation to another person carries. The emphasis I have placed on the risk, unpredictability, uncertainty, ambiguity, ambivalence, and spontaneity of our concrete relations creates a further difficulty for education, for it seems to suggest that we cannot control and therefore act responsibly within prescribed ways of being. That is, if responsibility is located in those responses that allow us to learn from the Other, that challenge us to exceed ourselves, and that alter us in ways we could not have predicted, then what do teaching and learning have to do with responsibility? How do we avoid creating a climate of hopelessness when we say that treating others with the dignity they deserve is rooted in a nonintentional being-for the Other, particularly when the whole project of social justice education is based on such ethical promise? Where do ethical possibilities lie, and how might we think about making such possibilities less rare?

These questions capture, it seems to me, two of the basic tensions arising in this work: first, that between our intentions to create and sustain relations of nonviolence and understanding that nonviolence does not arise out of intentionality; and, second, that between our institutionally defined roles as teachers and students and the way our personal histories, affects, and meanings are played out through those interpersonal relations that exceed these roles. These tensions, perhaps, make plain what is so troubling about discussing an ethics of responsibility as a relation across difference, because it becomes immediately evident that *what* teachers intentionally teach does not necessarily lead to more or better opportunities for ethical interaction (either for them or their students), and that in their relations, both with each other and to the curriculum, teachers and students are more than the predictable sum of their institutionally defined roles. Thus in seeing the conditions of responsibility in teaching as lying in surprising and unforeseeable encounters with difference, I am not suggesting here a list of principles that then can be codified and institutionalized through our teaching practice. Nor am I suggesting that we can ever fully prepare ourselves to be surprised by the strangeness of difference. What I am suggesting is a mindfulness and a sensitivity to the ways in which we participate in attending to difference within institutional contexts, on the one hand, and a vision of education as a practice that already participates in those conditions necessary for responsibility, on the other hand. Thus what I am proposing is an ethical orientation toward how we understand education more generally, and teaching and learning more specifically.

Responsibility needs to be rethought in terms of the pull teachers and students experience between their institutional duties and the personal, interhuman dimension of classroom relationships. In understanding ethics as always already about obedience to a set of rules or principles, the danger is that teacher responsibility is subsumed under institutional life, making it impossible to think seriously about how individuals not only supersede their institutional roles but also how such superseding is considered ethically exigent and morally worthy on occasion. Whether one takes an extreme case in point, such as the refusal to adhere to institutional regulations under Nazism or McCarthyism, for example, or a more common refusal to abide by rules to accommodate a student's particular needs (such as disobeying a school discipline policy in order to protect a student from further harm at the hands of potentially abusive peers), moral action cannot be subsumed under institutional life *in toto*. Teachers are more than institutional agents, and ethical conduct is irreducible to rule-bound behavior. In fact, viewing responsibility as a behavior that follows rules, codes of conduct, and ethical regulations raises serious questions about how we understand ethical conduct between people in the first place and how we understand the nature and function of institutional regulations in the second.

Zygmunt Bauman points out that there is moral confusion over the function of our institutional roles. Obeying institutional law alone depersonalizes our moral responsibility. Under these conditions, Bauman suggests, responsibility is "floated":[1] it becomes detached from the moral agent and is viewed only in relation to carrying out a job or a duty prescribed by the institution. Since our institutional roles cannot take in our full selves, "we console ourselves, and not without reason, when we find the task we have been asked to perform morally suspect or unpalatable."[2] In this sense, it is understood that if I do not obey the rules, someone else will. Bauman goes on to suggest, in a Levinasian vein, that it is precisely our capacity for individual acts of morality that holds in check the potential for institutions to erode our sense of individual responsibility.

Bauman's points are well taken here and speak directly to the issue of teacher responsibility as something that is not simply about fulfilling our obligations to rules or acting as institutional agents. That is, from an ethical point of view, responsibility cannot simply be a matter for policy but is fundamentally a personal, practical matter—a matter whereby our encounters with difference and otherness are brought fully to bear on each of us, and for which each of us is responsible. Indeed, teachers experience such responsibility every day, and in my classes on ethics, the most frequent way teachers articulate their struggles with doing what is "right" often is caught between what they are supposed to do as prescribed by institutional regulations and principles and what they feel they ought to do as persons in the face-to-face encounters they have with their students. Thus part of the project of coming to understand teaching as an ethical practice involves creating a vocabulary for teachers to better navigate through the institutional-personal tension that structures their professional lives.

This is not to suggest that roles, or the power dynamics that plague them, are unimportant, and that institutions do not play a central role in potentially mitigating against harm or in enshrining more just and equitable relations. For instance, in sexual harassment and abuse cases, policies, of course, are desperately needed to provide victims with recourse, and to ensure that institutions transparently recognize harm done to the persons within them. More than that, perhaps, such policies signify to potential harassers and abusers that such behavior is intolerable to the community at large, and thus they optimally function as preventative measures. Hence rules against harassment and abuse recognize the potentially aggressive nature of our interpersonal relations. In this regard, then, such regulations acknowledge that because of the vulnerability engendered in the pedagogical relation, there is also a capacity for teachers and students to do harm to each other.

However, in spite of the need for rules in mitigating against harm and creating more just social practices, my contention is that it is precisely because this vulnerability is present that rules cannot address satisfactorily the question of ethical responsibility. Drucilla Cornell points out in her study of justice, the law, and deconstruction that at times "violence masquerade[s] as the rule of law."[3] Not only can institutions such as schools and the judiciary enact a form of violence against those who are subjected to their rules but, as Cornell notes, justice is simply not reducible to any legal system, nor, therefore, to any institutional set of regulations.[4] Justice and ethics are greater than the cumulation of rules and regulations. Moreover, while Levinas, for instance, recognizes that justice is indeed *exercised* through institutions, ethical responsibility cannot be simply reduced to an adherence to institutional law. In fact, "justice ... must always be held in check by the initial interpersonal relation."[5] Again, to reiterate, it is not that obeying institutional rules is insignificant to just social relations and to protect persons from harm, the point is, rules cannot serve as a substitute for ethical response.

The assumption, then, that policies or codes of ethics are *the* institutional answers to predicaments of interpersonal relations masks the nature of responsibility, reducing it to a set of rule-bound behaviors divorced from the actual encounter with another person. That is, using policies as criteria against which moral judgments are made abstracts responsibility from the concrete human realities in and through which moral consideration is even relevant. Moreover, the risk here is that such abstraction may serve, in effect, to reify those policies and procedures around emotional contact to such an extent that teachers feel compelled to obey them, despite the possibility that they actually might, in some cases, cause more harm to the individuals involved when they are followed than when they are ignored. Policies within liberal institutions are based on treating everyone the same, and not necessarily equitably. Perhaps in the end we are simply asking too much of institutional rules when it comes to defining responsibility, for although they are necessary for the functioning of institutions, they cannot bear or adequately reflect the full burden for our personal responsibility to the other person. Rules cannot exempt us from acting responsibly toward the Other, nor can they replace responsibility with a call to follow orders.

For teachers, then, the difficulty becomes how to think about ethical responsibility as constituted through the ambiguity that structures our lives in institutions. There are two aspects to this. The first involves understanding that responsibility does not fully succumb to the lure of institutional law, while recognizing the inevitability and significance of such laws within institutions; the second involves recognizing the purely human and interpersonal dimension in which our responsibility is communicated, while acknowledging the necessary ways in which institutions are communal structures whose existence can never solely be about accommodating individual needs—and, indeed, alterity. Navigating through these tensions requires a vocabulary for understanding that our ethical response to the Other cannot be fully captured in the institutional language of rules and regulations.

The question remains, though, how to live well within this apparent aporia, and how to develop a vocabulary that might help us toward this end. The key to these questions, it seems to me, can only be elaborated with respect to the problem of intentionality, mentioned above. How might a vocabulary to live well within institutional contexts in a way that prizes the personal relationship not become transformed into an applied ethics but remain anchored in the nonintentionality of nonviolence? In other words, in rereading learning as an ethical attentiveness to the Other that comes prior to understanding, how might we open ourselves up to the strangeness of difference in ways that can be mindful without becoming overly deterministic or intentional? As I discussed with respect to Roger Simon's question, how can I awaken to an attending of my attending? I see a profound difference between acting with intention and being mindful of our responsibility. In the context of the classroom, intentionality suggests that one's response is premeditated, calculated, and voluntary. It means that one already knows what an appropriate response to another is, that one has reasonably considered options, and that one addresses the Other with these facts in mind. Such willfulness, however, cannot lead, it seems to me, to an engagement with difference that brings about learning, for what underlies such willful acts of behavior is a wish for control and, as Deborah Britzman claims, consolation. That is, intentionality reduces the risks so necessary for learning and ethical interaction and becomes a form of defense against the unpredictable challenges the Other brings to our sense of who we are and who we want to become.

On the other hand, being mindful, or reminding ourselves of our obligations to the Other, while admittedly a conscious activity, requires first that we are engaged in the ambiguity of communication with others. And such engagement is not simply an intellectual activity but is fundamentally rooted in our capacities for emotional involvement and attachment. Thus to be mindful is already to be engaged with someone who is before us, it is already to be engaged in a social relationship, it is already to be engaged in ethical possibility. What we therefore have to remind ourselves of only occurs in relation to an other who is present, whether through the narratives of texts or films or actual persons. That is, my awakening acts as a reminder that I am in this relation, here and now, and that this relation has put me in a position of responsibility that is not dependent on principles but on the Other's needs. What I have to be mindful of is the way in which my affect affects my capacity for response, affects my capacity to be confronted with the challenges to become altered in my encounter with the Other. As we have seen, this is no easy accomplishment. We respond unconsciously to the narratives of others, we form relationships to them outside the bounds of our best intentions. Thus to be awakened to my attending means risking nothing less than the security of my own self-identity. It means becoming awakened to *how* I listen.

What is at stake here is the development of a capacity for the continual renewal of the self in relation to another who signifies. The emphasis becomes not on embodying predefined images of what responsibility should look like, as though it were merely a performance of a code, but on the alertness and vigilance we bring to our own responses in the context of listening. Thus it is not so much that consciousness has no role to play in being vigilant, but that responsibility itself does not emerge from conscious intent. Our vigilance to attend to our attentiveness is an approach to communication that takes responsibility for itself *as* we encounter another person. Listening to the ways our own affect, as well as that of others, infuses our encounters makes listening to stories of suffering extremely difficult, but it also makes learning from them possible.

Where ethical possibility lies, then, is in the everyday social relations that make up our classroom life, and our reminders to ourselves that learning takes place through our attentiveness in those relations can, at best, help us attend to their occurrences in ways that remain responsive. When we introduce stories of suffering into our classrooms, when we attempt to move students to social awareness and commitment, we are perpetually confronted with emotional responses that become the starting point for our ethical adventure with the Other, and for our pedagogical work. Responding to students' responses is thereby infused with the hope that we may embody just those practices from which students can learn and develop insight. When we listen to students express their empathy, love, or guilt for another whose experiences they cannot share, we should not think that this is the end result of our pedagogical practices. Rather, this is the time in which we begin to help them make connections to their own implications in the lives of others. Thus every emotional response is pedagogically fruitful, since it reveals an implicit struggle with the ethical aspects of encountering difference.

It is not that responsibility, as I have so defined it here, is or ought to be the sole work of social justice education. Indeed, the interpersonal conditions of responsibility cannot serve as a replacement for the larger concerns of justice; responsibility, so conceived, does not replace the important struggle for a more inclusive curriculum, nor does it act as a panacea to the ills of social inequity and violence. However, what it does offer is a rethinking of social justice education as itself an ethical practice, one that must learn to work through the complex layers of affect that inform our responses to the Other so that it may offer alternatives to dealing with difference that better reflect its own intrinsic purpose.

NOTES

INTRODUCTION

1. Some mention should be made at the outset of how I am using the words other, Other, and "Other." "Other" refers to the more sociologically driven definitions that one finds in social justice education and cultural studies literature. As explored below, Levinas tends to use the term *Other* in relation to a specific, embodied individual, while *other* is used more as a generalization, and I will follow this convention as it is appropriate.

2. For a recent collection on the far-reaching nature of this ethical turn, see Marjorie Garber, Beatrice Hanssen, and Rebecca L. Walkowitz, eds. *The Turn to Ethics* (New York: Routledge, 2000).

3. Alain Badiou, *Ethics: An Essay on the Understanding of Evil*, trans. Peter Hallward (London: Verso, 2001), 20. His essential criticism is that difference holds no interest for thought, which is concerned only with truths, and that it is truths (in the plural), moreover, which can provide us with ethical insight. In terms of philosophical discourse, his critique of Levinas also is based on what he perceives to be the religious character of Levinas's ethical philosophy. For further discussion of Badiou's ethics, see Simon Critchley, "Demanding Approval: On the Ethics of Alain Badiou," *Radical Philosophy* 100 (2000): 16–27.

4. Jill Robbins suggests that the Holocaust should not be seen as a trope through which Levinas's writing might be singularly viewed. See her discussion of the many influences on Levinas's writing in her introduction to *Altered Reading: Levinas and Literature* (Chicago: Chicago University Press, 1999), esp. xv–xvi.

5. Emmanuel Levinas, *Time and the Other and Additional Essays,* trans. Richard A. Cohen (Pittsburgh: Duquesne University Press, 1987), 83.

6. My sense of encountering otherness as a condition of social justice pedagogies refers to the ways in which representations of inequity are discussed and utilized in classrooms in order to move students to reflection, action, and social awareness.

7. Yet such definitions cannot be treated as hard and fast when drawing on the work of Levinas, as this present work does. What Levinas means by ethics is not programmatic or systematic, nor does it only refer to a disciplinary field. Rather, Levinas's understanding of ethics is an approach to uncover those conditions necessary for the possibility of ethics and morality, conditions which make nonviolent relations to the other possible—what Robert Eaglestone refers to as the "ethics of ethics." *Ethical Crit-*

icism: Reading after Levinas. (Edinburgh: University of Edinburgh Press, 1997), 7. It is this understanding of ethics as that which is about conditions for nonviolence which will be my primary concern.

8. Zygmunt Bauman, *Life in Fragments: Essays in Postmodern Morality* (Oxford: Basil Blackwell, 1995), 11.

9. Jacques Derrida, "Violence and Metaphysics: An Essay on the Thought of Emmanuel Levinas," in *Writing and Difference,* trans. Alan Bass (Chicago: University of Chicago Press, 1978), 106.

10. As will be elaborated upon below, this de-"Othering" of the "Other" comes about via an understanding of "Other" as a socially constructed category resulting from social inequities. My understanding of Other follows Levinas, who declares it to be an absolute difference, a pure exteriority. Similarly, psychoanalysis calls our attention to the otherness of ourselves—the unconscious—as that which is unknowable. In this regard, for Levinas and psychoanalysis, de-Othering would be an unethical act in the extreme and an outright impossibility, respectively.

11. This comes out of an interview with François Poirié. See Poirié, "Entretiens," in *Emmanuel Levinas, Qui-êtes vous?* (Lyon: La Manufacture, 1987), 94.

12. Levinas claims, in an interview with Philippe Nemo, that "my task does not consist in constructing ethics; I only try to find its meaning. In fact I do not believe that all philosophy should be programmatic.... One can without a doubt construct an ethics in function of what I have just said, but this is not my own theme." *Ethics and Infinity,* trans. Richard A. Cohen (Pittsburgh: Duquesne University Press, 1985), 90.

13. Sigmund Freud, "On the Teaching of Psychoanalysis in Universities," 1919, in *The Standard Edition of the Complete Psychological Works of Sigmund Freud,* ed. and trans. James Strachey in collaboration with Anna Freud and assisted by Alix Strachey and Alan Tyson (London: Hogarth Press, 1953–1974), vol. 17, 169–173. (All further references to the Standard Edition will be cited as *SE* with the appropriate volume number).

14. Deborah Britzman, *Lost Subjects, Contested Objects* (Albany: State University of New York Press, 1998) and Adam Phillips, "Learning from Freud," in *Philosophers on Education: New Historical Perspectives,* ed. Amélie Oksenberg Rorty (New York: Routledge, 1998), 411–417.

15. Britzman, 117 and 118.

16. Ibid., 126. It is important to differentiate here between the ego of psychoanalysis and the ego of Levinas's philosophy. The Freudian ego is that which encompasses both a conscious self-identity and traces of unconscious affect; this allows the ego to be seen as that which is, by its very nature, a potential source of instability. The Levinasian ego, on the other hand, is really a Cartesian one: the self-same cogito. In this sense, Levinas views the ego as a totality, an ego that is always seeking to reduce the other to itself.

17. Simon Critchley, "The Original Traumatism: Levinas and Psychoanalysis," in *Questioning Ethics: Contemporary Debates in Philosophy,* ed. Richard Kearney and Mark Dooley (New York: Routledge, 1999), 239.

18. Levinas, *Time and the Other,* 82.

19. Ibid., 79.

20. See, in particular, Sigmund Freud and Josef Breuer, *Studies in Hysteria*, 1895, *SE*, vol. 2.

21. In terms of reading Levinas's work in relation to psychoanalysis, Simon Critchley has attempted a rapprochement between the two; see, in particular, "The Original Traumatism," and "*Das Ding:* Lacan and Levinas," in *Ethics, Politics, Subjectivity* (London: Verso, 1999), 198–216. See also Steven Gans, "Levinas and Freud: Talmudic Inflections in Ethics and Psychoanalysis," in *Facing the Other: The Ethics of Emmanuel Levinas*, ed. Seán Hand (London: Curzon, 1996), 45–61. The edited collection, *Levinas and Lacan: The Missed Encounter*, ed. Sarah Harasym (Albany: State University of New York Press, 1998), also deals with various tensions and offers productive readings of the work of Levinas and Lacan. There is little in the way of extensive discussion of Levinas's work from a clinical psychoanalytic perspective. Michael Eigen mentions Levinas's reading of the face for psychical development in "The Significance of the Face," in *The Electrified Tightrope* (Northvale, NJ: Jason Aronson, 1993), 49–60; and Paul Gordon, *Face-to-Face: Therapy as Ethics* (London: Constable, 1999) discusses Levinas within the context of psychotherapy. Levinas, on the other hand, has made many comments on psychoanalysis, often derogatory, to distinguish his own work from it. His words speak for themselves:

> Psychoanalysis is in its essence philosophical, the outcome of rationalism; it requires for reflection what reflection demanded for the thought that thinks naively. The non philosophical issue of psychoanalysis consists in a predilection for some fundamental, but elementary, fables—the libido, sadism, masochism, the Oedipus complex, repression of the origin, aggressivity—which, incomprehensibly, would alone be unequivocal, alone not translate (or mask or symbolize) a reality more profound than themselves, would be the terms of psychological intelligibility. That they have been collected from among the remnants of the most diverse civilizations and called myths adds nothing to their worth as clarifying ideas, and at most evinces a return to mythologies, astonishing when we recognize that forty centuries of monotheism had no other end in view than to liberate humanity from obsession with them. The petrifying effect of myths must all the same be distinguished from the assurance they are believed to give the understanding.

"The Ego and the Totality," in *Collected Philosophical Papers*, ed. and trans. Alphonso Lingis (The Hague: Martinus Nijhoff, 1987), 40.

22. Noreen O'Connor, "Who Suffers?" in *Re-Reading Levinas*, ed. Robert Bernasconi and Simon Critchley (Bloomington: Indiana University Press, 1991), 229.

23. Thomas Carl Wall, *Radical Passivity: Levinas, Blanchot and Agamben* (Albany: State University of New York Press, 1999), 32.

24. Cornelius Castoriadis, *The Imaginary Institution of Society*, trans. Kathleen Blamey (Cambridge: Polity Press, 1987).

25. Emmanuel Levinas, *Totality and Infinity: An Essay on Exteriority*, trans. Alphonso Lingis (Pittsburgh: Duquesne University Press, 1969), 51.

CHAPTER ONE

1. Simon Wiesenthal, "The Sunflower," Book One of *The Sunflower: On the Limits and Possibilities of Forgiveness* (New York: Schocken, 1997).

2. Many authors have discussed these difficulties in detail in relation to teaching literatures of trauma. See, for example, Deborah P. Britzman, *Lost Subjects, Contested Objects;* Claudia Eppert, "Relearning Questions: Responding to the Ethical Address of Past and Present Others," in *Between Hope and Despair: Pedagogy and the Remembrance of Historical Trauma,* ed. Sharon Rosenberg, Roger I. Simon, Claudia Eppert (Lanham, MD: Rowman and Littlefield, 2000), 213–230; Shoshana Felman, "Education and Crisis, or the Vicissitudes of Teaching," in *Crises of Witnessing in Literature, Psychoanalysis and History,* Shoshana Felman and Dori Laub (New York: Routledge, 1992), 1–56; and Judith Robertson, "Teaching about Worlds of Hurt Through Encounters with Literature." *Language Arts* 74, no. 6 (October,1997): 457–466.

3. Roger Simon, *Teaching Against the Grain: Texts for a Pedagogy of Possibility* (Toronto: Ontario Institute for Studies in Education Press, 1992), 56.

4. This is reminiscent of what Sandra Bartky has described in her concept of "ontological shock." *Femininity and Domination* (New York: Routledge, 1990).

5. Melanie Klein often uses the terms *ego* and *self* interchangeably, unlike Freudian and Lacanian analysis.

6. Cornelius Castoriadis, "Psychoanalysis and Politics," in *World in Fragments: Writings on Politics, Society, Psychoanalysis, and the Imagination,* ed. and trans. D.A. Curtis (Stanford: Stanford University Press, 1997), 129.

7. For the remainder of this chapter, I will be using the phrase "learning to become." While this is not a phrase that Castoriadis uses himself, I am indebted to his broad understanding of pedagogy in my use of it here and to his understanding of the ego as a social-historical institution.

8. Castoriadis writes, "The minimal requirement for this process to unfold is that the institution provide the psyche with *meaning.*" "Power, Politics, Autonomy," in *Philosophy, Politics, Autonomy: Essays in Political Philosophy,* ed. and trans. David Ames Curtis (Oxford: Oxford University Press, 1991), 149.

9. For a discussion on how education historically has performed coercively, see Alan A. Block, "'It's Alright, Ma (I'm Only Bleeding)': Education as the Practice of Social Violence against the Child," *Taboo: Journal of Culture and Education* 1, no. 1 (spring 1995): 123–142; also for a Foucaultian discussion of how children's bodies are disciplined in daycare settings, see Robin L. Leavitt and Martha Bauman Power, "Civilizing Bodies: Children in Day Care," in *Making a Place for Pleasure in Early Childhood Education,* ed. Joseph L. Tobin (New Haven: Yale University Press, 1997), 39–75. Both of these articles illustrate, in different ways, the type of violence that I am associating with "learning to become."

10. Castoriadis, *The Imaginary Institution of Society,* 104.

11. Plato, *Meno,* trans. G.M.A. Grube (Indianapolis: Hackett Publishing, 1981), 70a. All further references will be made in the text.

12. Shoshana Felman, *Jacques Lacan and the Adventure of Insight: Psychoanalysis in Contemporary Culture* (Cambridge: Harvard University Press, 1987), 69.

13. The full text from this section reads:

Socrates: A square then is a figure in which all these four sides are equal?—Yes indeed.

Socrates: And it also has these lines through the middle equal?—Yes.

Socrates: And such a figure could be larger or smaller?—Certainly.

Socrates: If then this side were two feet, and this other side two feet, how many feet would the whole be? Consider it this way: if it were two feet this way and only one foot that way, the figure would be once two feet?—Yes (82c).

14. This is particularly evident in Socrates' identification with the slave a little later on in the dialogue. In response to Meno's insistence that he answer the original question concerning whether virtue can be taught, Socrates states: "But as you think only of controlling me who am your slave, and never of controlling yourself—such being your notion of freedom—I must yield to you, for you are irresistible"(86d). The comment certainly raises questions about the erotic nature of the slave-teacher relation as Socrates seems to regard the performance of the question itself as exerting a demand beyond knowledge. This sentence appears in Jowett's translation of *Meno*, which generally is more playful and flirtatious than Grube's. See *The Dialogues of Plato*, trans. Benjamin Jowett (London: Sphere, 1970).

15. It is also evident that for the slave boy there is nowhere to hide from the question. It demands an answer, and with the right answer lies a glimmer of hope: reprieve from uncertainty—and further questioning.

16. Melanie Klein, "The Importance of Symbol-Formation in the Development of the Ego," 1930, in *Love, Guilt and Reparation and Other Works 1921–1945, the Writings of Melanie Klein*, vol. 1 (London: Karnac Books, 1992), 221.

17. Klein believes, following Ferenczi, that identification is a precursor to symbolism (which is echoed and developed further in Lacan's understanding of the imaginary and the symbolic). As will be evident below, however, Klein deviates from her initial view in her emphasis on the primary role anxiety plays in both identification and symbolization. It is this emphasis that makes her work, in my view, central for working through the anxieties attached to learning.

18. Britzman, *Lost Subjects*, 10.

19. Simon, *Teaching Against the Grain*, 62.

20. Zygmunt Bauman, *Postmodern Ethics* (Oxford: Blackwell, 1993), 20.

21. Ibid., 32.

22. Adam Phillips, "Learning from Freud," 412.

23. Drucilla Cornell offers a useful definition of the nonviolent nature of the ethical relation: "Again, by the ethical relation I mean to indicate the aspiration to a nonviolent relationship to the Other, and to otherness more generally, that assumes responsibility to guard the Other against the appropriation that would deny her difference and singularity." *The Philosophy of the Limit* (New York: Routledge, 1992), 62.

24. Emmanuel Levinas, *Time and the Other*, 83.

25. Thus Levinas is proposing something quite different from Buber's conception of the I-Thou, which is based on a symmetrical and shared subjectivity. Similarly, current conceptions of the ethic of care in education focus on the resemblance and reciprocity between ethical subjects, despite the fact that each subject may have a different role to play in the ethical relationship. This is clearly contrary to the emphasis that Levinas places on the radical alterity of the other person, whereby responsibility for the Other is nonreciprocal and does not anticipate any form of mutual interaction.

26. Levinas, *Totality and Infinity*, 51 (emphasis in original).

27. Levinas, *Ethics and Infinity*, 67.

28. I am following Levinas's usage of "I" and "ego" to refer to the structure of being that signifies the totality of the self over time. While in psychoanalytic theory, particularly that influenced by Lacanianism, the I is a fundamentally different structure than the ego, there is at times some slippage between the I and the ego in Levinas's work.

29. Levinas, *Totality and Infinity*, 43 (ellipses in original).

30. Levinas, *Ethics and Infinity*, 86.

31. Levinas, *Totality and Infinity*, 222.

32. Ibid., 66.

33. Britzman, *Lost Subjects*, 140 n. 16.

34. All further references to Klein's essay will be made in the text.

35. This shift in technique really becomes a redefinition of technique that seeps into all of Klein's clinical work after this point in time.

36. Mary Jacobus, *First Things: The Maternal Imaginary in Literature, Art, and Psychoanalysis* (New York: Routledge, 1995), 132.

37. Ibid., 137.

38. In Phyllis Grosskurth's 1986 biography of Klein, she mentions how as an adult "Dick" recalls Klein's affection to him in times of need. Klein, however, continued in her theoretical writing to deem such displays of affection as improper. *Melanie Klein: Her World and Her Work* (Cambridge, MA: Harvard University Press, 1986).

39. Levinas, *Totality and Infinity*, 66.

40. Lynda Stone, "Narrative in Philosophy of Education: A Feminist Tale of 'Uncertain' Knowledge," in *Critical Conversations in Philosophy of Education*, ed. Wendy Kohli (New York: Routledge, 1995), 184.

41. Shoshana Felman, "Psychoanalysis and Education: Teaching Terminable and Interminable," in *Learning Desire: Perspectives on Pedagogy, Culture, and the Unsaid*, ed. Sharon Todd (New York: Routledge, 1997), 28.

42. Sharon Todd, "Looking at Pedagogy in 3-D: Rethinking Difference, Disparity, and Desire," in *Learning Desire*, 237–260.

43. Phillips, "Learning from Freud," 412.

CHAPTER TWO

1. Megan Boler, *Feeling Power: Emotions and Education* (New York: Routledge, 1999), 156.

2. Richard Kearney writes, "It [empathy] is, as Kant noted in his account of 'representative thinking', a way of identifying with as many fellow-humans as possible—actors and sufferers alike—in order to participate in a common moral sense (*sensis communis*)." "Narrative and the Ethics of Remembrance," in *Questioning Ethics: Contemporary Debates in Philosophy*, ed. Richard Kearney and Mark Dooley (London: Routledge, 1999), 30.

3. Nel Noddings, *Caring: A Feminine Approach to Ethics and Moral Education* (Berkeley: University of California Press, 1984).

4. Obviously not all children whom we perceive, from our position of wealth and privilege, to be hungry are so. This is obviously not to say that hunger and famine are not urgent problems, but only that there are tropes of hunger that get played out in representations of the Third World, which in fact come to stand metonymically for the Third World in general. Moreover, understanding hunger as solely a Third World issue in the first place is deeply problematic given the state of poverty in the very city where these third graders live.

5. One such exercise reported to me on a couple of occasions by teachers involved dividing students in a classroom according to eye color; those with blue eyes received privileges, while those without received harsher treatment. The point was then to get the students to articulate what it is they felt and relate this to the historical treatment of Jews during the Holocaust.

6. See chapter 4 for an elaboration of guilt in the context of feeling responsible for harm that one has not directly committed.

7. Michel de Certeau, *The Practice of Everyday Life*, trans. Steven Rendall (Berkeley: University of California Press, 1984), 37–8.

8. See, for example, the essays in Rosenberg, Simon, and Eppert, eds., *Between Hope and Despair*.

9. Zygmunt Bauman, *Life in Fragments*, 44–49. All further references will be made in the text.

10. This is how Levinas characterizes Heidegger's being-with. Viewing it as a kind of being-aside, Levinas sees that this form of togetherness cannot lead to the emergence of responsibility and remains caught up in an individual's solitude.

11. Vetlesen states that "this commitment is unlike all others; it is not a product of the subject's intentionality; it is not wanted; it simply imposes itself as a property pertaining to the very structure of this dyad in proximity." *Perception, Empathy and Judgment: An Inquiry into the Preconditions of Moral Performance* (University Park, PA: Pennsylvania State University Press, 1994), 202.

12. Many authors attempt to make fine distinctions between sympathy and empathy. Megan Boler rightly notes, for instance, that philosophers do not agree on what goes under the name of empathy, *Feeling Power*, 158. As will be developed below, my own view of empathy as a mode of relationality refers specifically to the dynamics mentioned above: the act of putting oneself in the Other and that of putting the Other into oneself.

13. Max Scheler, *The Nature of Sympathy*, trans. Peter Heath (Hamden, CT: Archon, 1970), esp. 143.

14. Edith Stein, *On the Problem of Empathy*, trans. Waltraut Stein (Washington, DC: ICS Publications, 1989). See especially her discussion of Scheler's work where she claims that Scheler's definition of empathy is not her own, 27–34. See also Kathleen Haney's discussion of Stein's and Levinas's work. Haney argues, contrary to my own view here, that Levinas's understanding of the face-to-face relation requires empathy. "Empathy and Ethics," *Southwest Philosophy Review* 10, no. 1 (1994): 57–65.

15. Meyers also believes that a certain form of sympathy can be empathetic, but even this poses a tension: "empathetic sympathy is often morally significant, and it is not always morally desirable. Misplaced sympathy gives rise to sentimentality and worse." Diana Tietjens Meyers, *Subjection and Subjectivity: Psychoanalytic Feminism and Moral Philosophy* (New York: Routledge, 1994), 32. I will discuss Meyers's notion of empathy in more detail below.

16. Boler, *Feeling Power*, 158.

17. Carl Anders Säfström has put the question slightly differently and has noted three distinct kinds of emphases within educational research. *How* do we live with others? indicates identifying the processes of interaction; How do we live with *others?* asks us to consider social differences and identities; and How do we live *with* others? carries with it moral signification. "Identity and the Politics of Time" (seminar presentation, Uppsala Universitet, May 14, 2001).

18. John Llewelyn, *Emmanuel Levinas: The Genealogy of Ethics* (London: Routledge, 1995) 145.

19. Levinas, *Otherwise than Being or Beyond Essence*, trans. Alphonso Lingis (Pittsburgh: Duquesne University Press, 1998), 61.

20. See Luce Irigaray, "Women-Amongst-Themselves: Creating a Woman-to-Woman Sociality," in *The Irigaray Reader*, ed. Margaret Whitford (Oxford: Basil Blackwell, 1991), 190–197, and her discussion throughout *An Ethics of Sexual Difference*, trans. Carolyn Burke and Gillian C. Gill (Ithaca: Cornell University Press, 1993).

21. Levinas, *Totality and Infinity*, 75.

22. Ibid., 83.

23. Ibid., 121.

24. Ibid., 203.

25. Levinas, *Otherwise than Being*, 56.

26. See my discussion of passivity in relation to transcendence in chapter 4.

27. Levinas, *Otherwise than Being*, 62–3.

28. Ibid., 72.

29. This is not, of course, to say that the decisions we make regarding our treatment of others are without any significance. It is merely to say that the preconditions for such decisions to be made lie in the sentient, not conscious, subject.

30. Andrew Tallon, "Nonintentional Affectivity, Affective Intentionality, and the Ethical in Levinas's Philosophy," in *Ethics as First Philosophy*, ed. Adriaan Peperzak (New York: Routledge, 1995), 107–121.

31. Sigmund Freud, *Civilization and Its Discontents*, 1930, *SE*, vol. 21, 89.

32. Hanna Segal, *Introduction to the Work of Melanie Klein* (London: Hogarth Press, 1973), 27.

33. Jean-Michel Petot recognizes that Klein's notion of love derives from one's identification with an object and consequently it has its roots in narcissism. *Melanie Klein: The Ego and the Good Object 1932–1960*, vol. 2, trans. Christine Trollope (Madison, CT: International Universities Press, 1991), 41.

34. Melanie Klein, "Love, Guilt and Reparation," 1937, in *Love, Guilt and Reparation and Other Works 1921–1945, the Writings of Melanie Klein*, ed. Roger Money

Kyrle, in collaboration with Betty Joseph, Edna O'Shaughnessy, and Hanna Segal (London: Karnac Books, 1992), vol. 1, 311. On this same page she views, like Kant, sympathy as being bound to an other's happiness: "In the depths of the mind, the urge to make people happy is linked up with a strong feeling of responsibility and concern for them, which manifests itself in genuine sympathy with other people and in the ability to understand them, as they are and as they feel." Thus, Kleinian sympathy, in light of my discussion above, is a type of feeling-with the Other.

35. Klein, "On Identification," 1955, in *Envy and Gratitude and Other Works, 1946–1963, the Writings of Melanie Klein*, vol. 2, 143.

36. Segal, 36.

37. Meyers, *Subjection and Subjectivity*, 33. All further references to this work will be made in the text.

38. I wish to consider identification separately from projective identification; although one obviously "brings into the self" something from the outside in both, it is the explicitly projected nature of what is brought in that makes projective identification in my view quite distinct from other identificatory processes.

39. Elisabeth Young-Bruehl, "The Biographer's Empathy with Her Subject," in *Subject to Biography: Psychoanalysis, Feminism, and Writing Women's Lives* (Cambridge, MA: Harvard University Press, 1998), 22.

40. Freud, *Group Psychology and the Analysis of the Ego*, 1921, *SE*, vol. 8, 110 n. 2.

41. Reich, "On Countertransference," in *Psychoanalytic Contributions* (New York: International Universities Press, 1973), 136.

42. Reich, "Further Remarks on Countertransference," in *Psychoanalytic Contributions*, 277.

43. Ibid., 276, 277.

44. Reich warns of "pedagogic" attitudes: "The analyst feels tempted to fulfill thwarted infantile desires of patients and thus to teach them that the world is not as terrible as they in the childish ways of thinking assume. Thus anxiety is smoothed over; reassurance is given instead of real analysis of the anxiety." "On Countertransference," 145.

45. Reich, "Empathy and Countertransference," in *Psychoanalytic Contributions*, 348.

46. Ibid.

47. Young-Bruehl, 21.

48. Ibid., 22.

49. Interestingly, Vetlesen argues that this is precisely what makes empathy, as opposed to love, conducive to moral performance (*Perception, Empathy and Judgment*, esp. 204–218). I will take up his position more thoroughly in the following chapter.

CHAPTER THREE

1. As I am reading them, love refers to a particular feeling or quality of emotion whereas, following Levinas and Freud, eros refers to the more all-encompassing capac-

ity to love, which includes also the capacity for sensuality and passion and other erotic forms of communication between persons. In discussing eros further as a mode of communicative relationality between actual persons, I am deviating from the literature in education that discusses its role in the quest for knowledge. See, for instance, Kal Alston, "Teaching, Philosophy, and Eros: Love as a Relation to Truth," *Educational Theory* 41, no. 4 (1991): 385–395 and James Garrison, *Dewey and Eros: Wisdom and Desire in the Art of Teaching* (New York: Teachers College Press, 1997).

2. There has, of course, been much literature in education dealing with the nature of desire and erotic pleasure between embodied persons in the class, but this has not always been brought to the specific discussion of ethics within the orientation of social justice education. See, for example, Anne M. Phelan, "Classroom Management and the Erasure of Teacher Desire," in *Making a Place for Pleasure in Early Childhood Education*, ed. Joseph Tobin (New Haven: Yale University Press, 1997), 76–100; Jonathan G. Silin, *Sex, Death, and the Education of Children: Our Passion for Ignorance in the Age of Aids* (New York: Teachers College Press, 1995); and Erica McWilliam, "Beyond the Missionary Position: Teacher Desire and Radical Pedagogy," in *Learning Desire: Perspectives on Pedagogy, Culture, and the Unsaid*, ed. Sharon Todd (New York: Routledge, 1997), 217–236.

3. Kelly Oliver, *Witnessing: Beyond Recognition* (Minneapolis: University of Minnesota Press, 2001). She further acknowledges, with reference to bell hooks, that "there is no powerful discourse on love emerging either from politically progressive radicals or from the Left" (bell hooks, quoted in Oliver, 218). I discuss Oliver's advocacy of love below.

4. Max Scheler, *The Nature of Sympathy*, trans. Peter Heath (Hamden, CT: Archon, 1970), 71.

5. I discuss the tensions that love poses in terms of establishing a relation to a particular person, on the one hand, and to the generalized other, on the other hand. This cuts to the heart of the problem I will be discussing below in considering the limitations of love.

6. Freud, *Civilization and Its Discontents*, 102.

7. Levinas, *Otherwise than Being*, 120. All further references will be made in the text.

8. Vetlesen, *Perception, Empathy and Judgment*, 203. All further references will be made in the text.

9. For a detailed discussion of Levinas's changing views of love and eros, see my "A Fine Risk to be Run? The Ambiguity of Eros and Teacher Responsibility," *Studies in Philosophy and Education* 22, no. 1 (January 2003): 31–44. Also see Tina Chanter's discussion in *Ethics of Eros: Irigaray's Rewriting of the Philosophers* (New York: Routledge, 1995); Diane Perpich, "From the Caress to the Word: Transcendence and the Feminine in the Philosophy of Emmanuel Levinas" and Eva Płonowska Ziarek, "The Ethical Passions of Emmanuel Levinas," both in *Feminist Interpretations of Emmanuel Levinas*, ed. Tina Chanter, 28–52, 78–95, respectively (University Park, PA: Pennsylvania State University Press, 2001).

10. Emmanuel Levinas, *Time and the Other*, 88.

11. Ibid., 90.

12. Ibid., 86. The poet and classicist Anne Carson echoes this distinction in her study of eros,

> Eros is an issue of boundaries. He exists because certain boundaries do. In the interval between reach and grasp, between glance and counterglance, between 'I love you' and 'I love you too,' the absent presence of desire come alive. But the boundaries of time and glance and I love you are only aftershocks of the main, inevitable boundary that creates Eros: the boundary of flesh and self between you and me. And it is only, suddenly, at the moment when I would dissolve that boundary, I realize I never can.

Anne Carson, *Eros the Bittersweet* (Normal, IL: Dalkey Archive Press, 1998), 30.

13. Levinas, *Time and the Other*, 94.

14. Levinas, *Totality and Infinity*, 266.

15. Chanter, *Ethics of Eros*, 206.

16. Indeed, Vetlesen notes that Himmler was all too aware the moral power the face-to-face encounter had upon the perpetrators being able to carry out their murders, which is what led him to depersonalize killing and to organize a system of mass extermination. Vetlesen, 200.

17. It should be emphasized here that Vetlesen's project is not concerned with responsibility or moral action per se but about establishing the conditions of moral perception that involve our emotional capacities. However, this perception is connected to moral performance, and in this sense, how he grounds his understanding of perception carries relevance for responsibility as performance.

18. I will make all further references to this book in the text.

19. Freud's discussion of eros is an attempt to get underneath what affective attachments are necessary for the promotion of social life. Thus his references to love are, unlike those discussed above with respect to Vetlesen's position, not confined to the sphere of intimacy between two persons. Rather, Freud locates such intimacy along a continuum with the larger drive of eros. In this sense, my point here is to show how the feeling of love might be read as a manifestation of the social relations implied in eros.

20. His previous work, both in *Beyond the Pleasure Principle*, 1920, *SE*, vol. 18, 3–66—in which the death drive is given its first theoretical elaboration—and *The Ego and the Id*, 1923, *SE*, vol. 19, 3–68, discusses eros in terms of the sexual instincts which preserve life and form bonds to others, and the ego-instincts which seek to master the world for their own ends. His development of the closeness between eros and the death drive in terms of community with others, however, receives more elaborate treatment in *Civilization and Its Discontents*, to which I confine my discussion. All page references are from this text.

21. Jane Gallop offers a discussion of the complexity of the issues involved in her "Resisting Reasonableness" *Critical Inquiry* 25, (spring 1999): 599–609. Also see my own discussion in "A Fine Risk to be Run?" where I outline the tensions between erotic relations in the classroom and the institutional constraints and regulations in which they operate. I think such constraints are necessary in ensuring that there are procedures in place for mitigating against harm, yet when they are rigidly constructed (no-touch policies at schools are a good example), they often create a moral panic that drives these relations underground, producing an unhealthy climate of fear and suspicion.

CHAPTER FOUR

1. Elizabeth Spelman, drawing on Gabriele Taylor's *Pride, Shame, and Guilt: Emotions of Self-Assessment* (Oxford: Clarendon Press, 1985), views guilt as only being, in the end, self-referential; that is, it only recognizes that one has done harm, not that harm has had an effect on someone else. Thus she deems guilt an inadequate response to the suffering of others; *Fruits of Sorrow: Framing Our Attention to Suffering* (Boston: Beacon Press, 1997), 106–107. My own view is that guilt is very much about the recognition of harm experienced by others, and it is precisely this "awareness" that often causes us to feel guilt over deeds that we have not directly committed. In a similar vein to my own, Arne Johan Vetlesen states that "feelings of guilt . . . are bound up with being affected; and to be affected by the other, the other must appear to us as a 'real experience' that we have. In other words, the other must be perceived as a subject able to feel pain and be hurt." *Perception, Empathy and Judgment*, 197.

2. Emmanuel Levinas, "Useless Suffering," in *Entre-Nous: Thinking-of-the-Other*, trans. Michael. B. Smith and Barbara Harshav (New York: Columbia University Press, 1998), 91–102.

3. A psychoanalytic view of remorse is distinguished from the remorse that I am speaking of here. Freud is clear when he states that "when one has a sense of guilt after committing a misdeed, and because of it, the feeling should more properly be called *remorse*. It relates only to a deed that has been done, and, of course, it presupposes that a *conscience*—the readiness to feel guilty—is already in existence before the deed took place." *Civilization and Its Discontents*, 131. This idea that remorse can only be felt for something one is directly involved in seems to me to underestimate the power of fantasy in thinking that we are fully responsible for deeds that we consciously know not to have committed. Moreover, it also is the case that with regard to students talking about homelessness, there is no singular deed or act for which people feel responsibility, but their talk indicates a more generalized response to the ongoing forms of social contact that students have with homeless people. The idea of the readiness to feel guilty as an effect of conscience is discussed below.

4. Gabriele Taylor notes "that the deed of another (my child, my compatriot) may make me feel shame but not guilt. Guilt itself cannot be vicarious." *Pride, Shame and Guilt*, 91. I am pushing the point here to include that the guilt the self experiences necessarily implies a social relation.

5. See Leslie Roman's understanding of innocence as a form of white defensiveness in "White is a Color! White Defensiveness, Postmodernism, and Anti-racist Pedagogy," in *Race, Identity, and Representation in Education*, ed. Cameron McCarthy and Warren Crichlow (New York: Routledge, 1993), 71–88. Patricia Williams remarks on the futility and inadequacy of guilt in confronting an other's suffering. See in particular her chapter "Gilded Lilies and Liberal Guilt (Reflections on Law School Pedagogy)" in *The Alchemy of Race and Rights* (Cambridge: Harvard University Press, 1991), 15–43.

6. See the numerous examples in Spelman, *Fruits of Sorrow*; Williams, *Alchemy*; Julie Ellison, "A Short History of Liberal Guilt," *Critical Inquiry* 22 (winter 1996): 344–371; Gayatri Spivak, *The Post-Colonial Critic: Interviews, Strategies, Dialogues*, ed. Sarah Harasym (New York: Routledge, 1990); and Megan Boler, *Feeling Power*, to name just a few.

7. Ellison, "A Short History of Liberal Guilt," 344–371.

8. Ibid., 358.

9. Boler, *Feeling Power*, 172.

10. Ellison, 349.

11. Sandra Lee Bartky uses this phrase to denote the radical disjunction of subjectivity one experiences as a result of new awareness about one's self and world. See *Femininity and Domination*.

12. Shoshana Felman, "Education and Crisis," in *Testimony*, 53.

13. Ellison, 345.

14. Sigmund Freud, *Civilization and Its Discontents*, 124.

15. Williams, *Alchemy*, 22.

16. Felman, in *Testimony*, 196.

17. Judith Butler, *The Psychic Life of Power: Theories in Subjection* (Stanford, CA: Stanford University Press, 1997). All further references will be made in the text.

18. See in particular Freud, *The Ego and the Id* and *Civilization and Its Discontents* for an elaborated account of how guilt becomes a resolution of the Oedipal identification with the father.

19. See my discussion below on the complicated nature of guilt and fear of the loss of love. This relationship is not straightforward, and the differences between Freud and Klein on this matter have to do with the different emphases they place on love, authority, and aggression.

20. Levinas, *Totality and Infinity*, 51. See chapter 1 for a detailed account of this receptivity as a theory of learning.

21. Melanie Klein, "Love, Guilt and Reparation," 306. All further references to this work will appear in the text.

22. Zygmunt Bauman, *Postmodern Ethics*, esp. 10–13.

23. For example, see chapter 1 for a detailed account of her analysis with "Dick."

24. Freud identifies instincts, or more accurately, drives [*Trieb* in German] thus: "... an instinctual stimulus does not arise from the external world but from within the organism itself" and "moreover, since it impinges not from without but from within the organism, no flight can avail against it." "Instincts and Their Vicissitudes," 1918, *SE*, vol. 14, 118. A drive is inescapable. Thus Klein's discussion of how reparation is set into motion seems slightly at odds with the inevitability that conventionally marks an understanding of a drive.

25. Jacqueline Rose, *Why War? Psychoanalysis, Politics and the Return to Melanie Klein* (Oxford: Blackwell, 1993), esp. 166.

26. Freud, *Civilization and Its Discontents*, 124. Also, in her paper "On the Theory of Anxiety and Guilt," 1948, in *Envy and Gratitude*, esp. 26–27, Klein takes great pains to show how Freud has gestured to early formations of guilt, even as he put forth his ideas on guilt as an Oedipal process.

27. See Patricia Greenspan's elaborated argument in *Practical Guilt: Moral Dilemmas, Emotions, and Social Norms* (Oxford: Oxford University Press, 1995).

28. One can think of many examples where "living like the oppressed" or "putting oneself in the other's shoes" is seen as a strategy for mobilizing against injustice. But I want to caution against these as really being reparative in the Kleinian (and indeed moral) sense; instead, it is more a gesture of identification and projection, as discussed in chapter 2. While identification certainly can be a psychical strategy for defending against or resolving particular conflicts, it seems to me that in order to repair the harm that one imagines one has caused (which is one of the necessary components of guilt), one seeks reparation as an amendment to what has specifically caused the harm.

29. In a passage from *Otherwise than Being*, Levinas is clear about the problem of understanding egos as unique while subjecting them to universalizable theories. One cannot help but think of psychoanalysis here: "Obsession . . . does not simply figure as a relation among all the reciprocal or at least reversible relations that form the system of the intelligibility of being, and in which the ego, even in its uniqueness, is a universal subsuming a multiplicity of unique egos" (83). Instead, Levinas proposes that such thematization diminishes the ethical possibility of human relationality.

30. Lingis, "Translator's Introduction," *Otherwise than Being*, xix. All future references to this book will be made in the text.

31. Levinas also connects this "pre-originary" to the body and to maternity: "Subjectivity as flesh and blood . . . is the pre-original signifyingness that gives sense, because it gives. Not because, as pre-original, it would be more originary than the origin, but because the diachrony of sensibility, which cannot be assembled in a representational present, refers to an irrecuperable pre-ontological past, that of maternity" (*Otherwise than Being*, 78). While the whole subtext of the body and femininity cannot be addressed here, it is important to note that the pre-originary is precisely a non-beginning, what Levinas refers to as "an-archy." In capturing this time of "maternity," which is necessary for making sense and meaning, there is a close affiliation in my view with Klein's emphasis on the signifyingness of the mother's body, for it is the maternal body that gives birth to symbolism and the possibility, therefore, for making meaning.

32. See my discussion on transcendence in chapter 3.

33. Further, Levinas writes of exposure: "Exposure as a sensibility is more passive still; it is like . . . a having been offered without any holding back, a not finding any protection in any consistency of identity of a state. It is a having been offered without any holding back and not the generosity of offering oneself, which would be an act, and already presupposes the unlimited undergoing of the sensibility" (*Otherwise than Being*, 75).

34. Another translation of this appears in Levinas's works as: "We are all guilty before everyone for everyone, and I more than all the others." See, for example, Levinas, "Philosophy, Justice, and Love," in *Entre Nous: On Thinking-of-the-Other*, trans. Michael B. Smith and Barbara Harshav (New York: Columbia University Press, 1998), 105. However, the emphasis on "each of us," rather than "we," speaks more accurately to the issue of singularity and uniqueness I am discussing here.

35. Although the scope of this chapter prevents me from discussing this at length, the self also feels traumatized and persecuted because of the possibility of the other's death. Elisabeth Weber writes, "the trauma of the encounter with the other is trauma

of absolute responsibility, which is traumatic only because the one encountered can die." "The Notion of Persecution in Levinas's *Otherwise Than Being or Beyond Essence*," in *Ethics as First Philosophy*, ed. Adriaan Peperzak (New York: Routledge, 1995), 74. Levinas, moreover, is unequivocal in asserting that it is not only the possibility of one's death that is at stake, but the responsibility the I has towards the Other's death: "The proximity of the neighbour—the peace of proximity—is the responsibility of the *I* for the other, the impossibility of leaving him alone before the mystery of death." "Peace and Proximity," in *Alterity and Transcendence,* trans. Michael B. Smith (New York: Columbia University Press, 1999), 141. The theme of death and its relation to responsibility in Levinas's work is taken up more fully in Dennis Keenan King, *Death and Responsibility: The "Work" of Levinas* (Albany: State University of New York Press, 1999).

36. Simon Critchley offers a strong representation of what this trauma entails: "trauma is a 'non-intentional affectivity,' it tears into my subjectivity like an explosion, like a bomb that detonates without warning, like a bullet that hits me in the dark, fired from an unseen gun and by an unknown assailant." "The Original Traumatism: Levinas and Psychoanalysis," 236.

37. See chapter 5 for a more extended and developed discussion on listening.

38. I wish to emphasize again that this does not apply to those who "blame" victims for their own misfortunes or who espouse hatred and prejudice toward selected groups. These moves are not at all responsive nor responsible. Rather, I am discussing those expressions of guilt/innocence which articulate a genuine struggle to figure out one's own involvement in a harm committed. Moreover, they, like the other two types of guilt, also must be seen as a response to the teacher's pedagogical demand for students to take responsibility.

CHAPTER FIVE

1. *Jupiter's Wife*, dir. Michel Negroponte. New York: Artistic License Films, 1995. See also the web-site www.el.net/jupiters-wife/wife.html.

2. Gemma Corradi Fiumara, *The Symbolic Function: Psychoanalysis and the Philosophy of Language,* trans. Brian Keys (Oxford: Blackwell, 1992), 110.

3. I do not mean to suggest that all theories of dialogue embrace such a simplistic rendering of its purpose. Rather, I am trying to point out that more commonsense appraisals of the value of dialogue frequently focus on an epistemological assumption that speaking to each other will create a deepening of understanding for both involved.

4. Corradi Fiumara, *The Other Side of Language: A Philosophy of Listening,* trans. Charles Lambert (London: Routledge, 1990), 30.

5. Corradi Fiumara, *The Symbolic Function,* 110–111.

6. Ibid., 112.

7. Although in what follows I am distinctly moving away from Corradi Fiumara's midwife model, I think the issues she raises speak directly to the self-other relation and the question of learning I am addressing, particularly the three I have chosen to highlight here.

8. Corradi Fiumara, *The Other Side of Language*, 144. All other references will be made in the text.

9. Robert Gibbs, *Why Ethics? Signs of Responsibilities* (Princeton: Princeton University Press, 2000), 39.

10. Emmanuel Levinas, *Totality and Infinity*, 121.

11. There is some debate as to what extent psychosis can be treated; since the individual no longer partakes of a shared discourse, insight and interpretation become deeply problematic. For an interesting discussion on how psychosis is amenable to psychoanalysis, see Piera Aulagnier, *Un interprète en quête de sens* (Paris: Éditions Payots, 1991). Castoriadis also draws on Aulagnier's work in his discussion on psychosis.

12. Cornelius Castoriadis, "The State of the Subject Today," in *World in Fragments*, 141.

13. Ibid., 151.

14. Ibid., 161.

15. Cornelius Castoriadis, "The Construction of the World in Psychosis," in *World in Fragments*, 199.

16. Ibid., 198.

17. Castoriadis, "The State of the Subject Today," 149.

18. Emmanuel Levinas, "Is Ontology Fundamental?" in *Basic Philosophical Writings*, ed. Adriaan Peperzak, Simon Critchley and Robert Bernasconi (Bloomington: Indiana University Press, 1996), 6.

19. Gibbs, 29.

20. Levinas, *Totality and Infinity*, 171.

21. Ibid., 178.

22. Gibbs, 34.

23. Levinas, *Totality and Infinity*, 178.

24. Ibid., 171.

25. Ibid., 178.

26. Gibbs, 43.

27. Levinas, *Otherwise than Being*, 5.

28. Gibbs, 47.

29. Levinas, *Otherwise than Being*, 49.

30. Ibid., 50.

31. Ibid., 77.

32. Ibid., 120. See also my discussion in chapter 3.

33. Roger I. Simon, "The Paradoxical Practice of *Zakhor*: Memories of 'What Has Never Been My Fault or My Deed,'" in *Between Hope and Despair*, 19.

34. Deborah Britzman, "If the Story Cannot End: Deferred Action, Ambivalence and Difficult Knowledge" in *Between Hope and Despair*, 39.

POSTSCRIPT

1. Zygmunt Bauman, *Postmodern Ethics*, 18–19.
2. Ibid., 19.
3. Drucilla Cornell, *The Philosophy of the Limit*, 155.
4. Ibid., 116.
5. Levinas, *Ethics and Infinity*, 90.

BIBLIOGRAPHY

Alston, Kal. "Teaching, Philosophy, and Eros: Love as a Relation to Truth." *Educational Theory* 41, no. 4 (1991): 385–395.

Aulagnier, Piera. *Un interprète en quête de sens.* Paris: Éditions Payots, 1991.

Badiou, Alain. *Ethics: An Essay on the Understanding of Evil.* Translated by Peter Hallward. London: Verso, 2001.

Bartky, Sandra Lee. *Femininity and Domination.* New York: Routledge, 1990.

Bauman, Zygmunt. *Postmodern Ethics.* Oxford: Blackwell, 1993.

———. *Life in Fragments: Essays in Postmodern Morality.* Oxford: Basil Blackwell, 1995.

Block, Alan A. "'It's Alright, Ma (I'm Only Bleeding)': Education as the Practice of Social Violence against the Child." *Taboo: Journal of Culture and Education* 1, no. 1 (spring 1995): 123–142.

Boler, Megan. *Feeling Power: Emotions and Education.* New York: Routledge, 1999.

Britzman, Deborah P. *Lost Subjects, Contested Objects: Toward a Psychoanalytic Inquiry of Learning.* Albany: State University of New York Press, 1998.

———. "If the Story Cannot End: Deferred Action, Ambivalence and Difficult Knowledge." In *Between Hope and Despair: Pedagogy and the Remembrance of Historical Trauma,* edited by Sharon Rosenberg, Roger I. Simon, and Claudia Eppert, 27–57. Lanham, MD: Rowman and Littlefield, 2000.

Butler, Judith. *The Psychic Life of Power: Theories in Subjection.* Stanford: Stanford University Press, 1997.

Carson, Anne. *Eros the Bittersweet.* Normal, IL: Dalkey Archive Press, 1998.

Castoriadis, Cornelius. *The Imaginary Institution of Society.* Translated by Kathleen Blamey. Cambridge: Polity Press, 1987.

———. "Power, Politics, Autonomy." In *Philosophy, Politics, Autonomy: Essays in Political Philosophy.* Edited and translated by David Ames Curtis. 143–174. Oxford: Oxford University Press, 1991.

———. "Psychoanalysis and Politics." In *World in Fragments: Writings on Politics, Society, Psychoanalysis, and the Imagination.* Edited and translated by David Ames Curtis. 125–136. Stanford: Stanford University Press, 1997.

———. "The State of the Subject Today." In *World in Fragments: Writings on Politics, Society, Psychoanalysis, and the Imagination*. Edited and translated by David Ames Curtis. 137–171. Stanford: Stanford University Press, 1997.

———. "The Construction of the World in Psychosis." In *World in Fragments: Writings on Politics, Society, Psychoanalysis, and the Imagination*. Edited and translated by David Ames Curtis. 196–210. Stanford: Stanford University Press, 1997.

Certeau, Michel de. *The Practice of Everyday Life*. Translated by Steven Rendall. Berkeley: University of California Press, 1984.

Chancer, Lynn. *Sadomasochism in Everyday Life*. New Brunswick: Rutgers University Press, 1992.

Chanter, Tina. *Ethics of Eros: Irigaray's Rewriting of the Philosophers*. New York: Routledge, 1995.

Cornell, Drucilla. *The Philosophy of the Limit*. New York: Routledge, 1992.

Corradi Fiumara, Gemma. *The Other Side of Language: A Philosophy of Listening*. Translated by Charles Lambert. London: Routledge, 1990.

———. *The Symbolic Function: Psychoanalysis and the Philosophy of Language*. Translated by Brian Keys. Oxford: Blackwell, 1992.

Critchley, Simon. "*Das Ding:* Lacan and Levinas." In *Ethics, Politics, Subjectivity*, 198–216. London: Verso, 1999.

———. "The Original Traumatism: Levinas and Psychoanalysis." In *Questioning Ethics: Contemporary Debates in Philosophy,* edited by Richard Kearney and Mark Dooley, 230–242. New York: Routledge, 1999.

———. "Demanding Approval: On the Ethics of Alain Badiou." *Radical Philosophy* 100 (2000): 16–27.

Derrida, Jacques. "Violence and Metaphysics: An Essay on the Thought of Emmanuel Levinas." In *Writing and Difference*. Translated by Alan Bass. 79–153. Chicago: University of Chicago Press, 1978.

Eaglestone, Robert. *Ethical Criticism: Reading after Levinas*. Edinburgh: University of Edinburgh Press, 1997.

Eigen, Michael. "The Significance of the Face." In *The Electrified Tightrope*, 49–60. Northvale, N.J.: Jason Aronson, 1993.

Ellison, Julie. "A Short History of Liberal Guilt." *Critical Inquiry* 22 (winter 1996): 344–371.

Eppert, Claudia. "Relearning Questions: Responding to the Ethical Address of Past and Present Others." In *Between Hope and Despair: Pedagogy and the Remembrance of Historical Trauma,* edited by Sharon Rosenberg, Roger I. Simon, and Claudia Eppert, 213–230. Lanham, Md.: Rowman and Littlefield, 2000.

Felman, Shoshana. *Jacques Lacan and the Adventure of Insight: Psychoanalysis in Contemporary Culture*. Cambridge: Harvard University Press, 1987.

———. "Education and Crisis, or the Vicissitudes of Teaching." In *Testimony: Crises of Witnessing in Literature, Psychoanalysis and History*. Shoshana Felman and Dori Laub, 1–56. New York: Routledge, 1992.

———. "Psychoanalysis and Education: Teaching Terminable and Interminable." In *Learning Desire: Perspectives on Pedagogy, Culture, and the Unsaid*, edited by Sharon Todd, 17–43. New York: Routledge, 1997.

Felman, Shoshana and Dori Laub. *Testimony: Crises of Witnessing in Literature, Psychoanalysis, and History*. New York: Routledge, 1992.

Freud, Sigmund. *The Standard Edition of the Complete Psychological Works of Sigmund Freud*. Edited and translated by James Strachey. In collaboration with Anna Freud. Assisted by Alix Strachey and Alan Tyson. 24 vols. London: Hogarth Press, 1953–1974.

———. "Instincts and Their Vicissitudes." 1918. *SE*. Vol. 14. 117–140.

———. "On the Teaching of Psychoanalysis in Universities." 1919. *SE*. Vol. 17. 169–173.

———. *Beyond the Pleasure Principle*. 1920. *SE*. Vol. 18. 3–66.

———. *Group Psychology and the Analysis of the Ego*. 1921. *SE*. Vol. 18. 67–144.

———. *The Ego and the Id*. 1923. *SE*. Vol. 19. 3–68.

———. *Civilization and Its Discontents*. 1930. *SE*. Vol. 21. 59–148.

Freud, Sigmund and Josef Breuer. *Studies on Hysteria*. 1895. *SE*. Vol. 2.

Gallop, Jane. *Feminist Accused of Sexual Harassment*. Durham: Duke University Press, 1997.

———. "Resisting Reasonableness." *Critical Inquiry* 25 (spring 1999): 599–609.

Gans, Steven. "Levinas and Freud: Talmudic Inflections in Ethics and Psychoanalysis." In *Facing the Other: The Ethics of Emmanuel Levinas*, edited by Seán Hand, 45–61. London: Curzon, 1996.

Garber, Marjorie, Beatrice Hanssen, and Rebecca L. Walkowitz, eds. *The Turn to Ethics*. New York: Routledge, 2000.

Garrison, James. *Dewey and Eros: Wisdom and Desire in the Art of Teaching*. New York: Teachers College Press, 1997.

Gibbs, Robert. *Why Ethics? Signs of Responsibilities*. Princeton: Princeton University Press, 2000.

Gordon, Paul. *Face-to-Face: Therapy as Ethics*. London: Constable, 1999.

Greenspan, Patricia. *Practical Guilt: Moral Dilemmas, Emotions, and Social Norms*. Oxford: Oxford University Press, 1995.

Grosskurth, Phyllis. *Melanie Klein: Her World and Her Work*. Cambridge: Harvard University Press, 1986.

Haney, Kathleen. "Empathy and Ethics." *Southwest Philosophy Review* 10, no. 1 (1994): 57–65.

Harasym, Sarah, ed. *Levinas and Lacan: The Missed Encounter*. Albany: State University of New York Press, 1998.

Irigaray, Luce. "Women-Amongst-Themselves: Creating a Woman-to-Woman Sociality." In *The Irigaray Reader*. Edited by Margaret Whitford. 190–197. Oxford: Basil Blackwell, 1991.

———. "Questions to Emmanuel Levinas." In *Re-Reading Levinas,* edited by Robert Bernasconi and Simon Critchley, 109–118. Bloomington: Indiana University Press, 1991.

———. *An Ethics of Sexual Difference.* Translated by Carolyn Burke and Gillian C. Gill. Ithaca: Cornell University Press, 1993.

Jacobus, Mary. *First Things: The Maternal Imaginary in Literature, Art, and Psychoanalysis.* New York: Routledge, 1995.

Kearney, Richard. "Narrative and the Ethics of Remembrance." In *Questioning Ethics: Contemporary Debates in Philosophy,* edited by Richard Kearney and Mark Dooley, 18–32. London: Routledge, 1999.

Kelly, Ursula. *Schooling Desire: Literacy, Cultural Politics and Pedagogy.* New York: Routledge, 1997.

King, Dennis Keenan. *Death and Responsibility: The "Work" of Levinas.* Albany: State University of New York Press, 1999.

Klein, Melanie. "The Importance of Symbol-Formation in the Development of the Ego." 1930. In *Love, Guilt and Reparation and Other Works 1921–1945, the Writings of Melanie Klein.* Edited by Roger Money Kyrle. In collaboration with Betty Joseph, Edna O'Shaughnessy, and Hanna Segal. Vol. 1. 248–257. London: Karnac Books, 1992.

———. "The Early Development of Conscience in the Child." 1933. In *Love, Guilt and Reparation and Other Works.* 219–235.

———. "Love, Guilt and Reparation." 1937. In *Love, Guilt and Reparation and Other Works 1921–1945.* 306–343.

———. "On the Theory of Anxiety and Guilt." 1948. In *Envy and Gratitude and Other Works, 1946–1963, the Writings of Melanie Klein.* Vol. 2. 25–42.

———. "On Identification." 1955. In *Envy and Gratitude and Other Works, 1946–1963.* 141–175.

Leavitt, Robin L., and Martha Bauman Power. "Civilizing Bodies: Children in Day Care." In *Making a Place for Pleasure in Early Childhood Education,* edited by Joseph L. Tobin, 39–75. New Haven: Yale University Press, 1997.

Levinas, Emmanuel. *Totality and Infinity: An Essay on Exteriority.* Translated by Alphonso Lingis. Pittsburgh: Duquesne University Press, 1969.

———. *Ethics and Infinity.* Translated by Richard A. Cohen. Pittsburgh: Duquesne University Press, 1985.

———. *Time and the Other and Additional Essays.* Translated by Richard A. Cohen. Pittsburgh: Duquesne University Press, 1987.

———. "The Ego and the Totality." In *Collected Philosophical Papers.* Edited and translated by Alphonso Lingis. 25–45. The Hague: Martinus Nijhoff, 1987.

———. "Is Ontology Fundamental?" In *Basic Philosophical Writings.* Edited by Adriaan Peperzak, Simon Critchley and Robert Bernasconi, 1–10. Bloomington: Indiana University Press, 1996.

———. "Useless Suffering." In *Entre Nous: On Thinking-of-the-Other.* Translated by Michael B. Smith and Barbara Harshav. 91–102. New York: Columbia University Press, 1998.

———. "Philosophy, Justice, and Love." In *Entre Nous: On Thinking-of-the-Other*. Translated by Michael B. Smith and Barbara Harshav. 103–122. New York: Columbia University Press, 1998.

———. *Otherwise than Being or Beyond Essence*. Translated by Alphonso Lingis. Pittsburgh: Duquesne University Press, 1998.

———. "Peace and Proximity." In *Alterity and Transcendence*. Translated by Michael B. Smith. 131–144. New York: Columbia University Press, 1999.

Llewelyn, John. *Emmanuel Levinas: The Genealogy of Ethics*. London: Routledge, 1995.

McWilliam, Erica. "Beyond the Missionary Position: Teacher Desire and Radical Pedagogy." In *Learning Desire: Perspectives on Pedagogy, Culture, and the Unsaid*, edited by Sharon Todd, 217–236. New York: Routledge, 1997.

Meyers, Diana Tietjens. *Subjection and Subjectivity: Psychoanalytic Feminism and Moral Philosophy*. New York: Routledge, 1994.

Negroponte, Michel, director. *Jupiter's Wife*. New York: Artistic License Films, 1995.

Noddings, Nel. *Caring: A Feminine Approach to Ethics and Moral Education*. Berkeley: University of California Press, 1984.

O'Connor, Noreen. "Who Suffers?" In *Re-Reading Levinas*, edited by Robert Bernasconi and Simon Critchley, 229–233. Bloomington: Indiana University Press, 1991.

Oliver, Kelly. *Witnessing: Beyond Recognition*. Minneapolis: University of Minnesota Press, 2001.

Perpich, Diane. "From the Caress to the Word: Transcendence and the Feminine in the Philosophy of Emmanuel Levinas." In *Feminist Interpretations of Emmanuel Levinas*, edited by Tina Chanter, 28–52. University Park: Pennsylvania State University Press, 2001.

Petot, Jean-Michel. *Melanie Klein: The Ego and the Good Object 1932–1960*. Vol. 2. Translated by Christine Trollope. Madison, Conn.: International Universities Press, 1991.

Phelan, Anne M. "Classroom Management and the Erasure of Teacher Desire." In *Making a Place for Pleasure in Early Childhood Education*, edited by Joseph Tobin, 76–100. New Haven: Yale University Press, 1997.

Phillips, Adam. "Learning from Freud." In *Philosophers on Education: New Historical Perspectives*, edited by Amelie Oksenberg Rorty, 411–417. New York: Routledge, 1998.

Plato. *The Dialogues of Plato*. Translated by Benjamin Jowett. London: Sphere, 1970.

———. *Meno*. Translated by G.M.A. Grube. Indianapolis: Hackett Publishing, 1981.

Poirié, François. *Emmanuel Levinas: Qui-êtes vous?* Lyon: La Manufacture, 1987.

Reich, Annie. *Psychoanalytic Contributions*. New York: International Universities Press, 1973.

Robbins, Jill. *Altered Reading: Levinas and Literature*. Chicago: University of Chicago Press, 1999.

Roberston, Judith. "Teaching about Worlds of Hurt Through Encounters with Literature." *Language Arts* 74, no. 6 (October 1997): 457–466.

Roman, Leslie. "White is a Color! White Defensiveness, Postmodernism, and Antiracist Pedagogy." In *Race, Identity, and Representation in Education*, edited by Cameron McCarthy and Warren Crichlow, 71–88. New York: Routledge, 1993.

Rose, Jacqueline. *Why War? Psychoanalysis, Politics and the Return to Melanie Klein*. Oxford: Blackwell, 1993.

Rosenberg, Sharon, Roger I. Simon, and Claudia Eppert, eds. *Between Hope and Despair: Pedagogy and the Remembrance of Historical Trauma*. Lanham, Md.: Rowman and Littlefield, 2000.

Säfström, Carl Anders. "Identity and the Politics of Time." Seminar presentation. Uppsala Universitet. May 14, 2001.

Scheler, Max. *The Nature of Sympathy*. Translated by Peter Heath. Hamden, Conn.: Archon, 1970.

Segal, Hanna. *Introduction to the Work of Melanie Klein*. London: Hogarth Press, 1973.

Silin, Jonathan G. *Sex, Death, and the Education of Children: Our Passion for Ignorance in the Age of AIDS*. New York: Teachers College Press, 1995.

Simon, Roger I. *Teaching Against the Grain: Texts for a Pedagogy of Possibility*. Toronto: Ontario Institute for Studies in Education Press, 1992.

——. "The Paradoxical Practice of *Zakhor:* Memories of 'What Has Never Been My Fault or My Deed.'" In *Between Hope and Despair: Pedagogy and the Remembrance of Historical Trauma*, edited by Sharon Rosenberg, Roger I. Simon, and Claudia Eppert, 9–26. Lanham, Md.: Rowman and Littlefield, 2000.

Spelman, Elizabeth. *Fruits of Sorrow: Framing Our Attention to Suffering*. Boston: Beacon Press, 1997.

Spivak, Gayatri. *The Post-Colonial Critic: Interviews, Strategies, Dialogues*. Edited by Sarah Harasym. New York: Routledge, 1990.

Stein, Edith. *On the Problem of Empathy*. Translated by Waltraut Stein. Washington, D.C.: ICS Publications, 1989.

Stone, Lynda. "Narrative in Philosophy of Education: A Feminist Tale of 'Uncertain' Knowledge." In *Critical Conversations in Philosophy of Education*, edited by Wendy Kohli, 173–189. New York: Routledge, 1995.

Tallon, Andrew. "Nonintentional Affectivity, Affective Intentionality, and the Ethical in Levinas's Philosophy." In *Ethics as First Philosophy*, edited by Adriaan Peperzak, 107–121. New York: Routledge, 1995.

Taylor, Gabriele. *Pride, Shame and Guilt: Emotions of Self-Assessment*. Oxford: Clarendon Press, 1985.

Todd, Sharon. "Looking at Pedagogy in 3D: Rethinking Difference, Disparity, and Desire." In *Learning Desire: Perspectives on Pedagogy, Culture, and the Unsaid*, edited by Sharon Todd, 237–260. New York: Routledge, 1997.

——. "When Is Guilt More Than Just a Petty Face? Moving from Liberal Guilt Toward Reparation and Responsibility in Education." *Philosophy of Education 2000*, edited by Lynda Stone, 357–364. Urbana, Ill.: Philosophy of Education Society, 2000.

———. "'Bringing More than I Contain:' Ethics, Curriculum, and the Pedagogical Demand for Altered Egos." *Journal of Curriculum Studies* 33, no. 4 (July 2001): 431–450.

———. "A Fine Risk to be Run? The Ambiguity of Eros and Teacher Responsibility." *Studies in Philosophy and Education* 22, no. 1 (January 2003): 31–44.

Vetlesen, Arne Johan. *Perception, Empathy and Judgment: An Inquiry into the Preconditions of Moral Performance*. University Park: Pennsylvania State University Press, 1994.

Wall, Thomas Carl. *Radical Passivity: Levinas, Blanchot and Agamben*. Albany: State University of New York Press, 1999.

Weber, Elisabeth. "The Notion of Persecution in Levinas's *Otherwise Than Being or Beyond Essence*." In *Ethics as First Philosophy*, edited by Adriaan Peperzak, 69–76. New York: Routledge, 1995.

Wiesenthal, Simon. *The Sunflower: On the Limits and Possibilities of Forgiveness*. New York: Schocken, 1997.

Williams, Patricia. "Gilded Lilies and Liberal Guilt (Reflections on Law School Pedagogy)." In *The Alchemy of Race and Rights*. 15–43. Cambridge: Harvard University Press, 1991.

Young-Bruehl, Elisabeth. "The Biographer's Empathy with Her Subject." In *Subject to Biography: Psychoanalysis, Feminism, and Writing Women's Lives*. 17–25. Cambridge, MA: Harvard University Press, 1998.

Ziarek, Eva Płonowska. "The Ethical Passions of Emmanuel Levinas." In *Feminist Interpretations of Emmanuel Levinas*, edited by Tina Chanter, 78–95. University Park: Pennsylvania State University Press, 2001.

INDEX

affect, 4, 10, 11, 13, 137, 146
aggression
    fantasies of, 100–101, 103, 106
    in student responses, 104–106
Allen, Woody, 118
altered egos, 18
alterity, 11, 84
    preservation of, 3, 51, 52, 130
    and respecting singularity, 62
    revelation of, 51, 52, 61
    as unknowable, 107
    See also other, otherness, and difference
Althusser, Louis, 98–99, 107, 110
altruism, 84, 89
    as being-for, 84
ambiguity, 141
    of communication, 68–69, 125, 144, 145 (*see also* communicative risk and fine risk)
    of love, 67, 68, 71, 86
ambivalence, 141
    emotional, 104
    of life and death, 81, 83–84
    of love, 67, 85, 86
anxiety in learning, 32–37
Arendt, Hannah, 57
attending to difference, 142
attentiveness, 3, 9, 36, 37, 80 117,121, 124, 125, 130, 136
    awakening to attending to, 134–139, 145–146
    ethical, 14, 16, 63, 145
    in listening, 136–139
    to Other's meaning as learning from difference, 129, 131, 137
Aulagnier, Piera, 162n. 11
awareness, 98, 99, 100, 104

Badiou, Alain, 2
Bartky, Sandra Lee, 150n. 4, 159n. 11
Bauman, Zygmunt, 5, 28, 46–49, 50, 52, 101, 143
being-aside, 46
being-for, 48–49, 50–53, 59, 60, 62, 63, 66, 72, 135
being-with, 46–47, 72
Boler, Megan, 43, 50, 96
breakdown in common meaning, 128, 129
Britzman, Deborah, 10, 27, 32, 138, 145
broad empathy, 104
Butler, Judith, 98–99, 103, 107

care, 43, 66
Carson, Anne, 157n. 12
Castoriadis, Cornelius, 15, 29, 118, 136
    on learning to become, 19–21, 26
    on listening, 126–130
categorical imperative, 5
Chanter, Tina, 71
Cogan, Maggie, 117, 118–122, 123, 126, 127–128, 131, 132
commitment, 48–49, 62, 71, 73, 74–75, 76, 81, 84, 86–89
communicative openness, 60–61, 89
communicative risk, 68–72
consciousness, 59

Cornell, Drucilla, 144, 151n. 23
Corradi Fiumara, Gemma, 118,
    122–126, 132
creativity in language, 127–128
curriculum, 18, 141, 146
    and social justice education, 39
    as symbolization, 40
    via the Other, 39

de Certeau, Michel, 44
death drive, 83, 101–102, 157n. 20
"dense plots," 118, 120, 121
Derrida, Jacques, 7, 20
Dewey, John, 5
dialogic relation, 121, 122–123
    See also Socratic method
difference
    difficulties with, 114–115
    as manifest in communication, 130, 131, 138
Dostoevsky, Fyodor, 109, 110

Eaglestone, Robert, 147n. 7
education
    normative aspect of, 28
    as rhetoric, 7
    See also pedagogy and social justice education
ego, 19, 26, 31, 84
    in Kleinian terms, 18
    three movements in becoming, 32
ego-instincts, 83, 157n. 20
egoism, 12
Ellison, Julie, 96–97
empathy, 14, 43–63, 66–67, 73, 91, 118, 137, 141
    broad, 55–56
    definitions of, 49–50
    as a demand, 45, 47, 59
    feelings of, 49, 50 (*see also* feeling-for)
    imaginative reconstruction, 55–56
    incident specific, 55–56
    as key to analyst's role, 58
    putting oneself in the other's shoes, 53–57
    putting the other into oneself, 57–59
    recognition of, 59

eros, 65–89, 155n. 1
    and death drive, 83
    as life drive, 81–86
    as a quality of relationality, 69, 72
    and social cohesion, 82
    and social conflict, 82–83
    social control of, 82
    as a social relation, 86
    as type of relation, 70–71
ethics, 2, 142
    applied, 5, 6, 145
    as exceeding laws and rules, 144–145
    instrumentalizing, 6
    implied, 14–15, 29
    possibilities of in education, 13, 141–146
    as programmatic, 4, 28
    in relation to education 1, 2, 3,
    in relation to knowledge, 4–9
    thinking ethics through education, 29, 38
    the turn to, 2
exposure, 108, 134, 136, 160n. 33

face-to-face encounter, 18, 28, 51, 70, 130, 131, 143
Fanon, Frantz, 77–78
fantasy
    in empathy, 55
    in relation to guilt, 101–107
feeling-for, 53, 55, 57, 59, 60, 62, 73
feeling-with, 49, 50, 52, 62
fellow-feeling, 49–50
Felman, Shoshana, 38, 97, 98
fine risk of communication, 68–72, 86, 89, 133
forgiveness, 17
Freud, Anna, 57
Freud, Sigmund, 10, 55, 57, 67, 97, 99, 102, 103, 110
    feeling one's way into another, 53–54
    on empathy, 57–58
    on eros, 81–86, 157nn. 19, 20
    on guilt, 158n. 3

Gallop, Jane, 157n. 21
Gibbs, Robert, 126, 131, 133
Grosskurth, Phyllis, 152n. 38

guilt, 14, 91–115, 118, 137, 141
   and acknowledgement of harm, 92, 158n.1
   as declaration of innocence, 93–94, 105–106
   as declaration of lack of suffering, 93, 105
   as declaration of worry 93, 104–105
   and distancing, 93–94, 105–106
   and identity, 98–99, 103
   liberal, 95–97
   and loss of love, 99, 102, 103, 159n. 19
   and love, 101–103, 104, 106
   as moral failure, 96
   as moral orientation, 100–107
   as part of early development, 103
   as pedagogical problem, 92–95
   and pedagogy, 114–115
   and relation to innocence, 98, 99
   as responsible response, 111, 114
   as self-pity, 95
   as suffering, 110–111
   and time, 107

Haney, Kathleen, 153n. 14
hooks, bell, 79, 156n. 3
hope, 102–103, 125, 133, 137
   of education, 20
   of nonviolence, 25–27

identification, 57, 61, 160n. 28
   and imitation, 58, 61
   trial, 58–59
   See also projective identification
implied ethics, 14–15, 29
instincts, 159, n. 24
institutions, 85, 142–145
intentionality, 145
intimacy, 66
Irigaray, Luce, 51

Jacobus, Mary, 34, 35
Jupiter's Wife, 117, 118–122, 123, 126, 130, 133, 139
justice, 144

Kearney, Richard, 152n. 2
Klein, Melanie, 10, 92, 95, 99, 100–107, 110, 114, 160n.31
   "On the Importance of Symbol-Formation in the Development of the Ego," 32–37
   on guilt and reparation, 100–106
   on projective identification, 54–55
Kleinian subject, 101–102
knowledge about the Other, 8, 56, 106

Lacan, Jacques, 33, 38
language, 69
   See also listening as structural condition of speech and language
learning
   about the other, 3, 111
   and dynamics of empathy, 59–63
   as emotional labor, 113
   as a receiving, 29, 38
   riskiness of, 11, 130, 132
   three movements of in Meno, 22–25
   through listening, 118, 122
learning to become, 14, 18–21, 136
   in *Meno*, 22–25
   pedagogical demand for, 18, 24, 31, 32
   and student-teacher relations, 25–27
   as violent, 19, 27
learning from the other, 3, 9, 10, 15–16, 45, 67, 111, 112, 136, 137–139
Levinas, Emmanuel, 17, 20, 34, 36, 67, 86, 92, 95, 100, 114, 118, 126, 136
   on eros, 69–72, 73
   on fine risk, 68–69
   on the importance of the future, 13
   on otherness, 2, 9, 10, 11, 12, 13, 15, 29
   on responsibility, 11, 106–112
   on self-other relation in listening, 130–134
   on susceptibility, 106–112
   on teaching and learning, 29–32
liberal guilt, 95–97
listening, 14, 60, 111–112, 117–139, 141, 146
   as attending to alterity, 118, 126, 130–134

listening *(continued)*
   as attending to the Other, 126
   as attending to the Other's meaning, 118, 126–130
   as entering the speech of another, 124, 129, 131
   as ethical condition of language, 132
   ethical possibility of, 125
   as ethical response to suffering, 118, 137–138
   "maieutic," 123–124
   paradoxical nature of, 125, 129
   passivity of, 135
   as practice, 123–124
   as receiving alterity, 131
   in relation to narrative, 118, 123–126
   as response to Other, 117
   responsibility in, 135, 136, 138
   as saying, 133
   as selflessness, 124–125, 129, 131, 132
   as structural condition of speech and language, 122–123, 124, 125
   and teacher-student relations, 136–139
Llewelyn, John, 51
love, 65–89, 91, 118, 137, 141, 155n. 1
   as being-for, 73, 75
   between teachers and students, 87–88
   as a communicative relation, 71–72
   as connectedness, 76, 77–79, 80
   fantasies of in student responses, 104–106
   as a feeling, 65, 67, 75
   and guilt, 101–103, 104, 106
   limits of, 72–76
   as moral ideal, 75, 80, 81
   as political, 77–78, 79
   as response to the other, 79
   as responsibility, 76–77, 79
   singularity of, 67
   as a social relation, 67, 76–81 (*see also* eros)

maternity, 160n. 31
Meyers, Diana Tietjens, 50, 55–56, 62
mindfulness, 145–146
modes of relationality, 9, 59, 60, 63, 141
   See also empathy, eros, guilt, listening and love
moments of ethicality, 17
moral concern, 66, 72
moral relation
   love and guilt necessary for, 104
moral perception, 74–75
moral education, 5

narratives, 146
Nazi violence, 75–76
Negroponte, Michel, 117, 118–122, 123, 126, 131, 132, 139
Noddings, Nel, 5
nonintentional affectivity, 52, 60
nonintentionality, 145
nonviolence 3, 4, 9, 13, 14, 45, 53, 59, 86, 87, 130, 135, 136, 142, 145
   and teacher-student relations, 27, 31
nonviolent relations, 12, 14, 15,

O'Connor, Noreen, 13
object-instincts, 83
obligation, 139, 141, 145
Oedipus complex, 103, 159n. 26
Oliver, Kelly, 66, 82, 84, 87
   on love, 76–81
ontological difference, 8–9
openness, 68, 69, 79, 88, 92
Other and other
   approach to, 52, 68, 130–131, 133
   approach of, 69
   calling me into question, 131
   command from, 68, 109, 110, 132
   definition of, 147n. 1
   important for ethics, 2–3
   interminable response to, 133
   nonviolent relation to, 2
   as revealed through speech, 126, 132
   uniqueness of, 66–67
   unknowability of, 61
   See also alterity
"Other," 1–2, 8, 66, 147n. 1
otherness, 2
   as absolute, 2
   as a condition of learning, 30

as unknowable, 2, 3
See also alterity, other, and difference
"otherness," 77, 78, 79

passivity, 12, 52, 53, 60, 108, 130
   in attentiveness, 134
pedagogical relations, 4
pedagogical demand
   for learning to become, 18, 24, 31, 32
   for love, 87
   for togetherness, 47–49
   for empathy, 45, 47, 49
pedagogical encounter as possibility for ethics, 29
pedagogy, 18, 19
   violence of, 7
   and risk, 85, 87
   and love, 87
   and guilt, 114–115
      problems with, 92–95
   and listening, 136–139
   as self alteration, 19
   as hailing, 99–100
Petot, Jean-Michel, 154n. 33
Phillips, Adam, 10, 28, 40
Plato's *Meno*, 21–25
projection, 54–57, 60–61
projective identification, 54–55, 56–57
proximity, 70, 71, 133, 135
psychical implications, 4
psychoanalysis, 4, 10–13,
   importance of the past, 13
   tensions with Levinasian ethics, 10–13
psychoanalytic interpretation, 126–127, 129
psychosis, 126–127, 128, 129

quality of relationality, 15, 63, 135
quality of response, 36

radical imagination, 127
radical imaginary, 15
Rawlsian liberal democracy, 5
receptivity, 62
recognition, 66, 76
reparation, 95, 100–106

responsibility, 51, 52, 59, 62, 66, 69, 85, 89, 91, 92, 94–95, 100, 141–146
   birth of, 131
   conditions of, 79, 80, 141
   formation of, 95
   in listening, 126, 135, 136, 138
   and susceptibility, 106–112
   and risk, 132, 136 (*see also* fine risk)
   social and political, 66, 77, 78, 79, 80, 91, 94
   as subjectivity, 106–107
   and sustaining communicative openness, 131
   unavoidable, 11
   as unique, 109
responsiveness to the Other, 38–39, 122
risk, 141
   inherent in listening, 124–125, 129, 130, 132
Rose, Jacqueline, 102

sacrifice, 69, 86
Säfström, Carl Anders, 154n. 17
said, 133
saying, 133, 136
Scheler, Max, 49, 50, 67, 73, 75
Segal, Hanna, 54, 55
self
   inadequacy of, 110, 112
self-alteration, 124, 130
   See also learning to become
self-other relation, 38, 69
   and exceeding the self, 89
   and implied ethics, 38
   irreducibility of, 51, 60
   and listening, 124–136
   and love, 85
sensibility, 51, 52, 59, 160n. 33
sensible transcendental, 51
sexual harassment, 143–144
shame, 94, 95
Simon, Roger, 28, 145
Simon Critchley, 11, 161n. 36
social difference, 3
social justice education 1, 3, 8, 43–44, 65–66, 67, 86–87, 91, 93, 141, 146
Socrates, 7
   as teacher, 21–25

Socratic method, 30, 38
speech
   and psyche, 127–130
   See also listening as structural condition of speech and language
Stein, Edith, 50
Stone, Lynda, 37
subjectivity
   as a process, 19, 26
   as a suffering, 107
suffering, 66, 91, 92, 104, 110–112
   and hope, 133–134
   responses to, 92–95, 104–106, 112, 139
susceptibility, 92, 95, 98–100, 107–112, 138
   as passivity, 108
   and responsibility, 106–112
   as prior to knowledge, 113
symbolic relationship to knowledge, 18
symbolization, 26, 27
   act of, 18
   role in ego development, 32–37
sympathy, 50, 51, 52

tactics, 44
Tallon, Andrew, 52
Taylor, Gabriele, 158nn. 1, 4
teacher
   response to guilt, 114–115
   and student responses, 146
teacher and student relations
   tension between interpersonal and institutional relations, 142–145
teaching, 9
   delicacy of, 36–37
   and empathy, 60–61
   with ignorance and humility, 15, 138
   and learning as ethical relation, 30
   and love, 87
   as persuasion, 25
   thoughtfulness in, 138–139

time
   and change, 136
   of listening, 134–139
   of signification, 134
Todd, Sharon 157n. 21
togetherness, 45, 66
   demand for, 47–49
   forms of, 46
   modes of, 46–49, 52
   See also being-aside, being-with and being-for
transcendence, 48, 51, 52, 68–69, 71, 108
trauma, 160n. 35, 161n. 36
traumatism of astonishment, 11, 36
trust, 125, 129, 131, 133
type of relationality, 15, 126, 135, 136
types of communication, 71

uncertainty, 141
   of pedagogical encounter, 28, 37
   and implied ethics, 37
unconscious, 10, 13, 127, 129
   in learning, 28
   in making meaning, 118, 126
unshareable communication, 135–137

Vetlesen, Arne Johan, 48, 63, 69, 83
   on love, 72–76
vigilance, 80, 87, 146
violence, 7, 20
   of education, 20
vulnerability, 69, 89, 100, 113, 144
   of ego to violence, 20

Weber, Elisabeth, 160n. 35
welcoming the other, 131–132
Wiesenthal, Simon, 17–18, 41
Williams, Patricia, 98

Young-Bruehl, Elisabeth, 57, 59, 62

www.ingramcontent.com/pod-product-compliance
Lightning Source LLC
Chambersburg PA
CBHW021758230426
43669CB00006B/122